VW BEETLE

VW BEETLE

RESTORATION / PREPARATION / MAINTENANCE

JIM TYLER

OSPREY
AUTOMOTIVE

First published in 1994 in Great Britain by Osprey, an
imprint of Reed Consumer Books Limited. Michelin House.
81 Fulham Road, London SW3 6RB and Auckland.
Melbourne, Singapore and Toronto

A catalogue record for this book is available on request
from the British Library.

ISBN 1-85532-359-1

Editor: Shaun Barrington
Additional pictures by Dennis Baldry and Mike Key.
Diagrams courtesy Autodata.

Phototypeset by Keyspools Ltd., Newton le Willows.
Lancashire
Printed by The Bath Press, Avon.

CONTENTS

ACKNOWLEDGEMENTS

This book is very much the richer thanks to the help and goodwill of Simon, Barbara and Craig of the Beetle Specialist Workshop of Worcestershire, England, and most especially the encyclopaedic knowledge and vast experience of all things Volkswagen of BSW workshop chief Terry Ball. It is a rare privilege to be invited to spend a substantial length of time in such a quality professional restoration workshop.

The author would not have written this or any of the previous books in this Osprey restoration series had it not been for the help and encouragement of Em and Dave Fryer. Both trained in the motor industry; Em is the restorer of innumerable cars ranging from a turn of the century quadricycle to a Corvette Stingray, and his restoration work has featured (unsung) in other books; Dave his son is a very experienced vehicle technician.

Other of the author's friends have always proven valuable sources of information in addition to lending a much-needed hand from time to time! Chalkie and John, Alan Gosling of Martley Central Garage (whose signature adorns the author's various MOT certificates and who is always willing to help out with advice when needed).

Finally, thanks to the author's long-suffering neighbours and wife, Viv.

The Beetle of suburbia. Somewhat neglected, sans running boards and wheel covers, this 1973 VW1300 is untidy but sound. The Beetle is one of the easiest classic cars to restore, Mexican production ensuring that replacement body panels – even complete body shells – are reasonably cheap, plentiful and available through VW dealers and independent specialists.

INTRODUCTION

It is strange that the mainstream classic car movement, especially the classic car press in the UK, appears to lavish its attention on cars which were often dismal commercial failures, whilst largely ignoring more popular vehicles; even the most successful classic of all time – the Volkswagen Beetle. The most highly regarded classic cars are often those which originally sold in very limited quantities, survived in tiny numbers and are nowadays given values which far exceed their practical and aesthetic worth simply because of their rarity. The Beetle is a victim of its own success in this respect and, like its contemporaries the Morris Minor, Renault 4 and Citroën 2CV, is deemed too common by many classic enthusiasts to bother with or be seen in!

The Beetle makes up for this lack of acceptance from the classic world with the largest and most enthusiastic following to be enjoyed by any car, a following which is to a large extent isolated from the classic car movement and which treats the Beetle not so much as a revered and cosseted classic, but as a 'lifestyle' car to be driven and enjoyed.

This attitude is reflected in the way the majority of owners treat their Beetles; rather than religiously restoring them to original 'showroom' condition few can resist some degree of customisation. This can range from discreet to outrageous, from slightly lowering the ride height or replacing the rather utilitarian interior with plusher upholstery to drastically altering or replacing the bodywork. Modifications which would be regarded as heresy if applied to most mainstream classics are not only acceptable on a Beetle, they are considered positively admirable.

But even the most heavily customised Beetle can reflect a long pedigree; the style of California lookers dates back to the mid-1950s, Bajas and Beach Buggies are only slightly more recent. A seemingly (to many classic enthusiasts) outrageous customisation of the Beetle could in fact be a carbon copy of a car which was customised forty years ago – can it be considered anything other than a classic? The author thinks not.

The author believes that, of Beetles owned by enthusiasts, there are more customised examples (to whatever extent) than those cars restored to strictly original condition, based on the numbers of each seen advertised for sale here in the UK (which still leaves more authentic 'classic' Beetles on the roads of the UK than examples of just about any other classic car).

The Beetle is not only a classic and cult car, it is used world-wide as daily transport by millions of owners to whom it may just be 'the car'; nothing special, just turn the key and go from A to B. The simplicity of the air-cooled flat four and drivetrain give easy maintenance and generally fewer problems than more sophisticated alternatives. Allied to the rugged construction of the backbone chassis this gives the Beetle a higher survival rate than almost any other mass-produced car. Perhaps it is because the car is so prolific, rugged and long-lived that the prices realised by Beetles appear surprisingly stable in comparison with the volatile values of most classics.

However, the Beetle is not immune to the effects of old age and, like any other car, many older examples suffer extensive body rot and/or near-terminal mechanical problems which render them unfit for the road. Some of these cars are hastily smartened up for sale to an unsuspecting buyer, others will be given a thorough restoration which returns them to their former glory. A few of the Beetles which come to the market are unsafe for use on the road due to extensive, but expertly camouflaged, rot or uncorrected collision damage. It can be difficult for the aspiring Beetle buyer to establish which treatment a viewed car has received. This book should arm the prospective buyer with the knowledge needed to sort the bad from the good.

Because the Beetle has been subjected to literally tens of thousands of production modifications during its 47 year life, it is most unlikely that a single definitive work on the Volkswagen Beetle will ever be published – even books which specialise in a particular field such as mechanical repair or history usually run to two or more volumes, and the wider-ranging scope of this book unfortunately limits its coverage of any individual aspect.

This book is intended to help the would-be Beetle owner to find the right car, to bring it to the desired condition (whether the car is to be merely a work-horse, a classic or a custom) and to keep it in good condition and where it belongs – on the road. This is not a workshop manual (if anything, it is best thought of as a companion to a workshop manual, and it is strongly recommended that the book be used in conjunction with a good manual such as that published by Autodata) nor is it a general guide to the art of the classic car restorer or the customiser.

This book covers most aspects of buying, maintenance, restoration, modification and customisation although again, it does not purport to be the last word on these subjects and the reader is advised to use the book in conjunction with more specialised works where appropriate.

A 1967 VW 1500 ripe for restoration. Extensive welding or replacement of the sills and inner/outer wings will be required. The sills have an outer and inner panel with the heater channels running up the middle; if these have rotted the body must be unbolted and removed from the floorpan before effective repairs can be carried out. Less conscientious (or just downright incompetent) 'restorers' make the mistake of welding new sills directly to the floorpan – let the buyer beware!

1 · A SHORT HISTORY

There have been tens of thousands of factory modifications to the Beetle throughout its 50-year-plus production life, and the author includes no more than an abridged production history of the car, both for the interest of the newcomer to the Beetle scene, and as a guide to those readers who seek a particular year and model of the car. The following applies to UK imported cars; cars sold on other Volkswagen export markets may differ in many respects.

Having been designed by Ferdinand Porsche between 1934 and 1938, the 'Type 60' proved the ideal car to meet the requirements of Adolf Hitler, who had a vision that every German would possess motorised transport. The Volkswagen (People's Car) Beetle was intended to enter production in 1938 and, on 26th May of that year, the Volkswagen plant was officially opened.

Until 1946, the Volkswagen plant (called 'Strength Through Joy Town') was owned by the Nazis and was not a commercial company, rather a political creation. During the Second World War the Volkswagen factory was used for the manufacture of a limited number of Beetles (some authorities place war-time production at 1,500 cars) and also several types of military vehicle based on the Beetle platform and sharing its engine and running gear. The best known of these was the Kubelwagen, the German equivalent of the Allied Jeep. The factory was bombed intensively and nearly destroyed by the Allies as the war neared its end. After the cessation of hostilities, a group of British Army personnel from the Royal Electrical and Mechanical Engineers (REME) were dispatched to the plant to salvage what they could and – if possible – re-establish car production.

A single Beetle survived in the wreckage of the factory. The British Army personnel sent to the plant knew that the occupying forces were desperate for immediate and low cost motorised transport, and they painted it in military colours, demonstrated it to the Military Government and were rewarded with an order for 20,000 vehicles. A production target of 1,000 cars a month was set – for a factory which did not even have a roof – and through a mixture of hard work, innovative use of military and other available resources, and suffering (the first winter's production took place under a temporary tarpaulin roof), the 1,000th post-war Beetle was produced in March of 1946.

In fact, the Beetle in the form we know and love very nearly failed to appear, because those motor manufacturing company bosses who were offered the car turned it down in what many will nowadays perceive as a sadly typical display of British motor industry business acumen. Henry Ford was reputedly also offered the Volkswagen plant and Beetle, turning the offer down because the site was too near to the Russian border.

Finally a German management team, headed by Heinz Nordhoff, was assembled during the latter part of 1947, and in 1949 the factory was handed over to the regional government of Saxony.

By 1947, production was up to 2,500 cars per month, and the factory slowly gained momentum until in 1950 the company celebrated completing the 100,000th Beetle. Thereafter, production accelerated, and the one millionth Beetle milestone took only another five years to achieve. It is easy to gloss over this landmark without recognising its significance; in the mid-fifties, the total production figures of most cars were limited to a few thousands while a small number of runs reached the tens of thousands. Only a few particularly successful cars went on to reach hundreds of thousands. Million-sellers were as rare as hen's teeth. If ever a company could be stated to have risen phoenix-like from the ashes it was surely Volkswagen during the 1950s.

Despite attempts by the British Society of Motor Manufacturers and Traders to prevent Beetle exports (the car must by now have been seen as a serious threat to previously complacent UK manufacturers), exports began. The Beetle was not introduced to the UK until 1953 (fitted with a 1131cc engine, and until late 1953 characterised by a split rear window). Although over

500,000 of this version were manufactured. UK sales did not really begin in earnest until the following year with the introduction of the Type 1 (1200). Sold in both Standard and Deluxe versions, this model was fitted with an enlarged 1192cc engine which delivered 30 bhp. The new model featured vacuum ignition advance and improved cooling for the cylinder head. In total, over seven million examples of the 1200 Standard and Deluxe were to be sold world-wide.

In 1955, the first Karmann Cabriolet was offered on the UK market, four years after its introduction elsewhere. The following year, the exhaust system was altered to the now-familiar twin tail pipe set-up and the cars offered relative luxury with adjustable front seat backs. The battery capacity was increased to 66 amp hours and, along with interior cosmetic improvements, the bumper had over-riders.

In 1957, tubeless tyres were fitted in place of crossply. The following year, the front and rear screens were enlarged and larger drum brakes were fitted. In 1959, the chassis was strengthened, and in the following two years, the Beetle saw a host of improvements and modifications. In 1960, a front anti-roll mechanism was fitted, along with external door push buttons, and the generator output was increased. In 1962, the engine power was boosted to 34 bhp by increasing the compression ratio. An automatic choke and a windscreen washer were fitted. The fuel tank was altered. The Deluxe even had an all-synchromesh gearbox. In 1964, a folding rear seat appeared, and the Beetle became available in a new range of colours.

In 1965, the 1200A was introduced. The size of windscreens front and rear was increased. Late that year, the 1300 was introduced; basically this was a 1200 but fitted with a 1285cc, 40 bhp engine. Production of the 1300 was to run to some 2.7 million cars. The following year, a convertible became available for a short time, while in 1967 the 1200A acquired a reserve fuel tank and the 1300 rear suspension was altered to give a wider track. Late in the year, the 1500 was introduced with a 1493cc engine delivering 44 bhp. In its four years of production, some 1,800,000 1500s were manufactured.

In 1968, the 1200 gained fully independent suspension, some cosmetic improvements and an external fuel cap. The 1300 made the switch from 6 volt to 12 volt electrics, had dual circuit braking and a fuel gauge. The 1500 shared these improvements and had carburettor modifications. In 1969, the 1200 also received 12 volt electrics, plus hazard warning lights and a locking fuel cap. In addition, the 1300 came with a semi-automatic gearbox and radial ply tyres. The 1500 also acquired a steering column lock.

As the 1970s dawned, the 1200 received a modified carburettor and dual circuit braking, plus new style glass and the 1500 was discontinued. In 1971, the 1200 gained a larger windscreen while the 1300 also received greater power and was fitted with larger brakes. The 1600 Super was introduced late in '71 as the 1302S, fitted with the 1584cc unit. This car was the first to feature the new diagonal rear suspension, with double jointed drive shafts, and a McPherson strut front suspension. It also had front disc brakes. The following year, the 1200 gained a larger rear window. The 1300 and 1302S were fitted with an electronic diagnostic socket, but both 1300 models were discontinued in late '72. One point of especial note was that in 1972 the Beetle took the all-time car production record (15,007,034) from the Model T Ford, and this was celebrated with a limited edition 'World Champion' version.

In 1973, the gear lever and handbrake levers were re-positioned. The 1300A was introduced as an economy version, and was basically a 1200 car with 1300 engine. The 1303 (1285cc) and 1303S (1584cc) were introduced with the same basic bodyshell as the 1302S, but with a curved windscreen. The rear wings were enlarged, and disc brakes were fitted at the front end of the 1303S. The gear ratios were altered. A special Limited Edition GT Beetle was sold with a 1584cc engine.

In 1975, the 1303 and 1303S were fitted with rack and pinion steering, but in the same year, UK imports of both versions ceased. The following year, the 1200 became the 1200L. The extra De-luxe features were all in the interior of the car. In 1977, a convertible version of the 1303 made by Karmann was sold as the 1303 LS, and appears to have been imported into the UK until 1979. Sales to the UK of saloons ceased in 1977. European production of the saloon continued to 1978, and of the cabriolet until 1980.

But of course, production of the Beetle did not cease, but was merely transferred to other countries; Peru, Nigeria, Brazil, the Philippines and Mexico. In its place, Volkswagen offered the ill-fated K70 series for a short period before hitting gold again with the amazingly successful Golf series.

At the time of writing, the Beetle is still being manufactured in Mexico at the rate of 450 a day, and is in fact that country's best-selling car! In June of 1992, the twenty-one millionth Beetle rolled off the Mexican production line – a fact which was met with a resounding wave of indifference by at least the British motoring press. Perhaps this lack of recognition is not so surprising when you consider that the Beetle overtook the all-time production record (Model T Ford) twenty years previously, and that every single Beetle manufactured after that time sets a new production record!

The record is almost certainly unassailable now, because all manufacturers change their models substantially every few years, whereas the Beetle has been made in more or less the same form over 47 years' continuous production.

The Beetle has now returned to the shores of the UK with Mexican cars being imported in small numbers to sell to enthusiasts who want a new car, but a new car with more character than the efficient but often bland 1990s offerings. A convertible is also available (Bieber Cabriolet), giving the enthusiast the opportunity to acquire – at a far lower price than the likes of the Escort or Golf convertibles – a brand-new open four seater with bags of character but without any of the drawbacks inherent in running a classic.

During the latter part of 1993, rumours starting flying around the VW world that the company intended to import Mexican-built Beetles into Europe. So 'hot' was this news that it featured widely in the press.

Unfortunately, the rumours were repeatedly quashed by VW. Modern EEC legislation requires all new cars sold in Europe to be fitted with catalytic converters and to undergo ever-more rigorous crash and other testing – VW are not likely to wish to subject the Beetle to all that and sadly, it seems that the only way to obtain a brand-new Beetle will continue to be via personal import from Brazil or Mexico or by buying a Beetle from one of the few companies which do import small numbers. More 'The Beetle is Back!' type headlines appeared in 1994, but the concept car to which they referred had so little in common with the Beetle that the story was, like so many, without any real substance.

LIVING WITH A BEETLE

The first thing you tend to notice when driving a Beetle is that you have become enrolled – automatically – into the great and very friendly family of Beetle enthusiasts. The driver of virtually every other Beetle you see on the roads will acknowledge you with a wave or by a flash of the headlights. This camaraderie extends to drivers of other air-cooled Volkswagens; the drivers of Karmann Ghias, campers and vans. Type 3s and 4s will also almost universally acknowledge you. Before long you find yourself being drawn into the spirit of things, and you begin to wave back without conscious effort.

If you were unfortunate enough to suffer a roadside breakdown, it would be almost unthinkable for another driver of an air cooled VW to pass by without stopping to offer you assistance. Likewise, you will find that you will feel somehow under an unofficial obligation to stop and help if you see a fellow air-cooled VW driver in difficulties.

Something else you notice on your first Beetle drive is that it is fun. Cars today are smooth, quiet and have free-revving engines; the Beetle offers none of those qualities which modern drivers deem so essential, yet driving along with that torquey flat four chugging away in the 'boot' and making its presence felt in the passenger compartment both in vibration and decibels is actually a refreshing experience.

In these days of lean-burn engines and catalytic converters, some environmentally aware types might look upon the Beetle with some concern. The fuel consumption is hardly frugal by today's standards and the pollution from the average Beetle exhaust is higher than environmentalists would like. Yet in reality the Beetle is both economical and surprisingly 'green'.

The economy stems from the fact that, compared to almost any recent vehicle, the Beetle (new imported cars excepted) is essentially a non-depreciating car, so that, irrespective of fuel consumption, repair and other costs, Beetle ownership over a period of years is relatively cheap. For the price of two or three years' depreciation on a new modern family saloon car, you can buy and run a Beetle. For the price of five years' depreciation on the modern car, you should be able to buy, restore and run a Beetle and, after the five years are up, the modern car will have depreciated to the point at which it is practically worthless but the Beetle will still probably be worth a fair percentage of its purchase price and restoration costs.

The Beetle is also far more user-repairable than most, if not all, more recent cars; a fact which the DIY-inclined owner can use to bring down servicing and repair costs dramatically. Apart from any other consideration, all new cars sold on the UK market from January 1993 must be fitted with catalytic converters, which effectively means that the simple and easily repaired carburettor will probably be supplanted by sophisticated and anything but user-repairable fuel injection. The flat four engine can be removed in a fraction of the time it takes to remove the engines of most other cars (it takes minutes instead of hours), and the engine can be test-run on any suitable flat, hard surface before it is placed back in the car.

The car is ecologically 'friendlier' than many would have you believe. Most Beetles enjoy longer working lives than the average car, many out-lasting ordinary cars by a factor of two, three or even more. Since 40 per cent of the energy consumed by a vehicle occurs during its manufacture, the saving in pollution is obvious – catalytic converters and fuel consumption notwithstanding. In fact ecologists are slowly awakening to the idea that all cars should be manufactured to enjoy longer working lives in the interests of reduced pollution.

The Beetle can be a very reliable car, simply because

All Beetle interiors are spartan compared with those of modern cars, hardly surprising considering the age of the 'People's Car,' original design.

there is less to go wrong with it. The fact that the engine is cooled by air means that there will be none of the problems with cracked engine blocks and cylinder heads in cold weather due to the expansion of frozen liquid coolant, with leaking radiators and hoses or with non-functioning water pumps – all of which can afflict liquid-cooled engines and wreck some of them in a very short space of time.

Compare the Beetle with the average modern car. The modern car has by law to be fitted with a catalytic converter and hence normally fuel injection, and they also have to be fitted with electronic 'brains' (the dreaded Engine Control Units) which meter out the fuel precisely in order to avoid damaging the catalytic converter. All of this technology should pose no problems when the car is new, but when it is a few years old then each extra component represents something else which is likely to go wrong and cause a breakdown. Those electronic components will probably in many instances prove to be the most fault-prone parts of the modern car.

What is perhaps worse is that the mechanic is no longer dealing with repairable components, but is very often faced with sealed units or electronic components which are so hopelessly sophisticated that it takes a degree in computer science in order to understand how they function. In other words, problems within some of these units can only be dealt with by straight (and expensive) replacement. This increases repair costs but more importantly it means that a modern car which breaks down miles from anywhere due to a problem with one of its electronics systems cannot be repaired there and then. It must either be towed away or stay where it is until the necessary component can be sourced and transported to it. The Beetle is so simple that most roadside breakdowns can be dealt with there and then without need of special equipment beyond a normal motorist's tool kit.

Driving the Beetle

Driving a Beetle is very different from driving a more recent car. The seemingly lazy, slow revving engine which lacks straight bhp in fact delivers sufficient torque to get, and keep you, on the move without ever breaking into a sweat and, although the nought to sixty mph times are anything but impressive, the torque always seems to be there when you need it for overtaking. Ignore the speedometer reading at your peril; the slow engine revolutions are deceptive and can lull inexperienced Beetle drivers into driving far more quickly than they suspect.

The interiors of all Beetles are spartan in comparison with most modern cars. The seat bases are passably comfortable but the seat backs lack proper support, most noticeable when cornering. Instrumentation is kept to a bare minimum, displaying the speed and fuel tank contents but not the revs, oil pressure or engine temperature. Quite in keeping for a car which revels in being an anachronism in its own lifetime! Driver visibility is generally excellent, although all four wings are hidden from view, which perhaps explains the high numbers of town Beetles with dented wings!

The unnecessarily huge steering wheel coupled with the massive rear weight bias of the car makes the steering so light – even when manoeuvring at car park speed – that you could be forgiven for wondering whether Ferdinand Porsche cunningly hid a power steering pump within the steering box. Put a few too many psi in the front tyres, though, and the car feels as though the dampers at the front have failed; the eccentric bush-induced understeer is also increased which, coupled with the bouncing of the front end, can make cornering a little too exciting.

Correctly shod and with no weak points in the suspension and especially the dampers, Beetles can go around tight corners at considerable speed as sure-footedly as if they were – excuse the cliché – running on a pair of rails. Push the car a fraction too hard, though, and the rear end can break away into massive oversteer or in extreme cases a spin so quick and vicious that even the most experienced drivers can have trouble gaining control of the car.

The problem is one of weight distribution. Having the weight of the transaxle and engine over the rear wheels gives plenty of traction to get you moving on slippery surfaces, but when centrifugal forces become great enough during hard cornering, this mass possesses great potential energy which makes its presence felt the moment the rear wheels lose traction. Few people, though, ever drive so close to the limit for this – the so-called 'dumbbell effect' – to be a problem.

Swing axle cars are more prone to snap into oversteer than more recent semi-trailing arm cars because their rear wheels suffer constantly variable camber. Unlike the later Beetles which had universal joints at either end of their drive shafts, early 'swing axle' car drive shafts possessed only one UJ at the differential end. Because the transaxle which houses the differential rises and falls relative to the road (and thence the wheels) its angle alters that of the drive shafts and the hubs and wheels which were fixed to them. When the rear centre of gravity of these cars rises on a tight bend, the heavily loaded outside wheel develops a positive camber angle (which gives very poor grip). This rise in the centre of gravity is exacerbated if, for some reason, the driver lifts off the accelerator pedal – or worse, applies the brakes – part-way through the corner. When that happens at speed, the dumbbell effect is increased greatly.

Experienced Beetle drivers will be mindful of the potential dumbbell effect and will not rush headlong into blind corners which could conceal some obstacle which would force them to take avoiding action while the rear suspension was loaded.

The fact that the engine and gearbox of the Beetle are situated over the driving wheels brings one huge benefit; their weight gives those wheels great traction and hence the car excels when used on slippery surfaces and off-road. The Beetle will go where most other cars simply sit still and spin their driving wheels, and even the front-engined, front wheel drive car takes second place to the Beetle because, although its engine and

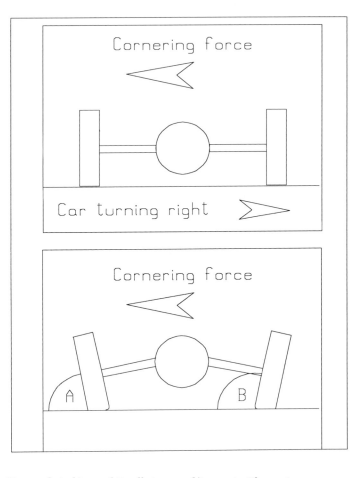

Transaxle jacking and its effect on road/tyre grip. The car is going around a right hand bend. When the transaxle lifts, the heavily loaded outer wheel develops positive camber 'A', whereas the lightly loaded inner wheel develops negative camber 'B'. Grip is greatly reduced.

gearbox might place weight over the driving wheels, the rearwards transfer of static mass which occurs when torque is applied to the wheels lessens their tyres' grip.

So, the Beetle is not especially rapid, comfortable nor well-behaved on the road when compared to modern cars; why then, do Beetle drivers gain more pleasure from driving their cars than those in more recent or more exotic machinery? The answer is simply that the Beetle driver can enjoy the Beetle experience. He or she wants to savour the sensations which only the Beetle can provide.

2 · BUYING A BEETLE

Because there are so many Beetles in existence, buying one is blindingly easy. Buying a good one is not. Although time-proven as a rugged and long-lived car, many examples (especially the older ones) will be suffering from advanced, often camouflaged, bodyrot or serious mechanical problems which render them unsafe for road use. Sometimes cars with dangerous bodyrot are sold honestly at low prices as 'restoration project' cars, but quite often the problems are hastily and shoddily covered up and the car sold dishonestly and sometimes at quite high prices as roadworthy. It can be difficult even for an experienced person to assess the true condition of a car with expertly camouflaged bodyrot, although mechanical problems are often self-evident, for example when they noticeably affect some aspect of the performance of the car, such as poor braking, road-holding or acceleration. Some mechanical faults, however, are less evident and demand an expert knowledge of the car and of how to properly appraise it.

Many of the Beetles which come onto the market may be advertised as restored and offered at an appropriately high price when in fact they have been incompetently repaired by a DIY enthusiast, or a back-street body shop. Price is no guarantee of quality. Many of the customised examples which are offered for sale may have been converted in a similarly slipshod manner, and even the best-looking and highest-priced of both restored and customised cars can actually be in poor condition. A few may even be death-traps.

Another pitfall awaits the unwary buyer: as the prices realised by Beetles continue to rise, the cars become more tempting targets for thieves who, using a variety of devices, fraudulently sell the cars on to honest buyers who will lose both their car and their money when the true identity of the car becomes known to the authorities.

So, despite the Beetle's exceptionally robust construction and reliability, finding a genuinely good example can be as problematic as finding a good example of any aged car.

WHICH BEETLE?

The first question to be addressed is which Beetle? The Beetle world appears to be split into two camps which might be summed up as the 'traditionalists' and the 'radicals' – both love the Beetle, but in different ways. The traditionalists like the Beetle just the way it is, and whilst some might view the whole subject of customisation as slightly *infra dig*, most will accept the custom enthusiast as a kindred spirit. The radicals favour one of the various schools of customisation, and might view the standard car as OK for those who like that sort of thing – but not for them.

The Beetle is all things to all men; some might require an honest, roadworthy and reasonably-priced example, demanding no more of it than reliable daily transport with a little more character than one finds in modern cars; others might seek an early car for restoration or customisation whilst yet another group may wish to by-pass the countless hours of hard labour which go into such projects and buy an already restored or customised example.

Amongst restored Beetles there is a choice between early and late, convertible or closed, original spec or mildly customised; amongst customised examples there are Cal lookers, Bajas, Beach Buggies and Rails, plus innumerable one-off specials – the range of available options is immense.

Restoration/re-shelling

If you seek a Beetle to be the basis of a restoration (or to re-shell or build up into a Buggy or other kit) then it will pay you to look for a particular type of car. This will be one with a predominance of excellent (recently replaced) mechanical components and good trim but with a shell/chassis which will be in need of some welding. Such cars usually come onto the UK market when they fail the MOT test on bodywork grounds, and they

ABOVE
Most restorers keep a small stock of project cars which they will have invariably have bought in at low prices and may be persuaded to sell at a small profit.

BELOW
This rot in the nearside doorstep (part of the heater channel/sill structure) is all too apparent, and proves beyond any doubt that new heater channels are needed. On some cars, rot like this will be camouflaged with GRP and/or body filler, so don't judge solely by appearances – use the magnet, probe with a sharp implement. This car would fail any roadworthiness test, yet if it has good mechanical components and only 'honest' bodyrot, it could make an excellent restoration project.

usually come very cheaply, even if the hapless vendor has recently spent much money renewing mechanical and electrical components. If the engine or gearbox is claimed to have been replaced recently, ask to see the invoice/receipt, to ensure that the reconditioning was carried out by a reputable company. The price paid for such a car should be a fraction of the sum of the costs of the new and usable components. The advertisements for these cars usually include the pitiful words 'some welding needed for MOT'.

If you intend to find a restoration car and repair its rotten bodyshell then be very careful when checking for previous collision damage. Restoring a straight bodyshell is usually within the capabilities of the enthusiastic amateur, but straightening out a bent one is most certainly the province of the professional. The Beetle spine chassis is particularly strong, although certain heavy collisions could cause mounting points for elements of the steering and suspension to be out of alignment – a front-end collision, for instance, can move the frame head and hence the majority of the suspension mounting points. This will make the handling and road-holding of the car unpredictable and in most cases will render the car unsafe and certainly unfit for use on the

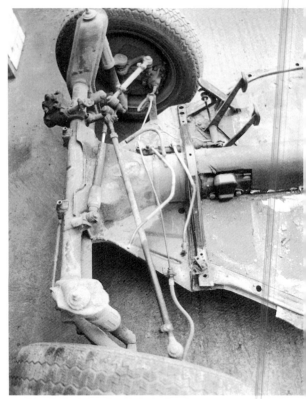

Forget it! This car is best considered a donor for a re-shell as far as the DIY restorer is concerned. Heavy frontal or rear collision can alter the positions of the sturdy chassis components which hold the suspension components. Unless you have a jig to ensure 100 per cent accurate rebuilding, a DIY restoration of such a car will probably be unroadworthy.

On torsion bar suspension cars, check the front beams for any signs of collision damage, because this can adversely affect the suspension geometry. You'll need to raise the front of the car and use a torch for illumination in order to see the beams. Another sure sign of front-end collision include corrugated flitch panels – turn the steering to full lock and take a look inside the front wings above and to the rear of the bumper mounts.

road. The costs of straightening out such a car would probably prove prohibitive, and a new chassis (floors and spine) might be the only option.

Whilst it is true to say that any car – no matter how badly the body has rotted – can be rebuilt, there is a degree of body and chassis rot which makes body restoration both uneconomic and so difficult that it is inadvisable to attempt a rebuild unless you have access to jigs to help align panels, a deep enough pocket to buy in a lot of quite expensive body repair and replacement panels. Such cars are best considered candidates for either re-shelling or conversion into one of the kit cars which come complete with their own chassis.

Check that the car has been maintained properly by examining the state of the oil, and checking whether the engine bay and engine ancillaries (especially the distributor cap and other elements of the ignition system) are covered in dirt or oil. A car on which maintenance has been skimped will furnish mainly dubious spares, and the last thing you want is a freshly

restored car which keeps breaking down whenever another component decides to fail. Engine oil plays an important role in preventing the engine from overheating. If a car has poor oil pressure or low oil level and has been run in that condition, then it will have run far too hot, and component wear will have been high.

If you want a quick and easy re-shell or kit car build-up, avoid cars which have been standing idle for any length of time. Many mechanical components appear to deteriorate more quickly when the car is left standing than they do if the car is kept in regular use. Another point against cars which have not run for some time is the likelihood that many of the nuts and bolts will have seized solid, making the initial strip-down far more difficult and frustrating than it need be and giving you no option but to cut, drill or grind away seized fittings, which must of course be replaced with new ones at mounting cost. Even worse, there is always the danger that whilst dealing with a recalcitrant fitting you will damage the associated component.

ABOVE
The rot in this car is extensive but no-one could have known just how bad the car was until the flitch panel had been cut out. This is approaching the limits of economic restoration, and cars in this sort of condition could best be considered as donors for other Beetles with better bodyshells.

RIGHT
This engine bay may look a little down at heel due to the poor condition of the pipes, but the fan belt was recent and correctly adjusted, the ignition components were in reasonable condition and the oil was clean – all pointing to a reasonably well looked-after engine.

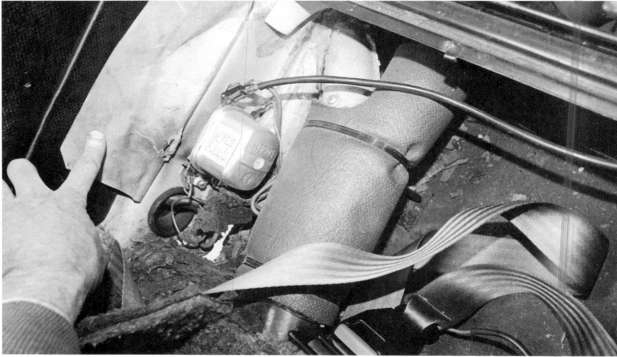

TOP

This – the author's car – may look like A Car To Be Avoided with obviously rotten sills, wings, jacking point and quarter panel, but at the right price it is a far better buy than an example which has been tarted-up. With a car like this, you can see exactly what you are getting, so there will be no nasty surprises part-way through the restoration!

ABOVE

Even more rot in the nearside heater channel and heelboard end on the author's car, but again this is honest rot. Many cars with this type of rot which are offered for sale will have extensive plating of such areas, camouflaged with lashings of body filler.

It is a good idea to seek a car which, although in poor bodily condition, is sound enough be used on the road for however short a period before the test certificate expires. Using the car on the road will help to highlight any looming mechanical problems which can then be dealt with at leisure during the restoration.

The very best Beetle for a restoration is one which, although it may have some bodyrot, has not previously been bodged. When the author asked the Beetle Specialist Workshop to keep an eye open for a Beetle for

himself, they managed to find a 1970 1500 (RVJ 403H – soon given the name 'Project') which had failed the MOT on bodywork but which had no previous evidence of bodywork repair excepting some body filler on external panels – a car which, in BSW workshop manager Terry Ball's own terminology, had 'not been got at'.

The rot on Project included the heater channel rear ends, sections of the floorpans, the rear body mounting points within the wheel arches and the rear bumper mounts. Plenty of rot – but honest rot. If you can find such a car then the restoration will be so much the easier.

The work-horse

If you seek a low-cost Beetle to put into immediate daily use, then the state of the mechanical and electrical components automatically assumes greater importance than it does in the case of the restoration car. If you were to buy an older car with a predominance of tired and worn components, then these would inevitably fail one by one at unpredictable intervals and the car would never prove reliable. The more recent the car, the better.

The best advice would be to concentrate on finding a low mileage recent car (1302, 1303 and S) which has a full service history (look for the letters FSH in advertisements), or one which has been owned for a long time by a competent and conscienscious DIY mechanic who has not skimped on regular servicing. Proper maintenance includes anticipating at what point in the near future various components are likely to give problems and replacing them before they fail. The vendors of such cars should be able to show you a series of invoices for spare parts (and labour charges if the maintenance has been carried out professionally) to prove that the car has been properly cared for.

The state of the bodywork in such cars is even more important than that of the mechanical components because, whilst a mechanical fault can mean taking the car off the road for perhaps one or two days whilst the fault is rectified, the rectification of bodyrot entails taking the car off the road for far longer – sometimes weeks, sometimes months, if the work has to be carried out on a DIY basis.

Most Beetles are now old enough to have received some degree of bodywork repair and you should assume that a viewed car will have had, or will soon require, such work. As with any other Beetle, you must be vigilant when looking for camouflaged bodyrot and poor repair.

It is advisable to accept from the outset that you are increasingly unlikely to be able to obtain a solid and reliable Beetle cheaply. The vendors of such cars will bear the maintenance plus any repair, new component or bodywork costs in mind when setting the price. In the long run, it is usually cheaper to pay a fair price for a good car than it is to buy the cheapest you can find and suffer a constant stream of repair bills when it breaks down.

Avoid cars which have been off the road for any length of time because as previously stated most mechanical, hydraulic and electrical components

actually age far less when the car is in regular use than they do if the car is left standing idle. Also best avoided are cars on which the vendor has recently spent a lot of money in mechanical repair; this indicates that a majority of components have reached the end of their useful life and hence that components not repaired or replaced recently will also need attention.

Most large motoring associations will – for a fee – undertake mechanical and body surveys on cars on behalf of members. Motor engineers usually offer the same service. Both will furnish you with a written report on the state of a viewed car and, if you are not confident in your own ability to properly assess the condition of cars then the fee involved in commissioning such a survey could repay itself many times over.

Be wary of cars with brand-new test certificates: some – by no means all – of these cars may have had a minimal amount of work carried out so that they can scrape through the test (which makes them easier to sell) but they could be on the market because either they are unreliable or because the owner wishes to avoid looming repair bills.

Several companies in the UK sell Beetles which they have 'sorted' the mechanics of in-house, and these usually come with a guarantee and can be safe buys. Other companies sell Beetles which they have fully restored and these, too, are a good option for those who want a reliable car. In both cases it pays to deal with companies which are situated fairly close to your home; you don't want to have to drive (or trailer) the car for miles if you have problems with it.

Restored cars

A good quality professional Beetle restoration will generally cost the owner more than the resultant value of the car. A full and conscientious DIY restoration not only costs a lot of money, it usually involves thousands of hours of work – not all of it pleasurable. It is little wonder that many would-be Beetle owners seek a ready-restored car, nor that the vendors of good restored cars very often set high prices.

The first fact to face is that you will not be able to buy a good restored car cheaply. If a restored car is offered at a low price then this in itself should arouse suspicion regarding the quality of workmanship and/or the extent of the restoration work – not to mention the possibility that the car could be stolen. Apart from the vendor's natural desire to recoup as much of the financial outlay involved in the restoration as possible, a genuinely good restored car will usually attract other potential purchasers, one of whom may want the car badly enough to try and outbid you.

You should also face the fact that a high price is no guarantee of quality, and that a number of 'bodged' cars will inevitably come to the market place dressed-up as restorations and priced accordingly.

Both with professional and amateur restorers it is now almost universal practice to keep a full photographic record of the work in progress, and it is recommended that you do not buy a 'restored' car unless you can see such a record (and satisfy yourself that the car pictured is the car you are buying).

Because there is usually so much money at stake when you are buying a restored car, it may be worth commissioning a Motor Engineer's survey before parting with your money. Alternatively, take along a knowledgeable friend when you view cars – if you don't have a knowledgeable friend then join the nearest Beetle owner's club and quickly make friends with the most knowledgeable person you meet there!

In addition to the points made in this chapter about assessing cars, there are a few extra checks to be made in the case of restored cars. A restoration basically comprises two parts; the bodywork and the mechanical elements. It is common for people commissioning a professional restoration to have the body restoration work carried out professionally, but to undertake the mechanical build-up themselves. It is vital that you attend to small details when examining the mechanical components and, more particularly, their fastenings. Look at the screw slots, the nuts and bolt heads. If the screw slots are distorted, if nuts and bolt heads are rounded, then the person who carried out the rebuild obviously did not possess a very good set of tools, and the state of the fastenings could well be reflected in more important, hidden areas.

Irrespective of whether the bodyshell restoration was carried out professionally or at home, it goes without saying that your inspection should be thorough. Rather than try to assess the body inch by inch, concentrate on the areas where repair panels (as opposed to full body panels) are commonly used. There is nothing wrong with the use of repair panels, but some people will try to weld them to existing metal which has thinned through rusting (and which will therefore be weak and/or will rust completely through in the fullness of time) instead of replacing the entire affected panel. Where you do find welded joints, assess them, and look for pores, poor penetration and the usual welded joint faults. (See Chapter Five).

Welded joints on external panels are usually well finished and should be invisible, so whenever possible, try to get a look at the inside of the seam. If you find rust there, then expect all repaired welded seams on the car to rust out before too long.

Customised cars

There is such a wide range of off-the-shelf customisations for Beetles that it is difficult to give advice which is strictly relevant to all types. The main concern must be the build quality (because many such cars are built by amateurs), not only of the bodywork but especially of fuel, brake, engine and electrical components. Bear in mind that these are all possible causes of fires, which are even more serious with GRP-bodied cars than with steel cars.

All Beetle-based kit cars fall into two basic groups. Some utilise the Beetle spine/floorpan assembly and others are built up onto a special chassis. When assessing the former, always pay special attention to the spine/floorpan assembly – it could have started to rot even before the kit body was bolted on, or in the case of a shortened chassis (Beach Buggy) the welding could be of a very low standard and the chassis spine consequently weak. The author has seen shortened chassis/floorpans on Buggies which appear to have been crudely 'stick'

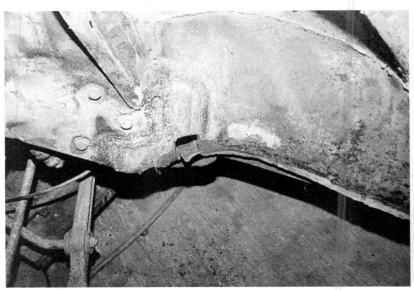

This flitch panel on a McPherson Strut Beetle has an obvious repair to the front end. What might not be quite so apparent is what lies underneath.

(Arc) welded, and which still showed evidence of burning through – the inappropriate welder burns holes through the steel which it is meant to be joining!

Begin by visiting a large Beetle gathering, so that you can see the various customs in the flesh and make a proper decision regarding which best suits your needs. This will also allow you to see both good and bad examples of the build quality of the custom, and enable you to quickly decide whether any car which you subsequently view is a badly or well-built example. Talk to the owners of any customs which take your fancy, because they will be able to give you valuable information on what specifically to look for when assessing the cars.

When viewing a customised car, be it a kit or a one-off special, try to establish whether the car meets all legal requirements, bearing in mind that in some countries these include the positioning of lights, number plates etc. Also, check the car over for anything which might cause it to fail the government roadworthiness test (MOT test in the UK), which can include any projections which the tester feels might pose a hazard to other road users or pedestrians, moving parts which are exposed or an insecure battery etc.

The available selection of any single type of custom Beetle is a fraction of that of standard cars, and the pressure to buy a viewed example 'before someone else gets it' is therefore stronger. Don't rush into a purchase because to do so is nearly always a mistake. If you have any cause for doubts about a viewed car and the vendor begins to get pushy to try and hasten you into a buying decision, leave the car alone and console yourself with the thoughts that you could probably build a better one yourself, there will probably be a better example available next week and pushy vendors want you to buy before you find the fault which lead to the car's being placed on the market!

Quite a few customised Beetles come onto the market

as un-finished projects. This can arise for a variety of reasons, and it is important to establish which. Many people simply run out of money before they complete the car, something which is a familiar occurrence in the kit car world, where those essential items which are sometimes listed by the kit manufacturers as 'optional extras' can add up to rather more than the cost of the kit and lead to financial embarrassment for the builder. Some unfinished projects are due to a lack of time to complete the build, others due to a lack of motivation to see the job through.

All of the above, perfectly plausible, pretexts for selling an unfinished project custom or Beetle-based kit could be given as a cover-up for a more sinister reason – the knowledge that the work done to date is in some indeterminate way inferior, or the fact that the kit or custom is based on a weak chassis.

When viewing an unfinished project custom car, you really have to be very careful when assessing the build quality of the job to date. Check the floorpan (and any standard body panels which have been retained) for rot and even for light rusting. Check any GRP panels for signs of damage and/or repair, because someone might have accidentally dropped something onto one.

Buying an unfinished project can save a lot of money in comparison with completing a build-up yourself, but it can also lead to heartache, so tread carefully.

In the case of kit cars, you might also care to obtain the manufacturer's build manual (most will sell this separately) in order to familiarise yourself with the kit and the way in which it is built. This should help you to properly appraise built examples.

Convertibles

Convertible Beetles come in three varieties; Karmann originals, professional conversions and DIY jobs.

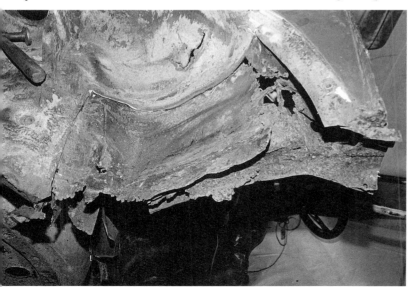

With the 'repair' panel cut away, the original flitch can be seen rotting happily away underneath, from which position of security, it can accelerate rot in the cover plate. The only real solution to this state of affairs is to weld on a new flitch – the complete panel – not recommended for beginners.

Karmann convertibles are always towards the very top end of the Beetle price range, so expect to have to pay a lot for one and assess the car as carefully as you can for the usual signs of accident damage and corrosion. Do check for authenticity, because there is money to be made from dressing up a DIY conversion as a Karmann original and selling it at a high price.

There are many companies which offer a professional conversion service for the standard Beetle and, whilst cars converted in this way will not be so expensive or exclusive as a Karmann, they offer exactly the same function at a far lower price. Because the roof panels of saloon cars generally contribute greatly to the strength and rigidity of the cars, it is vital that any saloon which is made into a convertible receives some extra strengthening. In the case of a Beetle, the immensely strong chassis/floorpan assembly arguably lessens the need for extra strengthening, but the author would recommend that widely available strengthening members are welded to the sill assembly and to the A post (to prevent scuttle shake). Professional conversion companies should do this as a matter of course, but it pays to check. The strength offered by the sill/heater channel assembly of converted cars is of the greatest importance in preventing the bodyshell from twisting, and so this area should be assessed very thoroughly.

Most DIY saloon to open top conversions will be based on a commercially manufactured kit. If you are looking for a car which is based on a particular kit then a visit to one of the larger Beetle events will enable you to talk to existing owners of converted cars and to learn enough about them to be able to assess the build quality. If you are thinking of buying any home-built convertible then the first thing you should ask is whether it is based on a kit and, if so, which? Treat non-kit DIY conversions with caution.

'Lookers'

By definition, a 'looker' will have a very smart external appearance, and some might appear to have an almost perfect finish both outside and in. Irrespective of the sumptuousness and quality of the interior and the deepness of the gloss of the paintwork, such cars can in fact be heavily bodged examples of basically rotten bodyshells. Because the cars look so good, the asking price, and therefore the stakes, are high. Try to ignore the flash and get down to the basics – give the car the most thorough bodywork and mechanical examination.

Check that beautiful bodywork with a magnet to discover whether it is steel or GRP and body filler! There is nothing wrong with the use of body filler, but if the magnet shows no attraction whatever to a panel then this tells you that the thickness of the filler is so great that the car has been bodged and the filler is likely to drop out at some time in the future because so great a thickness cannot flex with the panel.

The price asked for a looker which has a lot of expensive accessories will sometimes reflect the costs of those accessories, but there is generally no need to pay anything like such a high price. Apart from the very finest exceptions, the values realised by any non-standard Beetles rarely exceed and sometimes fall far below the value of a standard car in similar condition.

There is always a wide selection of custom Beetles offered for sale in the UK, and so there is no artificial pressure for you to hurry when making a buying decision.

Bajas

Because Bajas consist of the basic Beetle bodywork with sundry GRP bolt-on and bonded panels which contribute nothing to the strength of the body as a whole, the cars' body/chassis can be appraised using exactly the same routines as for a standard Beetle. The main point to bear in mind when looking for a Baja is that some – by no means all – will have seen some fairly heavy duty off-road use, and the worst of these could have camouflaged underbody/steering/suspension damage, in addition to which, breathing in dust-laden air will have done nothing for the engine unless good air filters were fitted. Check for off-road damage (including camouflaged damage to the roof and pillars which results if the car is rolled and, of course, damage to the floorpans, frame head, suspension and steering) and, because it is nigh-on impossible to clean all traces of fine dirt from a car, check for traces of this in nooks and crannies. Most Bajas are probably – like all off-road vehicles – never used other than on tarmac, and it is better to select such a car than one which has seen use in the rough. There is a good selection of cars with this popular modification, so don't be rushed into buying.

Because the Baja is usually raised to increase ground clearance, the effects of transaxle jacking on single-joint drive shaft cars are exaggerated, and the presence of a 'camber control' device should be reassuring! The so-called 'Z' bar fitted to the 1500cc Beetle is not, as widely supposed, an anti-roll bar nor is it an 'equaliser' (as the author has seen it erroneously described). The Z bar only acts when the transaxle tries to lift itself from the axle shafts and, as such, it is an anti-jacking device. The 1500cc Beetle is a good candidate for the Baja conversion because of this.

Be especially careful when assessing a Baja for road legality. In particular and with regard to the UK MOT roadworthiness test, the wheels must not protrude beyond the wheel arches and no moving part of the engine should be exposed.

WHERE TO LOOK

When you have decided which variety of Beetle you desire, the problem arises of where to begin looking for your dream car, who to buy it from and roughly how much to pay. Beetles are, of course, widely advertised in national magazines, and this might at first sight appear as good a place as any to begin your search. Unfortunately, because such magazines are distributed nationally, they attract advertisements from all over the country. If you are in the market for a comparatively rare original UK RHD Karmann convertible then the national press might offer the best (perhaps the only) solution because it will be the only place where you can find a reasonable selection to choose from, but if you seek one of the more common variants then you might as well begin looking nearer home, and with good reason.

Vendors of Beetles often arrive at their asking prices by following one of the published 'classic car value guides' in a classic car magazine (although some are misguided by agreed value insurance figures – more on this later). These can cause the buyer certain problems. Firstly, the guides often differ from each other in the values they ascribe to particular cars (the author has seen two guides which were published at the same time give one valuation of 50 per cent more than the other for the same car!) and secondly, they generally value the cars as belonging to one of three groups according to their condition. Group '1' or 'A' usually refers to very clean and original cars with little or no rust and reliable mechanical and electrical components (but not pristine concourse winners). Group '2' or 'B' usually refers to cars which run and possess the relevant certificate of roadworthiness (the MOT certificate in the UK) but which would benefit from a certain amount of mild mechanical repair and/or a small amount of bodywork attention. Group '3' or 'C' cars are described as those which may or may not be runners and may or may not possess a current certificate of roadworthiness, but which do require fairly extensive mechanical and body repair to make them really usable.

Problems arise because a vendor often wrongly assumes that his or her group 3 or C car is actually a group 2/B, and asks the appropriate price as indicated in a value guide. It will not be until you come to actually examine the car that the mistake, or sometimes the deliberate misrepresentation, will come to light. This is

not too annoying if you have travelled only a short distance to view the car, but following a long and totally wasted drive it can be infuriating.

If you are looking for a reasonably prolific Beetle variant then you will save much time, money and temper by only travelling to view cars situated fairly close to your home. In this case it is best to confine your search initially to local newspapers and other publications. Word of mouth is also an excellent way of finding a local car, because one of the people you inform that you want a Beetle might just know where one is available. Going out and finding a Beetle before it is advertised for sale also brings the benefit of allowing you to make an offer for the car without having other potential buyers hovering in the background ready to outbid you, which can often happen if you and they both answer an advertisement and turn up for a viewing at the same time.

Another advantage of viewing locally rather than in the national media is that many of the cars you see advertised will not be owned by Beetle enthusiasts, and the prices asked can sometimes be far more reasonable, because the non-enthusiast does not always attach any special 'classic' or other value to his or her Beetle; to such people, their Beetle is simply a car – not a classic, not a cult car.

In the UK, regional advertisement-only publications which specialise in used cars offer other useful media to study. These usually feature far more Beetles than local media, giving a far better selection at the cost of having to travel further within the region to view likely cars.

Instead of viewing advertisements for Beetles, you could always place a 'wanted' advert yourself, and this should generate a selection of available cars for you to choose from. The greatest benefit of placing a 'wanted' advert is that you will often attract responses from people who would not advertise their Beetle for sale but who would instead part-exchange the car or perhaps sell it to a relative or friend. You may also attract responses from people who were not previously thinking of selling their Beetle – in both cases, you alone will be viewing the car and there will not be the possibility of other potential buyers appearing on the scene to outbid you.

The author has noticed general pricing trends applying to cars according to which media they are advertised in. National magazine advertised cars tend towards the top end of their expected price range, especially cars which are advertised in the more 'up-market' magazines which have pages full of advertisements for affordable classic cars yet glossy editorial features on Ferraris and pre-war blown Bentleys. There are some 'man in the street' type classic magazines which seek to assure readers that their own car is a classic (and that therefore they should continue to buy the magazine), and the advertisements in these tend to feature less extravagantly priced cars. The UK Beetle/VW press appears at the time of writing to include the widest selection of sensibly priced cars, and is probably the best national shop window.

The prices asked for cars in regional advertisement-only publications, in common with local newspapers, are in general realistic, although the occasional silly price creeps in from time to time.

If you wish to see the very largest selection of Beetles for sale then visit one of the larger Beetle shows which are held throughout the summer months. Rather than having just a photograph by which to judge the car before embarking on a buying expedition, you have the cars there in the flesh. Don't, incidentally, hand over money at the show (unless you are buying from a known bona-fide dealer), but arrange to visit the vendor and carry out the transaction at his or her own house. The reasons for this advice will become clear later in this chapter.

There are five sources of Beetles. 1. The vast majority of Beetles which are bought and sold pass from one private vendor to another. 2. An increasing number of Beetles are sold by dealers who specialise in classic cars, a particular marque or preferably a particular model. 3. Relatively few Beetles nowadays find their way on to general car dealers' pitches. 4. The Classic Car auction is a relatively modern but growing phenomenon at which more and more classic cars seem to be traded. 5. General motor auctions very occasionally have a good Beetle.

Each potential source of Beetles has points both in and against its favour, and each will be briefly discussed in the order in which they appear above.

Private sale

The private vendor is often sought out by potential buyers because it is assumed that the prices involved in a private transaction will always be lower than those asked by dealers. Not necessarily so, for a variety of reasons. Many vendors, misinterpreting (genuinely or otherwise) classic car value guides or insurance agreed values, ascribe ridiculously high values to their cars. Many vendors are loathe to sell their beloved Beetles but are forced to by financial circumstances beyond their control and such people are prone to add a degree of 'sentimental' value to the actual value of the car when arriving at an asking price. Some private vendors are simply avaricious and are prepared to keep their Beetles on the market until they find a buyer foolish enough to pay their inflated asking prices.

Buying from a private vendor can sometimes result

in your getting a bargain, but the practice does carry huge risks. Private vendors of many products, certainly within the UK, are not subject to the stringent consumer protection laws by which a business selling the same item would have to abide. In the case of a privately sold motor vehicle it is still (at the time of writing) an offence to misrepresent it, but unless the misrepresentation has been published in an advertisement then there is no proof of any such offence. If the vendor gives you a verbal rather than a written assurance that the bodywork is sound yet the car breaks its back on the first hump back bridge you drive it over then you won't be able to claim that the car was misrepresented. It is, however, an offence in the UK to sell a motor vehicle which is in a dangerous, unroadworthy condition, but unless you can prove that the car in question was unroadworthy at the actual time of purchase then it is very difficult to take any action against the vendor.

A private vendor will usually assume that, once money has changed hands and the car is your property and you have driven it away, he or she has no further liability for the car. If you put your foot through the floor the first time you use the brakes then you may have great difficulty in gaining any form of redress without resorting to the legal system.

Beetles are now extremely tempting targets for thieves. Not only do the cars command attractive prices and usually find a ready market, but even broken down for spares they are worth real money. Most of the classic cars which are stolen and subsequently offered for sale (certainly in the UK) appear to be the subject of a type of organised crime called 'ringing'. In this, a car of a specific year and colour is stolen. In order to sell the car, the thief has to give it a new identity, which he can do in one of two ways. Firstly, he can take the registration document and number, engine and any other identification numbers of a scrapped example of the vehicle and merely replace the various identification plates on the stolen car (the 'ringer'). Secondly, he can apply for a duplicate registration document for an existing and perfectly legitimate example of the car (usually one which lives many miles away from the scene of the sale), then buy number plates and other identification plates to create another seemingly legitimate example.

Ringing is far more likely to be encountered with later cars in most of the Beetle's markets, because there are so many still in circulation that finding a ringer of a particular year and colour is not too difficult. Of course, with the prices of all Beetles likely to continue rising there could come a day when it would be financially attractive for a thief to go to the trouble of respraying a ringer (if he was unable to steal one in the right colour) to match the seemingly 'legitimate' documentation he possessed but, at the time of writing, the values of most Beetles are at such a level that this does not appear to be happening to any great extent.

Your best guard against buying a ringer is to ask to see not only the previous receipt of purchase but also a current or the last tax disc, test certificate and insurance document pertaining to the vehicle and owner respectively. A vendor who cannot immediately supply all of these for your perusal has obviously not used the vehicle in question for some considerable time, or he or she may never have run it at all if it is a ringer.

Perhaps the safest private vendor to buy from would be a member of a local Beetle club or a local branch of a national Volkswagen Owners' club. The enthusiasts who make up these clubs will often have already verified that the car was legitimate when they bought it. Alternatively, few thieves would risk advertising in club literature, so that cars offered for sale through advertisements in club magazines should also, in theory, be safer buys.

To summarise, buying from a private vendor rarely results in acquiring a car at a bargain price, and it can prove risky.

Specialist dealers

There are certain to be a few rogues amongst specialist Beetle dealers just as there are in any other trade or calling, although the dubious specialist car dealer is usually fairly easy to identify. A good dealer will have repair and possibly restoration facilities with which he can honour the terms of whatever guarantee he gives. A dubious dealer will not. A good dealer will usually have a proper premises whilst a dubious dealer will often be found operating from a barn or sometimes from a small lock-up or even his own front room.

A good dealer will usually specialise in a particular marque, model or type of car which he knows well enough to properly appraise, whilst a dubious dealer will take anything which comes his way. Without specialist knowledge, he will be vulnerable to being sold poorly restored cars, fakes and unroadworthy cars. A good dealer will avoid such cars, because he knows that to sell just one such vehicle on to a customer could cost him his reputation.

It is important to establish whether a dealer is honest and reputable. You also require the certainty of a worthwhile guarantee to the authenticity, legality and roadworthiness of a car before you part with money. If you bought off a seasoned rogue then you could find redress difficult.

There is another type of dealer who should be avoided at all costs. This is the person who trades in cars

from his own residential premises, usually unofficially. Such people often come from the ranks of classic car enthusiasts who, having bought and sold a few cars and made a profit from the activity, then try to build it up into a lucrative sideline. These people cannot offer guarantees and if they did then the guarantees would be worthless because they have no facilities for repairing the cars. These people are probably breaking various trading laws and avoiding taxes and, if they will happily defraud the authorities, they will just as happily cheat the customer. Avoid them at all costs.

Be guided in your choice of dealer by other Beetle enthusiasts, because there are a number of very competent and totally honest small businesses which restore Beetles which they then offer for sale. These companies are well known, and their reputation is a pretty good guarantee.

General car dealerships

General used car dealerships do not usually welcome having a Beetle on their forecourts or in their showrooms for the simple reason that it would probably be the only one amongst a sea of modern vehicles and hence very unlikely to sell. Beetles are taken in part exchange against newer cars by general dealers, but they are often disposed of through the trade, that is, they are sold on to a business which specialises in this type of car.

The fact that Beetles do enter the mainstream used car trade can be put to good use by anyone who lives in or near a large town. Simply visit or telephone the car dealers (especially VAG franchise holders) and explain that you wish to buy a particular type of Beetle. The dealer will be certain to let you know the moment he has one, because he can sell it to you for a far higher price than he could get through the trade. The price in question, incidentally, would almost certainly be negotiable and you may be able to haggle the price down and obtain a bargain in this way.

Classic car auctions

Classic car auctions have been going on for years, but it is only since the start of the 'classic car boom' of the 1980s that there have been so many auctions. In the UK there seems to be an auction taking place somewhere every summer's week-end. The drawbacks to buying from an auction are that you do not have the opportunity to have a test drive, nor the opportunity to place the car on ramps or over a pit to have a close inspection. However, a practised eye can rule out many cars on the grounds of poor bodywork with a minimal visual inspection, and most auctioneers seem to build a 'cooling off' period into their terms of business contract so that if the loom catches fire when you turn on the ignition to drive the car away, you can back out of the deal.

Classic car auctions attract many very knowledgeable people (and a great number who merely kick tyres and check to see whether the ash tray is full). By listening to the comments of the more expert appraisals, you can glean much useful information about individual cars. Be careful not to get caught doing this, just in case the person giving you a free lesson in car appraisal notices you and starts giving out false information!

Auctions are terrible places for impetuous people to shop. In the heat of the moment many buyers get completely carried away and really require a level headed assistant to help them keep their feet firmly on the ground. Try to take along an experienced Beetle enthusiast who can give you reasoned advice, just in case your enthusiasm takes over your own sense of reasoning.

General car auctions

Nobody visits general car auctions expecting to see good examples of the Beetle, and so nobody much bothers to enter them in general auctions. Occasionally, a company liquidation or the auctioning of goods and chattels from an estate might see a Beetle being entered into a general car auction, but in the main any Beetles at all which are found at an auction will be there simply because they proved impossible to sell elsewhere. Avoid these events.

Security

In the UK, a vehicle checking service long available to commercial business has, at the time of writing, been extended to private citizens. HPI Autodata (Tel. 0722 422422) will check the identity of a vehicle, they will check whether it is stolen or the subject of outstanding finance, and whether it has been involved in a major (recorded by insurance company) collision. If you have trouble getting through on the telephone number given here, your local Trading Standards Office should be able to furnish an up to date number.

HOW MUCH?

A Beetle, like any classic car, has three values. There is the value to the seller, the value to the buyer and, usually somewhere in between, the purchase price. Beetles cannot have such accurate published value guides as current and recent cars; Beetles are now old cars, and the value of the individual example will be most heavily influenced by its condition irrespective of any arbitrary figure which might be ascribed to its particular year and which model it is.

The entire classic/recreational car market is in a constant state of flux, so it is important that you base any cash offers for Beetles with current pricing trends in mind. There are several ways of obtaining current information. Some classic car magazines include value guides and, whilst these can sometimes prove mildly wrong, they do, over a period of some months, serve to show which way the market is moving.

Some vendors will base their asking price on an insurance valuation. Valuations which are carried out for insurance purposes are not to be taken too seriously. Some of the figures involved are arrived at by a valuer whose only experience of the individual car is a set of photographs – and you cannot tell the condition and hence the value of a car simply by looking at photographs. Apart from any other consideration, who is to say that the car in the photographs is not another example in better condition and only wearing the number plates from the actual vehicle? Some agreed values might be based on some kind of report prepared by a garage business or other valuer on behalf of the insurance company, but they cannot be relied upon as a true indication of the value of the car because you cannot rule out the possibility of some degree of collusion between the vendor and the valuer.

More accurate pricing information is usually available from owner's clubs, which may either be published by the club magazines or, in some circumstances, given out on request. Alternatively, a local club will doubtless contain some members who keep an eye on Beetle prices, and they may be persuaded to share their information with a fellow member.

If you have the time and inclination, then following advertisements across a wide range of advertising platforms (Beetle/VW magazines, local newspapers and regional advertisement-only publications) will enable you to build up a picture of what money is being asked for what cars. Concentrate only on the particular Beetle which interests you, and within a couple of months you could be as knowledgeable about Beetle values as any authority.

The author prefers to utilise the following method to value cars.

Firstly, he decides how much he can afford, then how much he would consider a fair price to pay for the car he is seeking in the condition he requires. When viewing a car, he lists all of the components which need renewal, plus any other work which needs carrying out (or which will require attention in the near future); he prices this and subtracts the total from the amount he considers a fair value for the car when all of the repairs have been carried out, to arrive at the value of the car to him.

Don't accept a receipt for your cheque or cash (pay by cheque if possible) from the vendor of the car if it includes the words 'sold as seen'. This is a rather tacky and not entirely effective get-out which some people employ when they want to shift a car which they know to have some serious (but undisclosed) fault, intended to put you off pursuing your complaint when said fault comes to light. In the UK, it is an offence for anyone to misrepresent an unroadworthy vehicle as fit for the road during a transaction, so keep hold of any published advertisement as proof of misrepresentation should a car described as being in 'good' condition turn out to be unsafe.

Do bear in mind that many of the Beetles which come to the market receive some sort of mechanical attention just before they are offered for sale. The work carried out could have been to a poor standard; in particular fixings might not be correctly torqued or perhaps fitted without shake-proof washers, and these can come loose in a short space of time – perhaps even whilst you drive the car to your home from the vendor's.

If, at this stage, you don't feel that you are yet qualified to carry out checks on the car yourself, get your local professional mechanic to give the car a once-over. An experienced mechanic should be able to spot any potentially dangerous fault on any car; alternatively, subjecting the car to an MOT roadworthiness test should not only unearth problems but also give you proof of their existence on the failure sheet, which will list any faults.

The checks and service routines recommended here are all covered in detail within the following chapters of this book. As ever, the author recommends that you also refer to a good workshop manual.

APPRAISING THE BEETLE – BODYWORK

Because the Beetle is blessed with that rugged spine chassis, the strength of many pressings and assemblies – particularly the sill/heater channel assemblies – is arguably not quite so vital as is the case with their

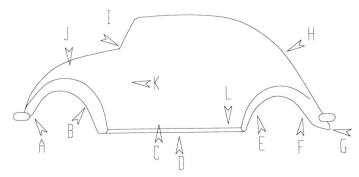

A quick tour of the Beetle rot spots.
A. Valance, spare wheel well, bumper mounting. B. Flitch, wing inner and outer edges, plus around headlamp bowls. C. 'B' post base. D. Sill/heater channel assembly. E. Rear body mounting. F. Bumper mounting. G. Valance. H. Air grille, windscreen surround. I. Roof pillars, scuttle. J. Luggage (also engine) bay sealing strip retainer. K. 'A' post. L. Heelboard (inside car).

equivalent on monocoque bodied cars. However, the only real difference between the two is that the Beetle with rotten sills but a sound spine chassis is unlikely to suffer any distortion capable of moving suspension mounting points, whereas the monocoque bodyshell with rotten sills can easily be bent to the point that the suspension mountings are moved – which makes the cars unsafe to drive and which means that repairs have to be carried out with the aid of a jig (McPherson strut Beetles do rely on the flitch panel for the top damper mounting, so the foregoing is not really applicable to them). The actual work entailed in rectifying bodyrot on the Beetle can be as difficult and time-consuming as the same work on any other car. When assessing the bodywork of a Beetle which you intend to buy, therefore, it pays to be as thorough as if it were any other car.

The suspension mounting points of the Beetle can, it should be pointed out, be bent in a frontal collision. A bent front axle is a sure sign that not only has the car been involved in a heavy collision but also that the damage rectification was less than thorough.

Do bear in mind that it is usually more difficult and time-consuming to repair bodged previous bodywork repairs than it is to deal with honest to goodness rot. Furthermore, there can be little more dispiriting than to discover that a car is heavily bodged only after you have started work on what you believed to be a straightforward restoration. Once you discover just one shoddy bodywork repair, then you really have no option but to strip the entire body down in order that you can find all similarly bodged panels.

One last point in this preamble; Beetles with sound

The base of the A post is a favourite area for rot to be bodged with ill-fitting plates and camouflaged with filler! Where the A post joins the sill is one of the more structurally important parts of the body. Apart from taking the weight of the door, they keep the basic shape of the body and prevent scuttle shake. But this one is honest, so you know what you're buying.

This car had failed the MOT – predictably – on rotten sills. A tentative attempt had been made to cut away the offending panelwork with an air chisel, but had been short-lived. This is not what is meant in the text by being 'got at' – that term would be applicable if the previous owner had hidden the rot with body filler or crudely patch repaired it.

BELOW RIGHT
The base of the heater channel has almost completely rotted away, showing the actual channel which carries the hot air to the front of the passenger compartment. Note the drain hole; moisture condenses out of the warm air from the heat exchangers when it passes down the heater channels. If you block up the drain hole, rusting will be rapid! New heater channel/sill assembly base repair panels are available, but be wary of buying a car repaired in this manner. The hidden heater channels will invariably be rusted and this would accelerate rusting of the new base plate.

floorpans, heelboards, A and B posts, rear body mounting panels, bumper brackets and heater channels etc. will never come cheaply, and, in the experience of the author (and this is confirmed by Terry Ball), Beetles which are offered at low prices always require welded repair or replacement of one or more of these components. Beetles which are sound in these vital areas but which may have poor paintwork and tatty interiors can often be found advertised at prices similar to cars with plenty of rot on the inside but gloss on the outside and plush interior trim. Given a choice between the two, take the former.

When you go to view a car, you will need to take the following: a notebook and pen to note down any faults which you find; this will furnish you with a list of faults which might – taken as a whole – put you off a car or perhaps give you a useful bargaining tool; a magnet to test for misuse of bodyfiller; a jack and a pair of axle stands; a torch to help you see into dark crevices and a sharp implement such as an old screwdriver which you can prod into suspect metal to see whether it is sound or rotting; a pair of goggles, gloves and overalls will be needed if the inspection gets serious and you climb under the car.

Before getting dirty, however, you might care to examine the external panels – what you discover there might rule the car out before you have to don overalls. Begin by examining the visible external body panels for signs of rivelling; this is corrugations usually caused by heat build-up during gas welding, but also possibly a sign of badly finished bodyfiller which is hiding collision damage. You can see rivelling best by viewing along the panel concerned with your eye positioned a few inches above its surface, and this will also allow you to see dents more clearly. If the paintwork is covered with a thin layer of grime (giving it a matt finish) then you will not be able to see any but the largest dents, so ask the vendor to give any dirty panels a wipe with a damp cloth in order for you to be able to examine them properly.

Pay particular attention to the roof panel and pillars. Because quite a few Beetles have been rolled onto their

ABOVE
This is a cross section through the heater channel/sill assembly, cut through at the base of the B post.

RIGHT
'Project' about to enter through the inviting doors of the workshop. Someone had to record this moment for posterity. From this angle, the car looks uninviting, and most buyers would turn the car down on its looks alone! Yet a few pounds of body filler and a quick respray could have made the car look quite smart enough to find an uninformed buyer.

The fact that the bumper is badly dented points to front end collision (confirmed by the body filler in the bonnet), which in this case had placed slight corrugations in the flitch panel – these were easily beaten out. The collision has to be fairly substantial for this damage to happen. Don't confuse this still light crash damage with the damage which results from a really heavy front-end shunt. The latter will destroy the front-end panelwork and bend the suspension beams. The car to avoid most of all is the one with new panelwork and bent beams – not always too easy to spot!

Rot like this is all too apparent, but any bodyfiller bodging specialist can make the wing look like new, so check carefully. Note that the wing beading is the same colour as the wings, indicating that the car has received an 'economy' respray. The stainless guard on the lower edge of the wing can actually trap water behind it, so that their value for rust-prevention is questionable.

roofs over the years, some cars will be found to have dents which have been roughly beaten out then filled up with bodyfiller. Some bodgers don't bother to beat out roof dents because this entails removing the head lining – and the worst won't even clean and key the surface for the filler. If there is more than the thinnest skim of filler on the roof panel (or, indeed, any other panel) then you should suspect that the work was carried out to a very poor standard. If you find any evidence of filler in the roof pillars other than a very thin skim covering a welded joint, then the car has probably been rolled and it has most certainly been bodged.

On de-seamed cars check for heavy use of filler around the areas where the seams used to be. If a thick layer of filler is found here, then the chances are that 'de-seaming' the car entailed hammering the seams inwards and flushing over with bodyfiller! A car treated thus has nothing to commend it.

Whilst checking the roof and pillars, check the metal near the window rubbers, because if the window has been replaced without sealant, water will have entered the rubber seal and caused rusting of the metal lip underneath. In time, this will spread under the paintwork surrounding the rubber. If this area is freshly-painted, incidentally, then it is probably to hide rusting of the metal lip – not too difficult a repair apart from re-fitting the screen afterwards, but nevertheless an indication that the car has been 'tarted-up' for sale. If

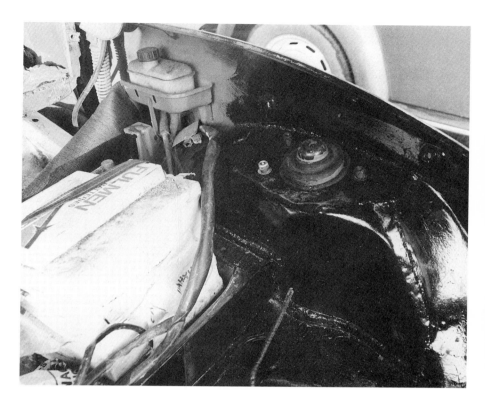

This flitch on a McPherson Strut car has been rebuilt – not necessarily a bad thing in itself as long as the patches are of sufficient strength to do the job – but the car should command a low price. The alternative to patching is to weld in a new flitch assembly; complicated, expensive and approaching the limits of practical restoration. With a new flitch, however, the car should command a reasonable price.

the window seals are in poor condition then you should expect to find some rusting from within on panels underneath; if the door window rubber is perished, for instance, then rusting out of the door skin and door bottom is likely. Whilst on the subject of doors, check for filler and GRP repairs right in the middle of the door skin, because there is a panel behind this which holds water against the skin. Carefully check door gaps and the hinges and their surrounds for evidence of brutality being employed to make the door fit – this can take the form of spacers or even washers hammered in front of the hinge to force it backwards, buckling of the skin adjacent to the hinge (either crash damage or extreme brutality when fitting the door) and obviously damaged paintwork on the hinges.

Lift the front (luggage compartment) lid: if you are immediately greeted with the aroma of petrol then either the fuel tank or line are leaking and the car should not be run until the problem has been identified and cured. Disconnect the battery immediately and inform the vendor of the problem and the dangers of using the car, smoking in its vicinity etc.

Check that the lid seal is in position and in good condition and examine the edge seams for rust; if you discover any, then you may well also find that the luggage floor and/or the side channels are rusted. If the rusting of the visible section of the luggage floor is bad then anticipate having to either patch or replace this

pressing (the latter is a difficult task, because only LHD versions appear to be available) and probably also the inner wing/flitch panels at the same time (a task for only advanced DIY'ers). The spare wheel well will normally also be rusted if the luggage floor is and, if you find that the spare wheel well has recently been replaced on a car which has bad rusting of the adjacent pressings then you will probably find that all bodywork repairs throughout the car have involved welding good metal next to bad, so that a total rebuild is called for.

On cars fitted with McPherson strut front suspension, the loadings from the concentric spring damper unit (i.e. the shocks transmitted from bumps in the road) are fed into the flitch panels. Any rusting or signs of patching/bodging in these panels – especially in the vicinity of the strut top mountings – is to be considered very serious. Don't go by looks alone, because it is not unknown for these vital areas to be smartened with GRP and bodyfiller – check for metal using a magnet and, if you have any cause for doubt regarding the strength of the area it is best to reject the car or to consider it as a restoration project only. Flitch panel replacement is one of the most difficult (and expensive) jobs in Beetle restoration, and in reality the province of the professional and specialist restorer.

Open the doors, and examine them for signs of rusting, in addition to the centre of the panel as already described, also check the lower quarter of the skin and

This A post lower repair was presumably hastily carried out prior to the MOT test, but it was welded onto rotten heater channels! Don't take signs of recent repair – however good they may look – as a guarantee that the rest of the car is sound. When new heater channel assemblies are fitted, this repair panel will have to be renewed. At least this repair – unlike most – is honest. Normally the welds would have been ground down and filler flushed over to hide the repair.

With Project raised and prodded in the right areas, the need for repairs to the lower part of the flitch – which rots in concert with the heater channel – became obvious. Check any repairs to the flitch lower section to ensure that the repair panels or patches are not welded on top of the originals – a practice guaranteed to rust the new steel in next to no time!

The rear section of the heater channel (on 'Project') was rotten enough for the author to push his fingers through it! This is, incidentally, almost unequalled as a method of severely slicing your fingers, so poke at rotten metal with an old screwdriver or similar implement. The author has seen many Beetles with this sort of rot which have had their heater channels patched – not good practice. Advanced rot of the heater channels invariably points toward rot in the floorpan edges.

the door base. Attempting to lift the doors will reveal whether there is too much play in the hinges. The A and B posts rot at their bases, so check for signs of rusting and for camouflaged rot and shoddy welded patch repairs. If the sill/heater channel assembly appears to be in better condition than the bottoms of the A and B posts, then this indicates that the heater channel was welded onto rusted steel and means that both will probably have to be renewed together – a time-consuming task. The side of the car between the B post and rear wheel arch (the quarter panel) tends to rot at its base and again, if the heater channel appears to be in better condition than this panel then the car has been bodged.

Inside the car, the most obvious areas to seek rust are the sill/heater channel assembly and the floor pans. It is common (though not good) practice to patch repair the heater channels, especially on cars which have rot in adjacent bodywork, such as the door posts and car side. If the heater channel is patch repaired, anticipate finding rot in the whole assembly and, if the heater channel alone has been replaced, count on having to rebuild the lot at a future date. If the heater channel has been repaired or replaced, look for signs of burnt rubber which will be the remains of the belly pan gasket! If the car is carpeted, then this will have to be lifted out and, if you discover that the carpet is glued to the heater channels, it is best to either seek permission from the vendor to remove it so that the channel can be examined thoroughly or to suspect that new heater channels will be required. The same goes for the floor pan and, if the carpet is glued down then at the very least you should be able to lift the edges (which is where rot is most likely).

Lift the carpet and/or sound-deadening material from the rear parcel shelf and check the state of the metal. Rust here indicates a long-term problem with a leaking rear window rubber, and is usually dealt with by patching – far from an ideal solution. The only really satisfactory way to deal with a rotted parcel shelf is complete replacement, along with the adjoining panels which will usually also have rotted – in other words, a bodyshell-off restoration.

If the floor is suspected of having weakness but a close inspection is not possible because of carpet glued to the topside and underseal underneath, then sit in each front seat in turn, hold the sides of the seat firmly and push downwards with your feet. A rotten floor pan will flex considerably under such provocation and you might even hear cracking sounds as rust flakes break loose. A rotten floorpan or even a partly rotten one means a bodyshell-off restoration.

Still on the subject of the sill/heater channel, one thing you can check without getting your hands dirty is the condition of the jacking point. When rotten, these collapse up into the sill structure. A common 'repair' is to weld a sturdy steel plate onto the sill above the jacking point; this panel will effectively have sealed off the drain hole and the sill can be expected to rust through in record time afterwards! Later in the examination of the car you will have to jack it up in order to see underneath; if you hear crunching sounds as the jack begins to take the weight of the car then it is better to find alternative jacking points than to risk being blamed for pushing up the jacking point and crushing the sill – which is likely.

Before leaving the subject of the heater channel assembly and floorpans, some people have been known to weld the two together, whereas they should really be bolted. If you discover that the heater channels are welded to the floorpans then this indicates that the car has been most horribly bodged and is worth very little because of the amount of work which will be required to put it right!

When heater channels are replaced, the correct method involves lifting off the bodyshell complete with

This rotten parcel shelf end has been treated to a lump of bodyfiller and, because the hole was so large, this was reinforced with chicken mesh (not an unusual combination of materials for 'repair' in rural areas – the car hailed from Herefordshire). Because the area was small, this was not too difficult an area to patch (but watch out for similar bodging in more important areas). More extensive rot in the parcel shelf can cause real restoration headaches.

Rot in the spine. You cannot usually see this until you have removed the seats and carpets, and also cleaned away paint, underseal or whatever else may have been painted on. Rot like this only occurs on the very worst of Beetles, so be guided by the condition of visible steel. The author would never buy a car with this sort of rot.

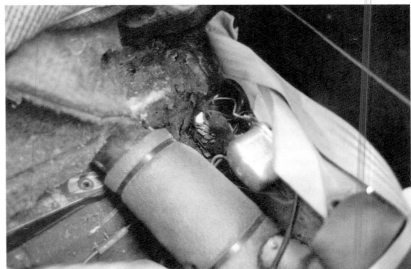

The heelboard outers are prime rust spots unless mud is regularly washed away from within the wheelarch.

This bracket is ideally placed to catch and hold mud, which naturally accelerates its rate of rusting. The 17 mm headed bolt cannot normally be seen until about a hundredweight of mud has been scraped away from the inside of the bracket, for which an old screwdriver seems the ideal implement. When appraising a car it is worth removing the rear wheels and taking a close look at this area. Many Beetles have rot here and, sadly, some are bodged.

This strange looking object is actually a section cut through what appeared to be a repair panel: as you can see, there are no less than four thicknesses of steel – the original panel plus three patches all welded one over the other. Again, this is one of those bodges which usually only come to light part-way through a restoration – be guided by the general state of the bodywork and any repairs which have been carried out and, if you have the slightest doubts about the car, reject it.

remnants of old channels, bolting new heater channels on the floorpan edges, then cutting the old channels from the bodyshell and lowering the shell back onto the chassis for welding to the heater channels. When this sequence is not followed, the holes in the floorpan and heater channel assembly don't line up, with the result that either the heater channels are welded to the floorpan as already described, or new holes are drilled in the floor edge to accept the heater channel fixing bolts. Some cars have extremely enlarged or multiple holes along the floorpan edge because of this; unfortunately these holes cannot be seen until the bolts and washers have been removed. This is not a problem in itself, but a sure sign of shoddy restoration which will be repeated throughout the rest of the car.

Still inside the car, examine the heelboard at its outer edges where the heater ducting is connected to the heater channel; this is one of the most frequently encountered Beetle Bodge areas, and rust here is commonly dealt with by GRP or even body filler and wire mesh! Welded repairs to this area would certainly destroy the belly pan gasket, and so for a proper repair, the body has to come off the car.

Lift the engine lid and examine the seal, then the folded lips for signs of rusting; also examine the air intake grille. The rear panel (valance) is prone to rot, so check for the use of filler and GRP. Check the fit of the engine bay to valance gasket – gaps indicate that a new rear valance has at some time been welded on in the wrong position!

Before jacking the car, clean all of the dirt from the rear body to damper casting mounting points within the rear wheel arches. This is a prime rot spot, so give it a good stabbing with a blunt instrument. If rot is found here, expect to also find it in the rear bumper mounts, the heater channel closing panels and most probably the heater channel/sill assemblies. Be extra careful when feeling for rot around the bumper mounting points, because sharp edges can make a mess of your hand!

Crumpled bumpers obviously indicate collision damage; perhaps less obviously, you should look for distortion of the flitch panels and engine bay/rear inner wing areas, which can also reveal collision damage. If you find evidence of collision damage then check the fit of the doors carefully, because heavy damage will have dictated that, if the door gaps are to look right, the hinges and in fact the door surround itself have to come in for some heavy-duty bodging.

Moving on to the underside of the car, apply the handbrake, chock the rear wheels and raise the front end of the car with a jack placed under the track control arm pressing, then support the car on axle stands. Examine the frame head. Rot here is very expensive and time-consuming to deal with and, in most cases, will entail a full strip down to a bare chassis before it can properly be dealt with. Any signs of collision damage on the frame head or axle (torsion bar cars) should be taken very seriously because suspension mounting points could have been disturbed. In such cases, it will pay to commission a motor engineer's report if you are still interested in the car.

Turn the wheels from lock to lock so that you can examine the flitch panels (inner wings); rotted flitch panels are not only a very difficult repair but also indicate that there is a strong likelihood that serious (and perhaps camouflaged) rot will be in adjacent panels.

Using a torch for illumination and a blunt instrument to stab with, check as best you can the underside of the luggage compartment/spare wheel well. Also check the insides of the front wings; if you find an area which appears to be thicker than the rest then it is filler.

Whilst the front of the car is raised check the wheel

bearings, brakes and steering (see mechanical examination).

Slacken the rear wheel nuts, transfer the chocks to the front wheels, raise the rear of the car and support it on axle stands, then remove the road wheels. Examine the inner wheelarch area closely, probing for rot and checking for body filler or GRP, and look for creases in the panels which indicate poorly corrected rear collision damage. Similarly check the outer heelboard and the underside of the decking (internal rear parcel shelf). Check the inside of the valance.

MECHANICAL/ELECTRICAL INSPECTION

Whether you undertake the mechanical examination or the test drive first is your own decision. In favour of test driving first is the fact that some mechanical faults might come to light so that you can rule out the car without getting your hands dirty! On a more serious note, the mechanical examination might reveal faults

This frame head is in a very sad state, and illustrates just how badly even very thick section steel components can rust if maintenance is skimped. The rotten cover plate should set alarm bells ringing, even if you were to fail to notice the rot on the off-side base plate. If you find rot here, the best advice is to find another car.

which would make a test drive risky if not dangerous and, for this reason, the author recommends that you check the car before taking it onto the road.

Begin your inspection inside the car where you can remain clean and (hopefully) dry. Check all of the electrical equipment; lights, wipers and horn. Grasp the steering wheel and try to lift and lower it; movement indicates poor mounting. Turn the steering wheel and try to ascertain how much the perimeter moves before the front wheels react. If the steering wheel turns by more than an inch or so then the problem could be cause by worn kingpins, a worn or maladjusted steering box/rack or a loose mounting. If you drive a car with a lot of null steering wheel movement, then the front wheels can react freely to bumps in the road and you have no way of knowing which way the car will jump when a front wheel hits a bump or pot-hole. Check that the windscreen is free of cracks and scratches (an MOT failure depending on country and current standards) and that all of the rubbers are in good condition (not perished and free from cracks).

Press the brake pedal and hold it down. If the pedal is spongy then there is air in the system, which will have to be bled and the cause of the air found and rectified. If the pedal sinks slowly to the toeboard then the master cylinder is faulty.

Remove the rear seat base and check the condition of the wiring and the battery. The wires' insulation must be intact and free from signs of scorching (indicating a short to earth fault which, if not cured, can result in the loom catching fire), and the battery should be clean, free

from spillage and securely fastened. Check the level of the electrolyte in each cell, and use a torch to see whether the plates are buckled, in which case the battery is on the way out.

Check all seat belt mounting points by tugging as violently on the belts as you can, check the condition of the seat belts and mechanism because frayed or damaged belts are an MOT failure point.

Check that window winders, screen washers and all instruments work.

'Bounce' each corner of the car, that is, push it sharply downwards and let go so that the suspension pushes upwards. If the corner rises, falls and rises again then the damper is faulty. This is a very un-scientific test, and damper problems are more easily detectable on the road. If, however, bouncing the car indicates ineffectual dampers, don't drive the car on the road, because worn dampers reduce tyre grip to an unbelievable degree.

Then move to the engine bay. Firstly, if there is a strong smell of petrol and the fuel delivery system is leaking then immediately disconnect the battery and don't run the engine until the cause has been found and dealt with. Grasp the crankshaft pulley firmly and try to move it backwards and forwards; if the movement (crankshaft end float) is much greater than five 'thou (.13mm) then the engine requires attention. Try to lift the crankshaft pulley to test for worn mains; if the pulley can be pulled up and down then the crankcase will have to be align bored and the crankshaft probably reground, an expensive repair.

If you have a compression tester, use it! Remove all four spark plugs (marking the leads if you are unsure of which goes where), and get an assistant to turn the engine over on the starter motor while you check the compression for each cylinder in turn. This normally runs in the range of 100–142 pounds per square inch. If one or more cylinders are lower than the others, apply a little engine oil through the plug hole (to seal the piston rings) and re-check. If the pressure is now OK then the problem lies with the piston rings and cylinder bores; if the low pressure persists than the leakage is past a valve stem, and a cylinder head overhaul will be needed.

Check the engine oil level and the condition of the oil; if you don't know what signs to look for then take along someone who does! Check the condition of the spark plugs, leads, distributor cap (look for minute splits) and the points (check that the surfaces are level and not pitted). The general condition of the engine bay can tell you a lot about a car. If it is dirty and covered with oil, then maintenance has obviously been skimped on – the Beetle engine is good for well over 100,000 miles if cared for, but a neglected engine will have a much shorter life span.

This close-up shows the rot more clearly. This car is dangerous to use in this condition. A new frame head costs very little less than a complete chassis assembly, so a car with such rot in the frame head is best dealt with by buying a new chassis. The car is worth very little because of this, and is best considered a spares donor.

Check the condition of the wiring, looking for burns and abrasions and, if your bodywork inspection revealed that the rear chassis/damper bracket mounts have been replaced, lift the sound deadening material from the engine bay side and check that the wiring underneath is not burned. Check that the wiring is original and that it has not been added to or otherwise tampered with.

Check that the tinware is all properly fastened into place. This might not seem to be terribly important, but the author has witnessed a shattered dynamo pedestal which was broken by violent vibrations caused by unfastened tinware.

Whilst the rear of the car is raised for the bodywork/chassis inspection, check the rear brakes, suspension and wheel bearings. There are small inspection holes in the brake backplate through which, with the aid of illumination from a torch, you can see the thickness of the brake lining. If there appears to be less than 0.1 in. of frictional material left on the brake shoes then they will have to be renewed. Using a screwdriver (preferably with an angled blade) or the proper tool, check that the brake adjusters are not seized and that the brakes are correctly adjusted (see Chapter Four). Maladjustment indicates shoddy maintenance; sticking adjusters indicates a total absence of maintenance!

Check the brake backplates for signs of brake fluid or, perhaps more commonly, oil contamination. The former means obtaining and fitting wheel cylinder seal kits; the latter entails obtaining and fitting a hub oil seal kit.

Check the rear tyres for uneven wear. Excessive wear in the centre or at the outside edges of the tread indicates over or under inflation respectively. If the tyres are worn on one side only, ask whether they have previously been fitted at the front of the car (indicating ill-adjusted front tracking). If not, then suspect that the spring plate has, at some time, been unbolted from the hub and replaced in a different position, which will cause toe in or out. In addition to increasing tyre wear, wrongly tracked rear tyres will suffer reduced grip, so this is a problem that needs sorting before the car is used on the road.

Check the condition of the handbrake cables and, if they are frayed or if they stick, make a note to that effect. Check the brake pipes for corrosion, kinks or damage, and the flexible hoses for any signs of damage or perishing. Check the condition of the drive shaft gaiters/boots. Splits are an MOT failure point – leaking gaiters on swing axle cars must be remedied before transaxle oil is lost.

Check the transaxle and the underside of the engine for obvious oil leaks, which must be traced and remedied. If the entire underside of these units is covered with oil and you are seriously interested in buying the car, wipe off as much of the oil as you can and re-check to establish the cause of the leakage following the test drive. An oil leak from the clutch housing could emanate from either the gearbox input shaft seal or the rear engine oil seal – the latter is more common but both require the removal of the engine and the latter the removal of the clutch as well.

Check the condition and correct adjustment of the clutch cable, and check that the clutch return spring is not broken.

Check all visible wiring – most especially the starter solenoid feed wire – for insulation damage. Check the bump stops and all visible bushes for perishing. Check the heater ducting for damage and the exhaust/heat exchangers for leakage and general condition. Exhausts are not too expensive but are an MOT failure point; good quality heat exchangers cost rather a lot.

Most importantly, use a torch to illuminate the visible section of the fuel line; if you have the slightest suspicion that it may be corroded then you must budget for immediate replacement. This is neither an inexpensive nor a pleasant task.

Whilst the front of the car is raised for bodywork/chassis inspection, take the opportunity to check the front brakes, wheel bearings, suspension and steering gear. Check drum brake backplates for fluid leakage, use a torch to check the shoe material thickness through the hole provided. Check the condition of the lines and flexible hoses, and check for fluid leakage at unions. Again using a torch, check the visible portion of the fuel line (see previous comments). Check the dampers for leakage and visually check for perishing of all rubber components.

Check the tyres for uneven wear. Wear concentrated on both sides of the tread pattern or in the middle of the tread pattern can indicate simple under or over inflation respectively; wear on one side of the pattern could indicate either that the tracking is wrongly set (an easy adjustment which should be carried out professionally) or that more serious problems lie elsewhere in the suspension.

On cars with torsion arm front suspension, check that the beam is not damaged, because it is possible for the suspension to be thrown out by frontal collisions. Check that the notches in the large hexagonal eccentric bushes located in the top of the stub axle assembles are both facing forwards; these set the front wheel camber, and if they are inserted wrongly then the handling will be adversely affected and tyre wear will be high.

Place a lever under each tyre and try to lift it – taking care not to unbalance the car from the axle stands supporting it! Vertical free movement indicates kingpin problems. Grasp each tyre at the nine o'clock and three o'clock positions, and try to rock it; movement indicates worn wheel bearings. Turn the wheels from lock to lock, feeling for roughness in the steering box (expensive) and either stiff or loose points probably caused by the steering damper (easy repair).

Test drive

If the car has passed all of the tests so far, then a road test will enable you to discover many of the potential drive/suspension faults without getting your hands dirty.

The author and publishers can assume no responsibility for the consequences of any of the following advice. It is up to the individual to ensure that the car is driven in a safe manner with full regard to the safety of other road users.

If you are to drive the car then ensure that you will be not inadvertently break any motoring laws in the process. This means that the car must be roadworthy and taxed and that you must be properly insured. If the vendor is to drive, ensure that he or she is acting within the law, because you could be regarded as an accomplice if the vendor is stopped and charged of an offence by the police during the test drive.

For the sake of safety, begin at moderate road speeds and do not try anything fancy until you are satisfied that the road holding, handling and brakes hold no nasty surprises. If you are not familiar with the on-road behaviour of the Beetle then it is recommended that, if possible, you arrange for an experienced Beetle driver to carry out part or all of the test drive. The experienced Beetle driver will be able to detect problems with the engine, unusual noises from the drive train, deficiencies in the handling and braking which may not be apparent to the inexperienced.

If the car shows signs of 'floating' at speed then the dampers are worn; if the front of the car nose-dives as the brakes are applied, if the bonnet pitches up and down as the car moves away from a standstill, expect to find worn or leaking dampers. Any car with worn dampers is unsafe to drive at speed, so continue the test, if at all, at slow speeds.

On an empty stretch of road, brake to a standstill from about 30 mph and note whether the car pulls to one side (worn or contaminated brakes). If the brakes have to be 'pumped' before they will operate properly then there is air in the system. A clonk on braking could indicate suspension problems or a loose brake calliper (disc braked models only). If a clonk can only be heard when the car is first braked when travelling either forwards or in reverse, the calliper pistons could be sticking. Repeat this test using the handbrake.

In all gears, accelerate and decelerate sharply to see whether the car can be encouraged (under provocation) to jump out of gear! If the car jumps out of first gear on the overrun then the chances are that the fault is due to incomplete gear engagement caused, in turn, by a wrongly positioned gear shift lever plate. Reverse the car a short distance and again brake to a halt, listening for clonks which could indicate suspension problems or a loose brake calliper.

If at any stage in these tests any doubts emerge regarding the brakes or suspension, then it is best to discontinue the road test on the grounds of safety.

Increase speed to normal road speeds and repeat the braking and gearchange tests, when any deficiencies in the engine, transmission or suspension not previously noted will be accentuated.

Stop somewhere off the public highway. Engage the handbrake, then slowly let the clutch out, depressing it again immediately the engine begins to labour. If the car begins to creep forwards then the handbrake is out of adjustment or the rear brakes are worn or contaminated. If the engine does not labour appreciably then the clutch is slipping and in need of attention.

Slow down to 25–30 mph in fourth gear and press the accelerator pedal fully down. If the engine misses or shows hesitancy then this could indicate a weak mixture, as could pinking – otherwise known as pre-ignition. Pinking has a host of other possible causes including wrongly set ignition timing, an overheated engine, air induction or pre-ignition caused by very hot carbon or tiny metal burrs on the cylinder head which ignite the mixture ahead of the appropriate time. The sound of pinking is that of the pistons tipping in the bores. In time, pinking wrecks an engine. If the engine knocks, then it is almost certainly due for new big-end bearings and a crankshaft re-grind – in effect, a 'bottom end' rebuild or an exchange engine.

When exiting a corner check that the steering wheel returns to the straight ahead position; if not, then suspect partial seizure in the kingpins.

After purchase

There is great temptation to load friends and family into a newly-acquired Beetle and set out on a long 'test' drive, but it is not the smartest way to begin your relationship with the car. It would be tragic if your car were to suffer a breakdown – or worse – a fault which leads to an accident on that first drive, and no matter how thorough your pre-purchase inspection of the car is, there is always a possibility that the car now possesses a serious fault or faults. For a start, you might have missed something so obvious that you will kick yourself when it leads to a breakdown in the future.

The vast majority of people are honest, but the vendor could turn out to have been a rogue. Perhaps Mister Vendor was less than scrupulous and forgot to mention the intermittent electrical fault which knocks the headlights out without warning or which used to occasionally blow a fuse which he up-rated so much that the fault is now fully capable of setting fire to the loom if the driver happens to switch on the wrong combination of electrical devices.

You could even discover that, during the period between your inspection and the collection of the car, the vendor has swapped some of the good components which passed your inspection standards for worn-out ones from another car – perhaps something as fundamental as brake pads or dampers. The components which might most typically attract this sharp practice are usually those which are reasonably easy to swap and fairly expensive to replace.

You could discover that the reason why the engine bay was spotless when you previously inspected it was because it had just been steam cleaned, and that plenty of fresh oil has by now found its way out of the engine during the drive home, leaving the engine oil level low.

It is better to begin your acquaintance with the new car in the workshop and give it a thorough check-over followed by a service. In addition to tools and consumables, you will need a good workshop manual.

Under the car

Begin by chocking one pair of wheels, loosening the wheelnuts and hub nut (drum brakes) on the other pair, disengaging the handbrake and taking the car out of gear, then raise the non-chocked side of the car and rest it on axle stands. Remove the road wheels and check the tyres for cuts, abrasions and bulges. Check the condition of the pads and examine the discs for scoring (disc brakes), back off the adjusters on drum brakes, remove the hub nuts and drums and check the shoes for wear, the drum for scoring, the backplate for oil or brake fluid contamination (hub seal or wheel cylinder seal kit needed) and (rear wheels) the handbrake components for free operation. With disc brakes, check for fluid leakage from the piston seals.

Check the dampers visually for signs of leakage and general condition. Check the brake hoses for bulges, cuts, abrasions or collapse. Gaiters on the drive shafts must be free from cuts, and will have to be replaced if they are damaged.

If you discover that any of these vital components have been swapped for worn-out alternatives following your inspection, then the best advice is to contact the vendor immediately and confront him/her with the facts, to contact your bank with a view to putting a stop on the cheque and, if the vendor denies any skullduggery, the trading standards office, police, any motoring organisation or owner's club to which you belong – anyone that you feel may be able to help.

Whilst the car is raised, take the opportunity to check the exhaust for signs of blowing, the visible sections of the fuel line for damage and the main battery/starter solenoid feed wire for signs of damage. Check any other wiring which runs under the car and inside the engine compartment. If you find any wires with damaged insulation then these need replacing before the car is used, and the battery earth should be disconnected there and then just to be sure that no wires can cause a short to earth.

Rear of the car

Whilst you have access to the rear underside of a Beetle, check the transaxle oil level and top up if necessary with the correct oil. If the oil level is low then keep an eye on it when you begin to use the car in case there is a serious leak.

Remove the thermostat cover (rear offside of the car) and measure the length of the thermostat both with the engine hot and cold. If the thermostat does not alter in length as the engine warms then the cold running flaps in the ducted air cooling system will not open, and the engine will overheat, causing accelerated wear and damage to the engine. (See Chapter Three for more details of this check.) Finally, check the torque of the nuts and bolts which hold the suspension together. Repeat the checks for the other side of the car.

Engine compartment

Check firstly that the engine compartment and the underside of the engine transaxle are in the same sort of state that they were in when you examined the car prior to buying it; if everything was spotlessly clean then but is now covered with oil then there can be little doubt that either the engine and transaxle were steam cleaned for your inspection and that the test run (if any) was too short, or that this is clear evidence of skulduggery such as the replacement of the engine which you saw during your inspection with another. It is easy to perform an engine transplant on the Beetle.

Check the generator drive belt for deflection. Check that the tinware set screws are all in position and that they have been tightened correctly.

Trace back any mysterious lengths of wire which do not appear on the circuit diagram in your workshop manual; they are probably add-ons and might well at some stage in the future overload the fuse for the circuit they are tapping. A blown fuse might not at first sight seem too dangerous, but were your lights to extinguish whilst you were driving at any sort of speed on unlit roads then the consequences could be terminal. If you really wish to be thorough then pay special attention to all earth connections – most intermittent electrical faults can be attributed to poor earths.

General

Move the front wheels to full lock in each direction, and check that they don't foul the bodywork; it may be as well to 'bounce' each corner of the car to simulate suspension travel when you check this. If the front wheels do foul the bodywork, then the chances are that larger or wider wheels and tyres have been fitted; if both prove to be standard, then either extremely poor bodywork repair has resulted in badly aligned panels, or the front suspension geometry has been altered because the car has been involved in a front-end collision. In either case, confront the vendor with the evidence.

Interior

Lift the rear seat base and check the battery for condition (ensure it is the one you saw during your inspection of the car) and especially for security. Were a battery to tip over then at best leaking electrolyte will make a mess of paintwork – at worst an electrical fire could be the result. Check the wiring in the vicinity.

Check the seat belts by tugging quite violently; these are anchored to the tops and bottoms of the B posts; it's better to discover that the mountings are weak with rust (or have been bodged) at this stage than when you're headed towards the windscreen following a head-on crash – or even part-way through an MOT. Weak seat belt mountings make a car unroadworthy, so seek redress with the vendor.

Check the steering by feeling for lost movement – that is, movement of the steering wheel perimeter which does not move the front wheels. If it is much more than about 1 in. then check that none of the fixings in the steering mechanism have come loose. This can happen when a car has received attention to the steering prior to sale, but nuts and bolts have come loose since. Void steering wheel travel can indicate that the steering box components require adjustments (this is covered in Chapter Four). Also pull and push the wheel to check for play, and lift it then push down to check that the steering column fixings have not come loose.

Sit in each front seat in turn, grab the seat firmly and push down on the floorpan with your feet to check that the seat fixings and floorpans are sound.

Service

The author would recommend that a full lubrication/ignition system service is carried out on any newly acquired car irrespective of any evidence of the fabled full service history or any claim by the vendor that the car is perfect and freshly serviced. Apart from giving you the peace of mind which comes from knowing that the job has been properly done, it might also unearth some latent fault which has so far escaped your attention. It also gives you a clean starting point for future servicing. (Details of how to carry out the various tasks are given in the following chapter.)

Change the engine oil and clean the strainer. Even better, clean the strainer then flush the system with a proprietary fluid before replacing the oil.

Top up the transaxle oil. Attack the car with a grease gun and fill every nipple until clean grease emerges, then wipe off any excess. Then get out the pumping oil can and attend to the hinges, locks, window winding mechanisms and so on.

It is advisable to change the brake fluid, not only to get new fluid pumping through the lines but also to check that the bleed nipples are not seized. Then adjust the handbrake and handbrake lever travel, and check the efficiency of the brakes against the engine before venturing out onto the public highway. To check the brakes you simply let the clutch pedal out slowly with the engine at tickover, the car in first gear and either the handbrake or footbrake engaged, ready to depress the clutch pedal the moment that the engine begins to labour. If the engine does not labour then the clutch is slipping, *unless* the car happens to be moving forward, in which case the brakes are not functioning. Finally the tracking should be checked at any service centre.

3 · MAINTENANCE

The Beetle is without doubt one of the easiest of all cars to maintain properly. The fact that the engine is air cooled means that there are no problems with sticking thermostats, leaky radiators and hoses, cylinder heads cracking when coolant freezes or worn water pump impellers. The mechanical components are simple, sturdy and long-lived; the ancillaries are often user-repairable or alternatively new or exchange reconditioned replacements can be obtained easily. Access to most of the components for servicing is better than on many cars, and in extreme cases when serious mechanical repair is found necessary, it is easier to get the engine and gearbox out of a Beetle than almost any other car.

Maintenance comprises a number of procedures which should be carried out at fixed intervals which are determined by either the number of miles travelled since the last service or the amount of time which has lapsed since then. Most maintenance procedures are concerned with preventative measures to prolong the life of the car and its components; some are concerned with making adjustments to maintain good fuel economy, smooth running and so on; many are checks to ensure that certain components (particularly the brakes, fuel and electrical systems) are functioning perfectly for safety reasons.

The price of ignoring proper service routines is that the car can become less safe to drive due to decreased braking efficiency, insulation breakdown on electrical wires or fuel leaks. A neglected car will also almost certainly show increased fuel consumption, and so skimping on maintenance does *not* save money! Furthermore, failure to check oil levels and to change the oil and clean the strainer, to check the ignition timing and carburation will shorten the useful working life of the engine. The engine oil is particularly important; with the air-cooled boxermotor, the oil plays a large part in cooling the engine and, if the oil level is allowed to drop then not only will lubrication suffer, but the resultant problems will be exacerbated by

overheating. Nearly all mechanical components will suffer increased wear and reduced life if maintenance is skimped.

The majority of Beetles in existence are now old cars, and so there can be no hard and fast service intervals (recent imports excepted), because too much will depend on the age and condition of the individual car and the way and the conditions in which it is driven. A car which lives in dusty, very hot or very wet conditions or a car which is driven hard will require more attention on a much more frequent basis than a car which is kept in a garage and driven carefully. The service intervals given in this chapter are a general recommendation which should be taken as a minimum requirement for a car which is driven hard or in adverse conditions, and as having a margin of safety for cars which are driven gently.

The most frequent recommended service routines are concerned mainly with checking the efficiency of components, that everything (especially the electrics) works, and maintaining lubricant and hydraulic fluid levels. These routines are intended to give a framework which will ensure that potential problems are spotted at the earliest opportunity. A small problem, left unattended, can often quickly develop into a large and expensive to rectify problem. The most obvious illustration of this is when the oil level is allowed to fall to the point at which the engine overheats and eventually the big ends start knocking. Do not worry if you do not understand the terminology at this stage, for all will be made clear later in the book. Suffice to say for now that for the sake of topping up the oil, the engine has to be removed from the car and stripped down for an expensive rebuild.

For weekly service checks, little specialised equipment is needed unless the checks reveal problems which have to be attended to. With each service interval, the list of necessary equipment grows a little. However, all of the tools and equipment necessary to carry out all servicing on a Beetle can be bought at a fraction of the cost of a 'full' service from many franchised garages, so the expenditure is easily justified.

Premises

It is a great help to have a warm, dry and well illuminated place in which to work, although all servicing can be carried out in the open. Avoid carrying out work in the rain, because water can cause problems with the ignition and electrical systems. A strong concrete surface over which you can park the car, raise it on a jack and support its weight with axle stands is essential.

Carrying out your own servicing at home can save a great amount of money compared with having it attended to by professionals. More importantly, you will be sure that all necessary jobs have been properly attended to, and that no unnecessary work or work which has not been done has been charged for. Many garages replace consumables such as brake shoes long before the components actually need replacing, and it is far from unknown for a few unscrupulous mechanics to charge the customer for certain work and parts but not to do the job because it is unnecessary.

MECHANICAL MAINTENANCE

The recommended six month/6000 mile service is quite involved, but within most people's capabilities. There is no harm whatever in attending to the more basic jobs yourself but leaving the more complicated tasks such as setting the ignition timing to professionals if you are unsure of your abilities. The more of the work you do yourself, the more money you will save.

Whenever you drive the car

In principle, you should check that the lighting system (including the brake lights and indicators) is functioning before driving on the public highway. You should also check that the windscreen wipers, washer and horn are functioning correctly. You should in theory check that the tyres – including the spare – are properly inflated, although most people just check by eye that none of the tyres have deflated. Without conscious thought, the author always checks the 'feel' of the brake pedal, just in case a hydraulic or mechanical problem has occurred since the car was last driven. It is a good practice to get into the habit of carrying out these simple checks before driving on the road, because the majority of car

breakdowns apparently occur within a few miles of the car's base, and would therefore not happen if the car was checked before being driven those few miles!

The more pessimistic amongst us also check that no new pool of oil has appeared underneath the car since it was last used. All engines hate being driven with low oil levels, and the Beetle will reward such abuse with a breakdown and possibly major engine damage within a very few miles!

Whilst you drive, listen to the sounds of the car on the move and, if you detect any new noises (or if an established noise suddenly stops) then investigate as soon as possible. Keep an eye on the oil pressure gauge or warning light as applicable, and if the warning light comes on (or the pressure gauge reading suddenly drops) then stop the car as soon as safe to do so and investigate.

You should always carry a small emergency tool kit in the car, even for short journeys. Many such kits can be found on the market, most coming in a handy tool roll or plastic container to keep all of the tools together. These should as a minimum requirement include pliers, side cutters, straight and cross-head screwdrivers, plus an adjustable spanner or a small selection of open-ended spanners (make sure you buy metric spanners). Always buy the best quality tools which you can afford. Supplement your in-car tool kit with a roll of self-adhesive insulating tape and perhaps a few short lengths of wire, plus consumables including spare 16 amp and 8 amp fuses and light bulbs. On long journeys, it is wise to also carry a quantity of engine oil, a spare generator drive belt and even spare ignition components.

Safety precautions

Never work on or under a car which is supported only by a jack or jacks – use axle stands to support the raised car, always on firm, level ground – and chock the wheels which remain on the ground to prevent the car from rolling off the axle stands. If you prefer to use a pair of ramps, make certain that they cannot topple before you climb under the car, and bear in mind that some ramps could be of poor quality or design and hence more likely to topple.

When using any combustible or flammable material or fluid (including paraffin, petrol and hydraulic fluid, bearing in mind that it is usually the fumes rather than the liquid which are the more dangerous) ensure firstly that there is no means of igniting it, such as cigarettes or electrical equipment which could cause a spark. Remember that most combustible fumes (note: petrol) are heavier than air and will quickly fill a pit.

Certain of the substances used in car maintenance

and repair are very harmful to skin, eyes or if swallowed. Always wear the appropriate protective clothing and treat everything with a degree of caution.

Electricity presents special dangers. Apart from the physical dangers of electrocution, a stray spark can ignite any fumes present.

Although every precaution has been taken in ensuring that the working methods given in this book are safe, the author and publishers can accept no responsibility for any injuries or losses incurred whilst carrying out the tasks detailed in this book.

Weekly maintenance

Weekly maintenance consists of a set of checks and does not necessarily involve any work being carried out. The tool list is minimal. A jack is vital; scissors jacks are not recommended, a bottle jack is acceptable and a small trolley jack is ideal. The author does not favour the use of scissors jacks because, although they have the advantages of being lightweight and cheap to buy, they are not usually stable enough for any work save a roadside wheel change; for this purpose, their chief advantage is that they take up very little room within the car.

A jack is a purely a lifting device and it is not intended to be used as a support – never work on or under a car which is supported only by a jack – so you will need a pair of axle stands. These are not too expensive and last a lifetime. You also require a tyre pressure gauge and a tread depth gauge. A small stock of consumables is recommended; these being battery electrolyte, engine oil in the specified grade and brake hydraulic fluid.

The oil filler cap. Use a one pint milk bottle not only to fill the engine with oil but also to help meter the oil. (Courtesy Autodata)

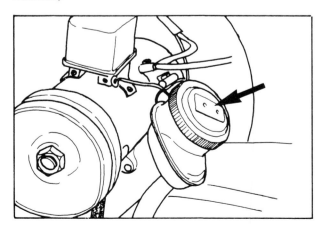

Firstly check the tyre pressures. Then chock both wheels on one side of the car, place the car in neutral and release the handbrake, then jack up the other side and support it on axle stands. Examine the tyres for cuts, bulges and tread depth. Look for the early signs of uneven tread wear; if the tread is wearing faster in the centre of the pattern than it is at the edges then the tyres have probably been over-inflated. If the tread wear is concentrated at both edges of the pattern then the tyre is probably under-inflated. If the tread wear is concentrated on one side of the pattern then the wheel alignment (tracking) requires adjustment, something which should be carried out professionally. If a tyre is faulty then replace it with the spare, and have the faulty tyre attended to. Repeat for the other side of the car.

Check the engine oil. The dipstick has two marks on it; one showing maximum level and the lower showing the minimum. Few people know the knack of pouring oil into a Beetle engine: decant the oil into a one pint milk bottle, offer it up to the filler neck then tip it up sharply. In addition to allowing you to fill the engine without covering the tinware with oil, this allows you to meter out precise quantities of oil. When pouring oil into the engine, bear in mind that the difference between the max and min marks represents just two pints of oil, so do not pour in too much at one go. Pour in a little, leave it for a couple of minutes to drain down into the sump, then re-check the level, topping up further if necessary. Take care not to over-fill the engine with oil, because too much oil can cause nearly as much damage as too little.

If the oil level is slightly low then top it up; if it has dropped substantially then the cause of the loss must be found at the earliest opportunity, and preferably before the car is used on the road. A car with a serious engine oil leak should not be used for any journey save the shortest run to a repair centre, and even for this it is advisable to tow the car in preference to driving it because engine damage can be very rapid once the oil level drops below a certain level. Remember that the oil in a Beetle engine is its liquid coolant; if the level is low then the engine will quickly overheat, which thins the oil and exacerbates the problems.

Check the fluid level in the brake reservoir (not applicable to early cars with mechanical brakes). If the level is very slightly down then top it up, if it is markedly low, then top it up but either trace and cure the leak yourself or have this done professionally at the earliest opportunity. If the level has dropped substantially then do not use the car on the road until the fault has been found and rectified. (See Chapter Four – Brakes).

Check the level of the water in the windscreen washer bottle (and the air pressure, which should be kept at around 40 psi in self-contained pressurised tanks – the spare wheel in cars which use the spare's

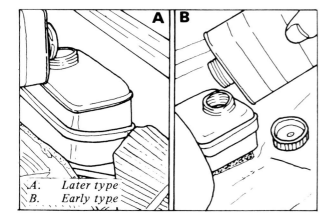

The brake fluid reservoir (A) later type and (B) early type. Take care not to spill the fluid onto paintwork – it's a very effective paint remover! (Courtesy Autodata)

compressed air to power the washer should also be kept at 40 psi) and top up if necessary. Do not use washing-up liquid in the bottle, because these liquids contain industrial salts which accelerate bodywork rusting. If desired, use a proprietary screen wash product.

Check the level of the battery electrolyte and top up if necessary. A substantial drop in the level (even in just one cell) means that the battery will have to be replaced.

Finally, check the tension of the generator drive belt. If this belt becomes too slack, it will not only fail to turn the generator (and so drain the battery), but it will also fail to turn the cooling fan and the engine will overheat. If the belt is too tight then it will place unnecessarily heavy loadings on the generator bearings. The belt should deflect by around ½ in. under firm pressure from your thumb. If the belt is too slack, adjust it as described later in this chapter.

Monthly maintenance

In addition to the checks already listed for weekly inspection, the author believes that it is worth taking the time to check the thermostat. This is situated on the underside of the engine, offside of the car. Remove the four set screws and the cover plate.

The purpose of the thermostat is to operate flaps in the ducted air cooling system; when the engine and thermostat are cold, the flaps remain in the closed position and limit the amount of cooling air delivered to the cylinders; when the engine and thermostat reach 65–70 degrees C then the thermostat should expand in length to 46 mm (1.8 in.), at which point the flaps will have fully opened and cooling air will be delivered to the cylinders. If the thermostat fails to operate, the engine will become overheated, which causes increased component wear in the short term and serious engine damage in the longer term.

If the thermostat does not appear to operate satisfactorily, remove the bolt at its base and then the bolt which secures its bracket to the crankcase. The thermostat may now be unscrewed from the end of the connecting rod. Immerse it in hot water and, if it fails to expand correctly, replace it. To fit a thermostat, screw it to the end of the operating rod and pull both fully downwards, at which point the flaps will be closed. Bolt the bracket to the crankcase so that it just touches the base of the thermostat with the latter in the lowest position. Bolt the thermostat to its bracket. Run and engine to normal operating temperature and check that the thermostat is functioning.

Six monthly maintenance

In addition to the tools listed previously, you will need a selection of straight and cross-headed screwdrivers, a grease gun, a selection of metric open-end or combination spanners (buy these as a set, preferably in a tool roll so that they can be kept in the car), and a spark plug spanner. You will need a feeler gauge; preferably one with a spark plug gap setter built-in. If you intend to check the ignition timing yourself then you will require a simple stroboscope. A pair of pliers and side cutters completes the tool list. If you can afford it, buy a ½ in. drive socket set in addition to spanners. Other tools may be required if some of the checks made in this service reveal problems.

You will also require the following consumables: engine oil in the recommended grade, brake hydraulic fluid, distilled water and general purpose lithium-based grease, oil strainer gaskets, drain plug washer.

Carry out every task and check listed previously.

MAINTENANCE CHECKLIST

Engine

The engine oil and strainer should be attended to (never change the oil without also cleaning the strainer). The textbook method of changing the engine oil starts with the advice to warm the engine thoroughly in order to thin the oil and so help more of it drain. The author sees two drawbacks to this working method. Firstly, the oil (which plays a part in cooling the engine) will be very hot indeed and quite capable of burning you. Old engine

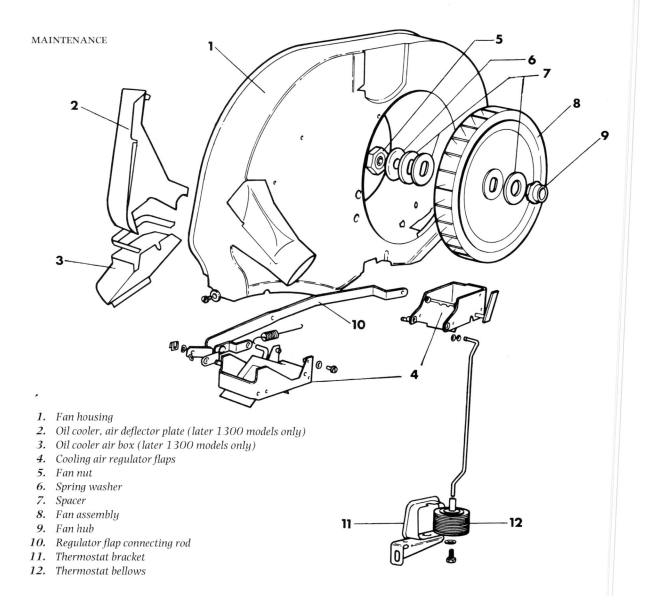

1. Fan housing
2. Oil cooler, air deflector plate (later 1300 models only)
3. Oil cooler air box (later 1300 models only)
4. Cooling air regulator flaps
5. Fan nut
6. Spring washer
7. Spacer
8. Fan assembly
9. Fan hub
10. Regulator flap connecting rod
11. Thermostat bracket
12. Thermostat bellows

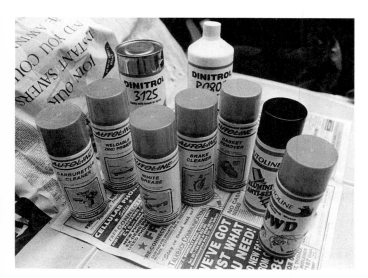

ABOVE
The fan shroud and its contents. If the thermostat (12) fails to expand when the engine warms, then the flaps (4) will remain shut so that the engine overheats. When this happens, the engine can seize within a few miles. (Courtesy Autodata)

LEFT
There are a host of lotions and potions available to make life easier for the DIY-inclined motorist. This is just a sample of products from the Autoline range; the Aluminium Anti Seize, PWD and brake cleaner would prove very useful for maintenance.

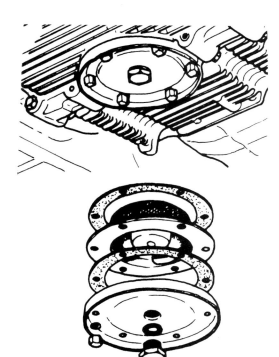

The engine oil drain plug and strainer. Always clean the strainer when changing the oil, and use a new gasket. (Courtesy Autodata)

The oil strainer (removed for this photograph) should be removed and cleaned out regularly.

oil can cause problems if it is allowed to come into contact with your skin; these will probably be exacerbated if you pre-heat the oil! Secondly, if the oil change is carried out after the car has been standing idle overnight, then the oil will have had plenty of time to drain down to the sump. Whichever method you choose is up to you.

You will need a receptacle for the old engine oil. You can buy special containers with deeply dished sides for this purpose, and they do offer you the advantage of being able to seal them once the oil has drained. However, an old five litre oil can, with one side cut away, serves just as well. Old engine oil is a very good rust preventative when painted onto steel surfaces. If you can find no use for the old oil, however, then dispose of it properly; most garages will accept it on your behalf for recycling.

To drain the oil, place the receptacle underneath the sump drain plug and then undo the plug. The oil will start to drain. To increase the flow rate, unscrew the oil filler cap. Leave the oil draining for fifteen minutes or longer if possible.

When the bulk of the oil has drained, you can attend to the strainer. The strainer assembly is to be found underneath the centre of the crankcase, where it is secured by six nuts. Place an oil receptacle under the strainer base plate (it will already be in the correct position on some cars, because the drain plug is situated

in the centre of the base plate) and undo the nuts, taking care to keep oil off your hands.

Remove the strainer assembly. Clean off any of the old gasket material and wash the strainer in neat petrol. When refitting, use new gaskets.

Check the tension of the generator drive belt and, if it deflects more than ½ in. under firm thumb pressure, tighten it. To do this, lock the generator by inserting a thin screwdriver through the hole in the front pulley half against one of the screws in the generator, then remove the pulley nut. There should be a number of shims between the two halves of the pulley, and removing some of these will increase the belt tension (and vice versa). Keep the spare shims under the pulley

When removing shims to tighten the generator drive belt, replace them on the outside of the pulley, so that they are ready to hand when you have to fit a new belt. Check the condition of the belt frequently, and replace it (you'll have to use all the shims) with a new one if it shows any signs of cracks or fraying. (Courtesy Autodata)

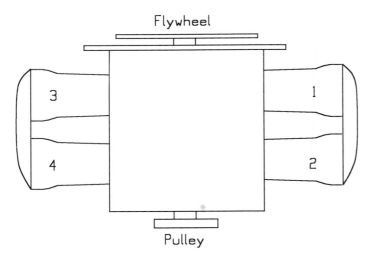

Flywheel

3 1

4 2

Pulley

The firing order is 1, 4, 3, 2. The crankshaft pulley is nearest the rear of the car.

nut on the outside of the pulley. If you do not save the shims and decide to fit a new belt (if the existing one becomes frayed or cut) then you will have to obtain and fit shims; otherwise the belt would be too highly tensioned and it would place unacceptably high strain on the generator bearings.

Disconnect the high tension (HT) leads from their respective spark plugs; if you are unsure about which plug connects with which lead then either place a folded masking tape tag on each lead and write onto this the relevant cylinder number, or mark 1,2,3 or 4 bands on each lead (according to which cylinder it runs to) itself using typist's correction fluid. The illustration shows the cylinder numbers (the pulley end is at the rear of the car, the flywheel is inboard) and the firing order.

The valve clearances have to be adjusted – happily, this is one of the few tasks which can be accomplished easily with the engine still in the car. Chock the front wheels, raise the rear of the car and support it on axle stands.

The engine should be cold. Begin by cleaning all dirt from the two rocker covers, and ensure that no dirt from nearby components can fall onto the valve mechanism. Disconnect the HT leads (mark them if appropriate with the relevant cylinder number to aid correct replacement) and remove the spark plugs. The rocker covers are held by spring clips, prise these away and lift out the covers. Take the car out of gear.

Remove the distributor cap, then turn the engine until the rotor arm is pointing where the number one cylinder HT lead terminates in the distributor cap – do this either by pulling the generator drive belt or with a spanner on the generator pulley bolt (if the engine will not turn over then the drive belt is slipping and should be tightened before carrying on). The rotor arm should be pointing at a notch in the distributor body rim. The

notch in the crankshaft pulley should be pointing upwards, in line with the crankcase centre join or, if there are two notches, they should be slightly to the right of this line.

Check the valve clearances for number one cylinder. Try to gently place a feeler gauge of 0.006 in. (0.15 mm) in between the rocker arm and the top of the valve stem; if it will not go in or if it is very slack then the clearance has to be adjusted. Undo the locknut on the adjuster screw, then place the feeler gauge in position and tighten the adjuster screw until very slight drag can be felt on the gauge when it is moved. Remove the gauge, hold the adjuster in position with a screwdriver and tighten the locknut using a ring spanner. Re-check and re-adjust if necessary.

Turn the engine anti-clockwise until the crankshaft has gone through 180 degrees (the rotor arm will have travelled through 90 degrees and be pointing at the position of number two HT lead within the distributor cap). Check and, if necessary, adjust the clearances for number two cylinder. Repeat the anti-clockwise movement as before (rotor arm 90 degrees, crankshaft 180 degrees) and check and adjust the clearances for cylinder number three, then repeat the process for cylinder four.

There is also a quicker method, which must only ever be used when the engine is stone cold. Turn the engine over until the crankshaft pulley notch is at top dead centre. On one cylinder head, three rockers will have movement, on the other, just one. Adjust those valve clearances, then turn the crank pulley through a complete rotation, when the previously engaged rockers will now have movement; adjust the valve clearances of these.

Re-fit the rocker box covers, using new gaskets.

Ignition

The ignition system is one of those areas where the Beetle has a vast number of permutations regarding timing, points gap etc. A book which is primarily concerned with the subject of restoration cannot possibly cover all eventualities. Because of this, the author describes the principles of carrying out the work and advises the reader to obtain a good workshop manual to find the precise details for the car in question. Be very careful when ordering the manual; some publishers produce up to four different manuals for different years of Beetles.

Remove the sparking plugs and examine them. The nose should be a light fawn colour; if it is covered with a dry sooty layer then the engine has been running too rich, if it is covered with a sticky black layer then the

RIGHT
The Beetle cylinder head. Expect to find the valve gear on your own car covered in oil, unlike this one, which is on a freshly rebuilt engine

BELOW
Don't waste the opportunities afforded for a little maintenance when the engine is out. Here. Terry is checking the rocker to valve stem clearances. The feeler gauge should be gripped reasonably firmly when inserted. If the engine is in the car, you'll have to raise the rear of the car and work lying on your back!

The distributor with its cap removed. Check the condition of the cap and the rotor arm. Remove the rotor arm to check the points condition and gap.

Various distributors are fitted to the Beetle; all share much the same design. (Courtesy Autodata)

1. Condenser
2. Contact breaker arm
3. Securing screw with flat and spring washers
4. Insulating washer
5. Contact breaker point
6. Return spring
7. Breaker plate with earth cable
8. Plastic washer
9. Low tension cable
10. Distributor cap
11. Rotor
12. Distributor shaft
13. Steel washer
14. Fibre washer
15. Distributor housing
16. Vacuum unit
17. Distributor retainer
18. Sealing ring
19. Fibre washer
20. Shims
21. Driving dog
22. Pin
23. Circlip for driving dog
24. Shim

engine is burning oil, probably from the gap between a valve and its stem or past worn piston rings. If the plug ends have a glazed appearance then the engine is overheating and should not be run until the cause has been found and rectified. Check out the ignition timing and the fuel mixture for the cause of most overheating problems, and check especially for the usual causes of pre-ignition – air induction, weak mixture or timing too far advanced. Sooty or oil-fouled plugs may be cleaned and re-used; glazed plugs must be scrapped and replaced.

Clean the spark plug electrodes using a wire brush. The gap should be set using the appropriate tool at 0.23 in. (0.6 mm).

Next check the condition of the points. Remove the distributor cap and lift off the rotor arm. The points should be clean and should present flat surfaces to each other; if they are dirty then they may be gently cleaned; if they are pitted or if one has a hollow and the other a matching protrusion, they should be changed. In either case, the gap will have to be re-set.

Remove the spark plugs and take the car out of gear so that the engine may be turned over by hand. Turn the engine until the points cam is directly on top of a lobe

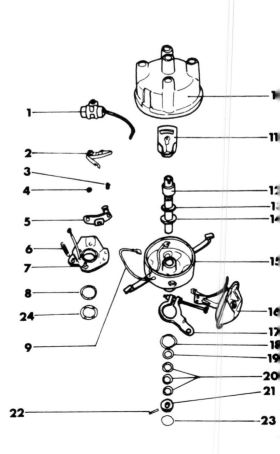

and the points gap is consequently at its greatest. Place a 0.016 in. (0.4 mm) feeler gauge in the gap; it should enter easily with the tiniest amount of drag. If adjustment proves necessary, slacken the securing screw and adjust the points using a screwdriver in the notch provided. Tighten the securing screw then re-check.

It is advisable to check the ignition timing, and it is essential that the timing is checked after the points gap has been re-set. There are two methods of doing this; static and dynamic. The advantage of static timing is that no special tools save a 12V bulb test lamp are needed; the advantages of dynamic timing is that it also checks (where applicable) both the mechanical and the vacuum advance mechanisms, and it is inherently more accurate. To carry out a dynamic timing check you will require a stroboscope. These are low-cost items, but always try to obtain one which will give a reasonably bright light; some are so dim that you cannot see the timing marks by their light in normal daylight. You will also need some typists' correction fluid.

Static timing

Remove the sparking plugs, place the car in neutral and remove the distributor cap. Mark the plug leads as already described if you are unsure of which goes where.

Turn the engine over until the rotor arm is pointing where number one cylinder HT lead terminates in the distributor cap (it will also be pointing at the notch in the distributor body rim). Place the two wires from your test lamp across the points. Turn on the ignition (NOTE; do not leave the ignition turned on for too long, because

ultimately this practice burns out the coil), then turn the engine backwards and forwards until you find the exact point at which the bulb lights. This is the point at which electricity flows to number one plug. At this point, the notch in the crankshaft pulley (single notch cars pre-1971) should be in line with the crankcase split, and the rotor arm should be in line with the distributor body rim notch. Cars made after 1971 which have a single crankshaft pulley notch are not so straightforward. The 1200 and 1300 notch denotes top dead centre (TDC) and there is no notch or other mark to indicate where the timing should be set. It is recommended that owners of these cars either consult a specialised workshop manual or, preferably, have the timing set professionally. The person who undertakes this work will make a temporary timing mark, which you can later make permanent (use a centre punch) for future reference! For cars with three notches on the crankshaft pulley, the centre notch should be used.

If the timing is incorrect, turn the engine until the appropriate notch lines up with the crankcase joint, then slacken the distributor clamp bolt. Attach the test lamp and switch on the ignition. Turn the distributor until you find the exact point at which the lamp lights, and fasten the clamp bolt whilst keeping the distributor in this position. Test and re-set if necessary.

Dynamic timing

The points made regarding the crankshaft pulley timing marks (or lack of the same) are equally appropriate to dynamic timing. If you are unable to establish where the timing mark should be then consult a good workshop

Using a feeler gauge to measure the points gap. (Courtesy Autodata)

The location of the timing marks on the crankshaft pulley. (Courtesy Autodata)

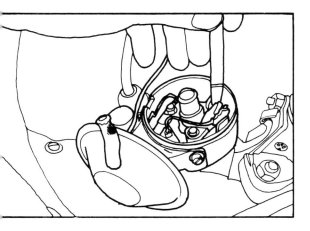

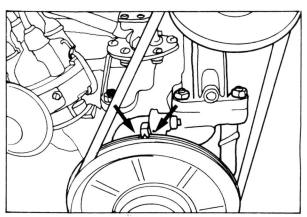

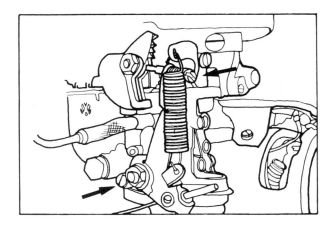

Adjustment of the early carburettor. (Courtesy Autodata)

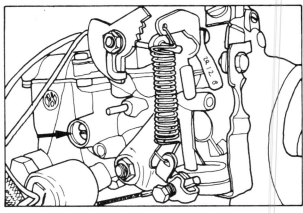

Adjustment of the later carburettor. (Courtesy Autodata)

manual or preferably have the job attended to professionally. If you take the latter course then the person who carries out the test will make a timing mark on the crankshaft pulley, which you can later make permanent with a centre punch for future reference!

Assuming that you can establish the correct timing mark, proceed as follows. Disconnect the vacuum advance pipe from the carburettor. Highlight the timing mark using typists' correction fluid. Disconnect plug lead number one and connect the two leads from the stroboscope to the lead and plug respectively. Start the engine and shine the strobe onto the spinning crankshaft pulley. The stroboscopic light will flash every time number one spark plug fires, and appear to arrest the motion of the crankshaft pulley so that you can easily compare its position relative to the crankcase joint. If the notch or other timing mark appears to the left of the crankcase joint then switch off the engine and retard the ignition by moving the distributor slightly in the direction of the rotor arms travel, or vice versa.

Carburation

The problem with attempting to adjust the air/fuel mixture at home is that there is no accurate method of objectively testing the results of your efforts unless you possess one of the small exhaust gas analysers which are today available for the DIY motorist. Now that exhaust gas is measured as part of the UK annual MOT test, it may be as well to ask that the mixture is set by the tester before your car is tested. Otherwise, it should not take too long nor cost too much to have this small job carried out professionally every six months. Even accurately setting the tickover (750 rpm for most models and 850 rpm for cars with semi-automatic gearboxes) requires

the use of specialist equipment. However, if you wish to do the work at home, these are the basic principles. Begin by warming the engine then adjust the throttle adjusting screw (which bears against the throttle lever) until the revolutions rise to just under 1000 rpm (fast idle). Then turn the mixture control screw slowly clockwise until the point at which the engine begins to run erratically (the mixture is weak) and turn back by 60 degrees (one third of a complete turn). Re-set the tickover. As stated, it is best to have this work carried out by a professional with the aid of an exhaust gas analyser, and you would normally only carry out this adjustment following an engine or carburettor rebuild, in order to get the engine running well enough to make it to your local garage!

In addition to the home exhaust gas analyser machines now available, a number of devices are advertised to make setting mixture easier. Chief amongst these is the Colourtune system, which uses a special spark plug which allows you to see the combustion colour and adjust the mixture to obtain the correct colour and hence the appropriate mixture.

Still on the subject of fuel, check the fuel tank and lines for leakage.

Transmission

Check the transaxle oil level. Park the car on level ground then remove the 17 mm hexagonal transaxle filler plug. If you don't have the correct tool for this, try making your own by bolting or preferably welding a 17 mm bolt to a length of steel. If this is the first time you have attempted to remove the plug, you may find that it is very tight, in which case a hexagonal drive will probably be needed to start it. The oil should be level

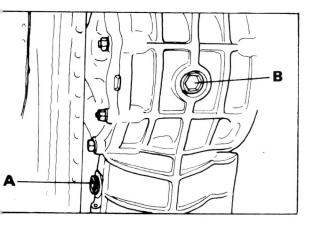

LEFT
The transaxle filler plug (A) and drain plug (B). When the transaxle appears full, leave it for a few minutes and then try again – it takes time for the oil to work its way into the unit. (Courtesy Autodata)

BELOW
The author welded a shortened 17 mm headed bolt to a length of steel to make this drain/filler plug tool. The filler plug was so tight that the bolt sheared, and eventually a proper hexagonal drive had to be used. With regular maintenance, the tool (repaired) should be able to start the plug!

with this and, if not, top up. In the case of Stickshift models, a dipstick is provided to show the oil level: if this is low, then top it up using the correct fluid – Dexron 1 or Dexron 2.

The clutch travel should be checked and adjusted if necessary. There should be half an inch of free play. To adjust pedal travel, turn the large wing nut on the clutch operating lever, which can be found in front of the engine on the nearside of the car.

Grease the nipples on the front suspension (beam axle). Using a pumping oil can, lubricate the door, bonnet and engine lid hinges and locks.

Check the condition of the drive shaft joint gaiters and renew if necessary. In addition to being an MOT test failure point, split gaiters will allow water and dirt into the joints, where it will cause accelerated wear.

Brakes

Check the fluid level in the brake master cylinder; if this is a little low then top up with new brake fluid. If the level is very low then fluid has been lost and the car should not be used until the cause has been identified and dealt with. (See Chapter Four.)

Check the thickness of the lining of the pads/shoes. The minimum acceptable thickness is ⅛ in. (3 mm) for pads, and ¹⁄₁₀ in. (2.5 mm) for shoes.

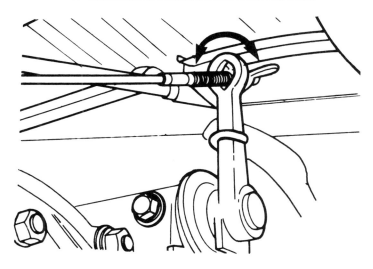

If approaching this thickness then it is as well to renew them. There are inspection holes in the brake backplate for checking the shoe thickness.

If the brake pedal travel is too great and the handbrake is inefficient, the rear drum brakes will have to be adjusted. Note that later cars have self-adjusting rear drum brakes, and poor braking performance usually means that either the pads and shoes are contaminated or worn, or that some part of the mechanism is sticking.

Drum brake shoes are supported at one end by the

This large wing nut is used to set the cable adjustment. (Courtesy Autodata)

wheel cylinder pistons; these are pushed outwards so that the shoe presses against the drum when the brake pedal is pressed. At the other end the shoes are located in the adjusting screws. Adjustment is carried out by removing the two blanking plugs in each backplate, and using a straight-bladed screwdriver (an old screwdriver with a cranked end is better) to turn the star adjuster wheel for each shoe in turn. Adjust each shoe until the wheel is locked, then back it off until the wheel will turn freely.

Operate both the handbrake and foot brake to centralise the shoes, then re-adjust the brakes if necessary; sometimes this process will have to be repeated several times before the shoes are correctly adjusted.

Check the handbrake travel and adjust if necessary. When the handbrake is pulled up onto the fourth notch, the rear wheels should be locked. If not, then adjust as follows. If you have just adjusted the brakes, then pump the pedal to centralise the shoes. Pull the handbrake onto the second notch then remove the rubber gaiter from the bottom of the handbrake lever. Slacken off the locknuts on the cable ends, then insert a screwdriver into each cable end slot in turn to prevent it from turning whilst you tighten the nut. Adjust the cable end nuts so that equal pressure is felt on both, then test the handbrake by pulling it up to notch four and seeing whether the wheels are locked. Repeat if necessary and finish by tightening the locknuts and re-fitting the gaiter.

If, in common with the author, you have difficulty in remembering which way to turn the adjusters in order to spread the shoes, try holding a nut and bolt by the adjuster so that the bolt head takes the place of the shoe end and the nut imitates the adjuster. By turning the nut you will see (there are no left-hand threads) which way the bolt head moves and deduct whether to turn the adjuster up or down. The front adjusters are the more difficult to get at, and a cranked screwdriver will be a positive aid.

Annual service

Carry out every task and check listed previously. The brake shoes and pads (disc brakes only) have to be checked for wear. Even if the car has passed the MOT braking test, this gives no indication of brake *wear*, only of braking efficiency. In the case of drum brakes, rather than peer through the hole in the backplate, remove the drum to permit a more thorough inspection. The brake drums should be cleaned. (See Chapter Four for more details of these operations.) Renew the sparking plugs and points. Renew the engine breather filter. Every eighteen months renew the brake hydraulic fluid (see Chapter Four). Every three years renew the brake hydraulic seals.

BODYWORK PREVENTATIVE MAINTENANCE

You can extend the useful working life of your Beetle greatly by looking after the bodywork on a regular basis. Whilst it is true to say that no matter how badly rotted a car becomes, it can still be rebuilt (albeit at considerable cost), there can be no doubting that prevention is always less expensive and traumatic than cure, and this section of the book looks at ways of extending the life of the bodywork in order to put off that time when extensive bodywork rebuilding will be required.

The rear brake mechanism. As a matter of course, always clean the drum, shoes and other components of dust (out of doors, and most important, wear a dust mask because the dust is dangerous to breathe in), strip and grease the adjuster mechanisms and check for fluid leakage whenever the drums come off.

General care

In order for metal to rust it needs only to be exposed to the slightest amount of moisture (including moisture in humid air). Paint scratches and chips which expose bare metal will obviously permit this to happen, and so any such breaches of the paintwork should receive immediate attention, preferably before any moisture which comes into contact with the metal has sufficient time to let rust gain a foothold.

Very shallow scratches which do not go through to the metal may be gently cleaned out and hand painted with a small brush. If bare metal has been exposed (to all intents and purposes corrosion begins the moment metal comes into contact with air which contains moisture) then it is usually best to take a small area of the surrounding paintwork down with wet 'n' dry (used wet) to reveal a little more metal than was originally exposed. The existing paint at the edges should be 'feathered', that is, there should not be a discernible shoulder around the area. This should be dried and thoroughly de-greased before being treated with Bondaglass Voss 'Bonda Prima' or a similar rust-retarding paint. Use of this product should stop any tiny traces of rust which remain on the surface of the metal from spreading. If necessary, high-build primer can then be applied and flatted down before top coating. Before applying any paint or rust-resistant product, check that it is compatible with the existing surrounding paintwork of the car. *Do not* use cellulose-based products on other types of paint, because the powerful thinners will lift them.

Old paintwork will usually be faded, so that the new paint stands out from the surrounding area. If this is the case then cutting the old and new paint (allowing a suitable period for the new paint to harden first, which varies according to the type of paint used) with a proprietary mild cutting compound will remove accumulated road dirt and take a very thin layer off the old paint to lessen the difference, as well as improving the surface of the new paint. It is best to leave any new paint to harden for at least a fortnight before cutting it back.

Underneath the car, particularly within the wheel arches but also along the floor outer edges and heater channels, mud accumulates and should be cleaned off at regular intervals. Mud not only holds moisture in contact with the car body for long periods but it holds the salt which is used on roads in the UK in winter. Little accelerates rusting faster than salt.

Steam cleaning is the very best way in which to remove mud from the underside of the car, although most people make do with a powerful jet of water. High pressure cleaners can also remove underseal which no longer adheres to the metal due to the spread of rust underneath. Far from being a problem, this is a great help because it gives you a fighting chance of dealing with the rust at the earliest opportunity. You can hire such washers by the hour or day from many DIY and equipment hire businesses. If you do use one then make sure you have rust-arresting primer and some underseal to deal with the rusted areas which will be exposed.

Washing the car regularly not only keeps it looking good but also helps to show up any scratches or minor dents which could, if left untreated, lead to the onset of corrosion. It is a good idea to begin by washing the underside of the car and the wheels, because the use of a hose or high-pressure water device can splatter mud all over the place, including onto the paintwork you have just washed if you did things in the wrong order. The head of a stiff broom can be a help in removing mud from under the floorpan/heater channel areas, where it can be difficult to direct a jet of water. After cleaning the underside, switch your attentions to the roof and then work downwards.

Never use ordinary washing-up liquid to wash the car, because many liquids contain industrial salts! (Do not use them in the windscreen washer bottle, either, because some of this soapy water will find its way onto the paintwork). It is always safest to use a proper car shampoo. Begin by hosing the car down with fresh water to get as much dirt as possible into suspension and off the body. If you take the wash leather or even a sponge to bodywork covered in gritty dirt then the dirt will grind at the surface of the paint. Begin with the roof, work along the bonnet, down the back and sides and lastly do the valances.

After this initial hosing or washing down it is as well to use a chamois leather and repeat the exercise, gently helping dirt from the surface with the leather, before applying the car shampoo and then rinsing this off.

At this stage you should thoroughly inspect the paintwork for any signs of damage and attend to these before polishing. If the paintwork is very dull then you might consider cutting it back before you polish it, using one of the several products for the purpose which are widely available from motor factors. Finally, polish the paintwork. Car polish repels water, so that water which is kicked up from the road (and which contains dirt) will wash away before the majority of the dirt has an opportunity to come out of suspension and stick to the paint.

Preventing rust

Whenever a replacement panel which is a part of a box section has to be welded into position, the opportunity should be taken to give as much protection first to the side which will end up inside the section. Obviously, the area of metal which is to be the actual join will have to be cleaned bright and de-greased, but most of the panel can be treated to several layers of primer. Some of this paint protection will probably burn off during the welding process, but any protection is better than none.

The maximum protection against rusting will be gained by using one of the better 'rust arresting' primers rather than normal primer. In the author's experience, the rust-arresting primer previously mentioned also performs very well on clean metal; better, in fact, than normal primers.

The Beetle has a number of box sections, most of which can (and usually do) rust from the inside. When a panel or panels from a box section is repaired the opportunity to give further protection to the metal should not be missed. As soon as the welding is finished and the metal has cooled, a wax-based product such as Dinitrol 3125 should be applied. This will often entail drilling a ⅜ in. hole in order to gain access to the enclosed section, and the hole should afterwards be sealed with a rubber grommet.

The wax is applied either with one of the hand pumps supplied by the manufacturer or via a compressor-driven 'paraffin' or underseal spray gun. When cold, most wax-based products are of too thick a consistency to spray properly, and so they should be warmed until they become thin enough by standing the tin in a bowl of hot water. A cheap though less effective alternative to wax is old sump oil, which will have to be thinned in order to get a fine spray and to which some people add a little creosote.

Underneath the car, not only the bodywork but also items from the suspension benefit from protection against corrosion. There are various ways in which the suspension and associated components may be protected.

If the underside of the car is steam cleaned, then components previously covered in a layer of mud will be revealed to possess a covering of rust underneath. It is not always practical to clean and re-paint such components nor to partially clean and then use a proprietary rust arrester. Many people slow the corrosive process in such cases by painting on old engine oil.

When oil is applied to a ferrous surface, it spreads to form a thin protective layer which offers the considerable advantage of remaining 'self healing' for a period of time—that is, as if the layer is breached by a scratch then the oil will again spread to re-cover it as long as it remains thin enough to do so. In time, the oil not only thickens of its own accord but also because it is absorbed by dirt, so that in order to work consistently the process should be repeated from time to time. If oil is used thus then be very careful not to let any come into contact with the brakes.

Proprietary wax products such as Dinitrol 3125 are used by many in place of oil (which can be very messy to apply), mainly in the protection of the underbody. Waxes remain reasonably fluid during the summer months and so can be self-healing, but in colder winter climates this will not happen.

Underseal is the usual product utilised for underbody protection. It is a very thick substance which can go some way towards absorbing the impact of stones kicked up by the road wheels which would otherwise expose bare metal to the elements. Underseal forms a thick and hard 'skin' over the metal, and here lies its greatest drawback. Any rust which exists before the application of underseal or rust which forms afterwards can spread rapidly and virtually unopposed, unseen under the surface of the underseal.

Underseal works best on new panels which already have some form of rust protection, and is best considered a form of protection for the actual anti-rust protection.

Arresting rust

When rust is discovered on thin body metal or even on sturdy chassis or suspension components there are two options for dealing with it. Preferable is the complete removal of all traces of rust from the surface of the metal, followed by primering and top-coating. This can be a time-consuming process, however, and many people prefer to utilise rust arresting products. Sometimes, the body panel metal can be so badly rusted and thin that completely removing the rust might result in a hole. In such circumstances a good rust arresting product can help to prolong the life of the metal, provided that it is not a structurally important panel.

The car accessory market usually offers a wide range of chemical treatments which are all 'guaranteed' to arrest existing rust and ensure that the metal never rusts again. Not all appear to actually work in the experience of the author and also according to various published reports of independent testing. Rather than list the many products which do not reportedly work, the two which in the author's experience do work and which he uses are Bondaglass Gloss 'Bonda Prima' and Dinitrol RC800.

Unlike many other products, Bonda Prima is not claimed to chemically alter the composition of rust. The manufacturers state that it works by infiltrating and encapsulating rust particles in a resin. Dinitrol RC800 converts rust into an inert organic compound which can be primed. Both certainly work.

In order to work properly, rust arresters should be applied only to flake-free, grease-free and dry surfaces, which should ideally have no more than a thin coating of corrosion.

It is useless, incidentally, to use any rust arresting primer on metal which is to be filled. If you are straightening out a dent, for instance, then you have to remove all traces of rust before applying the filler straight onto clean metal, because if you were to apply a rust-resistant primer first then the filler would adhere strongly only to the primer, which does not itself possess sufficient adhesion to the metal, and both filler and paint will drop off in next to no time. If you apply filler over rusted metal, the rust will rapidly spread underneath the filler, which will eventually drop out.

To arrest rust, you should begin by thoroughly cleaning and de-greasing the section in question. When it has dried then it may be firstly wire-brushed and finally rubbed with emery cloth or paper in order to remove any loose rust and to key the surface. Follow the instructions with whichever product you choose to the letter. In the case of Dinitrol RC800, this entails merely painting on one or more coats (12 hours between coats) and then applying any primer paint. The work should be carried out in a warm, dust-free and dry building if possible; otherwise on a hot and dry day outside. Bonda Prima is available in a spray can or a tin for brushing or spraying with a compressor. After treatment, cellulose should be applied either within 6 to 24 hours or after seven days; other paints may be applied after four hours.

Areas which can really benefit from rust arresting maintenance are those body panels on the underside of the car, such as the heater channel closing panels and the floorpans. If underseal on such panels shows any signs of lifting then the following can greatly increase their life-span (assuming that they have not rusted right through).

Firstly, all traces of old underseal and paint have to be removed. The easiest way in which to achieve this is to scrape away the underseal and then use paraffin and a rag to remove the remnants. You can use an electric drill (or an air drill powered by a compressor) fitted with one of a selection of wire brushes and 'flap wheels' or, alternatively, an angle grinder fitted with a cup brush.

Beware the lengths of wire which become detached from the cup (which rotates at 10,000 or more rpm) and fly off at high speed – but these will tend to rip away filaments of underseal which stick to whatever they hit. Protective clothing, especially goggles, must be worn to avoid personal injury from flying rust flakes and the aforementioned lengths of wire from cup brushes. If the panel being treated is anywhere near the petrol tank then this should firstly be removed.

Next, as much rust as possible should be removed using emery cloth or paper (to work right into corners) in addition to the drill and wire brushes and flap wheels. No more than a very thin coating of rust should remain. Apply the rust arrester, followed by a second coat and a topcoat at the recommended intervals. Underseal may then be re-applied if desired to finish the job.

General bodywork preventative maintenance

On the hottest, driest day of the summer it is a good idea to remove the seats, carpets and interior trim from the car, and to give as much of the newly exposed metal as possible anti-corrosion protection.

A thin coating of a moisture-inhibiting wax or oil may be applied under footwell rubber mats to protect the floor and heater channel sections. Even with this protection, if the carpets (where fitted) get wet then they should immediately be removed and dried out.

Chrome work presents special problems. The tiniest pin-hole will enable rust to become established under the surface of the chrome, and it spreads unseen until large areas begin to 'bubble' and eventually to flake off. New chrome work can be polished to provide some protection, but because the bumpers and other items with a chrome finish are vulnerable to stone chipping, there remains very little which can be done in the way of long term protection. The non-chromed side of such fittings does benefit from either wax or oil protection.

Where small chrome fittings meet painted bodywork, problems with rusting can arise. The chrome light surrounds and other fittings are all able to trap and hold water in contact with the bodywork, and furthermore, the bodywork paint is often breached as the pieces of trim are fitted into place. Wax or oil may be used to help prevent this if care is taken not to allow either to run onto surrounding paintwork.

4 · REPAIR AND RESTORATION – MECHANICAL

Workshop manuals are usually based on work which is carried out on recent examples of the car concerned, examples on which nuts and bolts are not seized solid, on which screw slots, nuts and bolt heads have not previously been distorted by some ham-fisted and ill-equipped incompetent, on which clean components come apart easily and the use of brute force and ignorance is never a tempting – though dangerous – option. With old cars of all types, life is rarely so easy, and the author has attempted to include as many of the typical problems encountered when working on old Beetles as possible, and to give the best solutions to those problems.

Occasionally, a workshop manual will advise a particular course of action without explaining how the item in question works, why it is there, or without giving background information on why the work should be done. The author believes that if the reader understands how a mechanical item works and what it does, then he or she will be better equipped to deal with any problems which arise concerning it.

This book approaches mechanical repair work as though the individual jobs were being encountered during a restoration rather than as one-off running repairs. As far as possible, the chapter is written so as to be of benefit to those who do have to tackle a particular repair in isolation, although space dictates that in this respect this book should be viewed as a companion to a workshop manual.

As with the previous chapter, the number and variety of specifications of Beetles prevents any single work on mechanical repair from being truly comprehensive, and readers are strongly advised to obtain a good workshop manual specific to their own Beetle. Bear in mind that the more limited the scope of the manual (the fewer varieties of Beetle it covers) the more comprehensive it will be. A manual which covers half a dozen different models will be very limited in specific detail on any of them.

The author strongly recommends that novices use a camera to record stages in the strip-down of mechanical components as a reminder of how they fit together during re-assembly! Not even the most detailed of workshop manuals – let alone a restoration guide – can illustrate absolutely everything and, although the author and editor have included as many illustrations as

There are times when it's best to sit and think the job through instead of launching headlong into it and risk making mistakes. The author at full ponder.

possible, the 80,000 or so production modifications to the Beetle preclude the chance of any book ever being truly comprehensive in this respect.

WORKPLACE AND TOOLS

More so than with maintenance, a dry and warm place of work is very desirable for mechanical repair because the work is much more involved and therefore time-consuming, and your own comfort has to be a priority. In addition, you will be dissembling components which will be susceptible to rusting if left for any length of time in a damp workshop.

The ideal premises will be fitted with a bench and have lots of dry storage, yet still leave ample room for you to work on the car. One metre clearance all around the car is really an absolute minimum, and a clearance of two metres is preferable.

Your basic maintenance tool set will be found wanting for many mechanical repair tasks. Not only will the number of different tools that you need grow with the range of repairs you undertake, but some of the tools will have to be fairly heavy-duty if they are to survive the rigours of mechanical repair. In addition to a normal socket set it pays to obtain a set of deep sockets (preferably hexagonal), perhaps a speed brace and extension bars if your current set does not have these, and a torque wrench is vital.

Many of the fasteners (screws, nuts and bolts) which you will have to remove will prove to be seized almost solid and are best dealt with by using an impact wrench which will come with a set of screwdriver bit heads but which should have a detachable ½ in. square drive adaptor which allows you to use it with hexagonal impact sockets when necessary (if you have a large enough air compressor, then an air impact wrench is obviously better). The Beetle, in common with most cars, has a small number of large and usually stubborn nuts ranging up to 42 mm in size, and the author always prefers to buy hexagonal rather than twelve-point sockets in larger sizes, because these are far less likely to 'round' the nut or burst in use.

Still with heavy-duty tools, a set of general-purpose pullers (2 and 3 legged) will be necessary, along with a ball joint splitter, a coil spring compressor (McPherson strut cars only) and perhaps a nut splitter.

A number of less heavy tools are also needed, including internal and external circlip pliers, a vernier calliper, Allen keys, an inspection lamp, electrical crimping tool and a selection of electrical connectors.

Depending on the extent of work which you wish to carry out, you may also require a number of highly

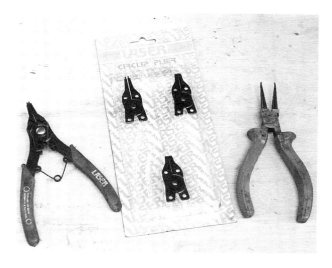

Circlip pliers. The pair on the right are for internal circlips and useless for removing external ones. The pair on the left have interchangeable jaws and will handle all types of circlips – even those which are difficult to get to.

ABOVE
This wedge-type ball joint splitter did not cost too much, and has given many years of service.

BELOW
If you buy cheap tools, they'll cost you more in the long run. This budget scissors-type ball joint splitter broke after very little use.

specialised tools which are specific to the Beetle or perhaps even to a particular model or year. These tools are not all essential but they can make life very much easier when working on the engine, drive train and suspension. In the UK, VW Tools of West Yorkshire (address at the back of this book) feature most of these specialised tools in their mail order catalogue.

As ever, buy the very best tools which you can afford, because poor quality tools will cost you more in the long run. This does not mean that you should blow half of your budget on a set of top-end spanners and not have enough money left to buy a decent socket set! If your budget is limited, then ensure that you get all of the basic tools mentioned above, and borrow or hire more specialised tools as and when necessary.

Safety

Always carefully consider safety before starting work. Disconnect the battery earth strap and for bigger jobs preferably remove the battery from the car. If you have to work under the car, ensure that it is properly held aloft by solid axle stands and that the wheels which are left in contact with the ground are properly chocked so that the car cannot roll and tumble off the axle stands. If you are starting work on a job which may involve using a naked flame anywhere on the front of the car (welding or using heat to help 'start' a reluctant nut or bolt) then begin by removing the fuel tank and line. Before using a naked flame or generating great heat (as in welding) anywhere on the car remove the fuel line or any brake hose or pipe in the vicinity.

Petrol is not the only highly flammable substance to present hazards; brake fluid is equally dangerous and apparently more easily set on fire; plastics and rubber also burn well. The greater danger from petrol is posed by its fumes rather than by the liquid itself; the fumes are heavier than air and can fall to fill a pit with a potentially explosive mixture – so no smoking, welding nor naked flames in the pit.

Always make full use of appropriate safety clothing. You only have one pair of eyes and you cannot obtain replacements if you damage them so it pays to protect them with goggles whenever you are working under the car or doing anything which causes sparks or rust flakes to fly through the air.

When replacing components which are held by bolts, it is good practice to put a little copper-based grease or alternative aluminium-based products on the bolt threads, because this will make their subsequent removal much easier. Do not, however, use such greases on fittings which have to be torqued, because they reduce the natural friction to the point that the fitting can be over-stressed when torque is applied. On nuts and bolts which are to be torqued, use a light oil instead.

The author and publishers can accept no responsibility for any loss, injury or mishap which occurs whilst any of the instructions in this book are being followed; it is up to the reader to at all times accept responsibility for his or her safety.

FUEL TANK REMOVAL

The first step on a restoration or indeed any major mechanical job is to make the car safe, not only disconnecting and preferably removing the battery, but also the fuel tank and lines, as well as bleeding the brakes to remove all highly flammable liquids. (Brake bleeding is covered in detail in the section dealing with the braking system.)

The fuel tank is situated within the front luggage compartment, usually covered with carpeting or trim. Its removal usually precedes a full restoration, although it may prove necessary to remove it to check suspected leakage. Disconnect the battery, and pull the petrol gauge wire connector from the terminal on the sender unit.

If possible, the tank should be drained of as much petrol as possible, and this can be accomplished in two ways. It is feasible to clamp the flexible line under the tank, to disconnect the fuel line and to connect up another line which is lead to a suitable receptacle. Most people will opt to siphon the fuel out. Whichever method is used, the author would strongly advise that the tank and receptacle are earthed; that they are connected by a length of wire which will prevent any chance of static electrical discharges between the two, which could ignite the fuel/air mixture.

Undo the fitting which holds the fuel filler pipe to the tank and pull this from the tank, then stuff the tank filler hole with rag to prevent accidental spillage. Undo the set screws which secure the tank and lift it just high enough to get a clamp (a brake hose clamp is ideal) onto the flexible hose on the outlet. The tank may now be lifted out carefully, and is best stored in a separate outbuilding.

Examine the fuel tank minutely (especially the underside and seams) for signs of rust or even tiny perforations. Never attempt to repair a fuel tank; if it leaks, replace it and ask your local garage to dispose of the old one safely for you.

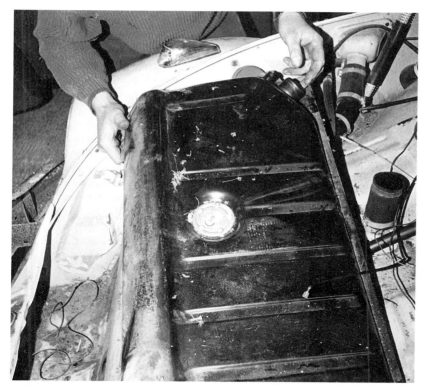

The first step in a restoration is always to disconnect the battery. The second is always to remove the fuel tank. Drain as much fuel from it as you can, disconnect the filler pipe and stuff the tank filler hole with a rag, then lift the tank sufficiently to be able to get a hose clamp onto the outlet underneath before lifting it clear.

On McPherson Strut cars, tank is tucked under the wiper motor box at the rear. Clamp the fuel line from underneath the car, because in some instances it is too short to allow you to pull the tank up to clamp it.

This is what you'll see after removing the fuel tank from a torsion bar car. The next step in the stripdown will be to disconnect the steering column flanges.

ENGINE REMOVAL

The Beetle has to be the most DIY enthusiast-friendly car of all, because engine removal can be accomplished more quickly and easily than with any other car. In fact, so easy is it to drop out the Beetle's engine, that it is tempting to remove it for some jobs which can be accomplished – albeit with some difficulty – with the engine in situ. In addition to a trolley jack and either axle stands or ramps, the tools needed are a 17 mm open end and ring spanner, an 8 mm combination spanner, straight and cross-head screwdrivers and a fuel pipe clamp.

Basically, engine removal involves raising the rear of the car, disconnecting everything which connects the engine to the rest of the car (wiring, fuel line, throttle linkage etc.), supporting the engine on a trolley jack, unbolting the four engine mounting bolts, then pulling the engine back clear of the gearbox input (first motion) shaft, then lowering it on the trolley jack and pulling it out from under the car.

Begin by disconnecting the battery earth strap. Because engine removal becomes easier the higher the rear of the car is raised, you may prefer to disconnect both battery terminals and remove the battery to prevent spillage. You can remove the engine lid if required, although this is not essential. Chock the front wheels fore and aft (it is good practice to engage the steering lock where fitted to prevent the wheels from turning side to side), raise the rear of the car as high as possible (using a baulk of timber to protect the sump) and support the car on axle stands placed under the side members, again using wood packing. Check that the car is raised high enough for the engine, when balanced on top of the (lowered) trolley jack, to be drawn out from under the rear valance. Check that the axle stands are secure by lowering the jack until the stands are taking the combined weight of the engine and body, then raise the jack so that it takes the engine's weight but does not lift the bodywork off the axle stands.

Remove the air filter assembly, pre heater and oil breather hoses. You can drain the oil if desired, although this is optional. Use masking tape and a biro to make up tags for wires as you remove them if you are not 100 per cent sure that you will be able to remember where each goes, and remove the wire from the oil pressure switch, the low tension lead, any wires attached to the carburettor, plus wiring which runs to the generator.

Remove the accelerator cable from the carburettor, and push it back through the hole in the fan cowling. Remove the heater hoses from the exhaust shield plate, then remove the exhaust shield plate itself.

From underneath the car, disconnect the flexible fuel line from the rigid fuel line, plugging both to minimise

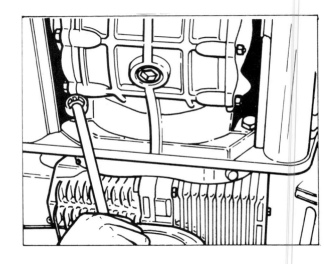

The lower engine mounting bolts are not too difficult to get at. (Courtesy Autodata)

fuel leakage. The potential for fuel leakage is potentially far less if the fuel tank has already been removed.

Disconnect the heater control cables. Disconnect the heater ducting from the heat exchangers.

Ensure that the jack is taking the weight of the engine but not of the bodywork. Remove the top engine mounting nuts and bolts. These cannot normally be seen and you'll have to work by 'feel' alone (the car in the photographs has its bodyshell raised from the chassis which obviously improves access). On pre-1971 Beetles there is a nut on each bolt and removal is a two-person job. On later cars the bolts run into captive threads and the task can be accomplished single-handed. Check again that the engine is fully supported by the jack before removing the lower engine mounting bolts – it is essential that no weight is allowed to fall on the gearbox first motion (input) shaft. Check that no wires, cables or hoses connect the engine to the rest of the car. Pull the engine rearwards until it is clear of the input shaft, then lower it and drag it out from underneath the car.

Re-fitting is the reverse of removal, and the same cardinal rule of not allowing the engine's weight to hang on the gearbox first motion shaft applies. The engine bay side seal may need replacing, and this is one of the less pleasant tasks in Beetle restoration! The rubber locates in rails and, whilst in theory it should be possible to work its lips into the rail, in practice you may succumb to the temptation to open up one of the metal lips, slip in the rubber then tap the lip back down.

If you have previously removed the sound deadening material from within the engine bay then replace this before the engine goes back in. The panels have wire reinforcing and this is all too easy to stab your hand with, so be careful! Whilst on the subject of trim, the engine lid seal can either be clipped or fed into place; in either case be sure to leave plenty of slack so that the

On this later Beetle, one engine mounting bolt also serves to hold the starter motor, and the bolt has a flat machined onto the head so that it won't turn when the nut is undone or tightened.

With the bodyshell off, it is far easier to get at the engine mounting bolts.

The engine bay side sound proofing panels have internal wire reinforcing, the ends of which are almost guaranteed to spike your hand. They locate under the folding tabs which – incidentally – make good earths if you have problems with the rear light earth connection.

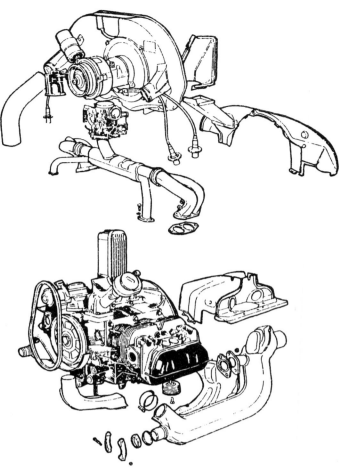

Tin ware, inlet manifold and heat exchangers have to come off. (Courtesy Autodata)

When the rotor arm lines up with number one plug lead terminal, it will also be in line with the notch in the distributor rim and the crankshaft pulley notch should be at the top. (Courtesy Autodata)

trim lies flat and does its job.

Do remember to feed the throttle cable through the hole in the fan casing before fitting the engine, and ensure that it cannot kink to become trapped in between the engine back plate and the bell housing. Raise the car just high enough to allow the engine on a trolley jack under the valance then, with an assistant to help balance the engine, raise it up to the same height as the first motion shaft, align it correctly and ease it backwards. Take care not to rip out the engine bay seal!

ENGINE STRIP

Having a split crankcase and cylinder barrels gives the flat four more in common with a motorcycle engine than the average car engine, and the stripping and rebuilding of the Beetle engine is much easier than working on most other car engines. To properly inspect the internals, however, requires that you have access to highly accurate measuring equipment which is expensive to buy. This measuring equipment can reveal a need for certain engineering operations to be carried out, again using equipment which is unlikely to be available.

Before starting a restoration, it is worth while borrowing a compression tester and using this on all four cylinders to ascertain whether any are low. The desired compression varies between 100–142 psi according to the engine type, but if all four cylinders give similar readings in excess of 100–110 psi and within 10 psi of each other then compression is OK. If one or more cylinders give low readings then expect to find leakage either past the piston rings (worn or damaged rings or bores), past the barrel and /cylinder head or a valve (burnt valves/seats). If one or more readings are low, then try putting a little engine oil into the bore via the spark plug hole and re-test. If the reading is now normal, the chances are that the leakage is past the piston rings; if it is unaltered, look for burnt valves. Also, try pulling and pushing the crankshaft pulley to check for excessive end float (over 0.005 inch) and lifting and lowering it to check for play in the mains – if you can feel any play here then a bottom-end overhaul is called for.

If you were to strip your engine and then take the components to a professional engineering shop for inspection and for any machining work found necessary to be carried out, you could discover that the costs of the work plus any components which prove essential by far exceeds the cost of a straight replacement reconditioned unit.

Because of this, it is strongly recommended that you give serious consideration to replacing your own engine with a reconditioned unit. In addition to a straight swap, this gives you the option of buying a more powerful unit or one built to withstand use with unleaded fuel.

A clean work area is vital, and cleanliness is of the greatest importance generally when working on an engine. You can strip the Beetle engine on any flat surface such as a workbench or even on the floor, but the task is much easier if you can buy or borrow one of the special bench or floor standing mounts which bolt onto one half of the crankcase and allow the unit to be swivelled for improved access. Before starting to strip the engine, drain the oil.

Remove the spark plugs then turn the engine over by pulling the generator belt until the notch in the front half of the pulley aligns with the screw in the generator.

Use a screwdriver between the two to lock the generator, then undo the pulley nut, remove the drive belt and replace the pulley nut with its shims. Undo the clamp which holds the generator and the set screws which hold the fan shroud, then lift the assembly clear of the crankcase.

Undo the inlet manifold nuts and lift the manifold and carburettor clear. Unbolt and remove the oil cooler, then blank off the oil feed and return holes in the crankcase to prevent anything from entering it.

Remove the thermostat. Remove the distributor and fuel pump.

Unbolt the heat exchangers/exhaust assembly complete. Remove the crankshaft pulley bolt, and use a puller to remove the pulley. Remove the clutch.

To remove the clutch, slacken the bolts in a diagonal pattern. When fitting a new clutch, ensure that it is correctly aligned as described in the text. Take the opportunity to check the condition of the ring gear teeth.

With the tinware removed, unbolt the inlet manifold ends and remove the central pipe and carburettor.

ABOVE
With the bulk of the tinware off, it remains to remove the oil cooler, distributor, generator pedestal and fuel pump; finally remove the heat exchangers.

BELOW
Removing the flywheel using a two-legged puller.

The flywheel nut should be tightened to 200 ft lbs, and can take some shifting! The flywheel has to be locked before the nut can be undone, and this is best achieved by using a steel bar of at least four feet in length with two holes drilled to correspond with clutch bolt holes, to which the bar is bolted. Using a 36 mm, three-quarter inch drive hexagonal socket and the best leverage you can obtain, slacken the nut. It may prove necessary to have an assistant or two to hold the engine still while force is applied; a better method is to arrange the two levers so that you can push them together. If one lever end rests firmly on the workshop floor, the second can be pressed downwards without any of the force being applied moving the engine. It is still advisable to have an assistant to hold the engine still.

If this fails, it may be as well to take the engine to a garage and ask a mechanic to start the nut – a powerful air impact driver can sometimes work.

Mark one dowel peg and the adjacent area of the flywheel with a dab of paint so that the latter can be replaced in the same relative position, then remove the flywheel. A little help from a rubber mallet may prove necessary.

Clean then remove the rocker box covers by prising off their spring clips. Clean away all traces of the gaskets (which, like all other gaskets, must be renewed). Undo, as evenly as possible, the two rocker gear retaining bolts then lift the rocker gear clear and mark it in some way to show which cylinder it corresponds to. From now on, all components must be marked or stored in such a way that they can be replaced in the correct location. Remove and mark the pushrods, or (alternatively) place them in a piece of stiff cardboard with suitable holes and make your marks on this.

Slacken then remove the cylinder head nuts in the sequence shown, turning each nut a fraction before progressing to the next, then repeating the process until all are loose and can be removed. Lift the cylinder head from the cylinders, giving the underside of the head a tap or three with a rawhide mallet if necessary (it usually is). *Never* use any kind of lever in between the head and the cylinders, because this would ruin the seal between them. As the head comes free, remove the pushrod tubes and mark them.

Pull each cylinder in turn away from the crankcase until the piston pin and gudgeon clip can be seen. Remove the gudgeon clip, gently drift the pin until it is free of the connecting rod small end, then remove the cylinder and piston complete. You can remove the cylinder first and then the piston if you wish, but removing both together lessens the chances of cylinders and pistons becoming mixed up!

Remove the oil pump cover plate. The oil pump is gripped between the two crankcase halves and its

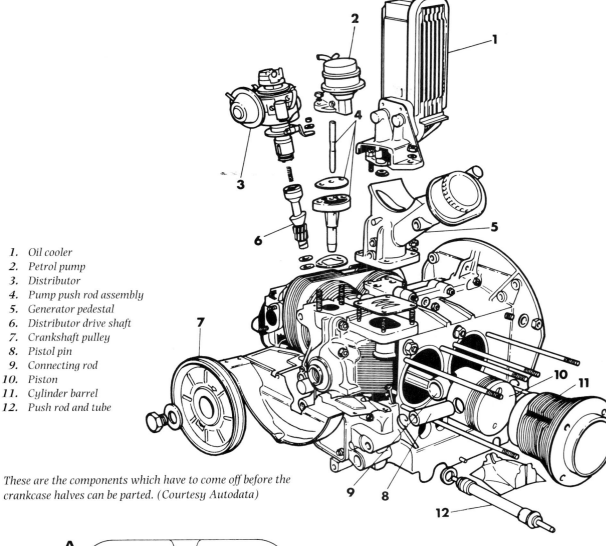

1. Oil cooler
2. Petrol pump
3. Distributor
4. Pump push rod assembly
5. Generator pedestal
6. Distributor drive shaft
7. Crankshaft pulley
8. Pistol pin
9. Connecting rod
10. Piston
11. Cylinder barrel
12. Push rod and tube

These are the components which have to come off before the crankcase halves can be parted. (Courtesy Autodata)

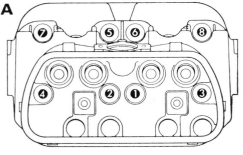

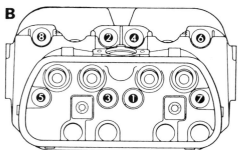

A. Initial tightening and
   final loosening order
B. Final tightening and
   initial loosening order

Follow these sequences for slackening and tightening the cylinder head nuts. Turn each by one flat on the first pass, then by two on the next, then slacken them fully. Tightening is also progressive. (Courtesy Autodata)

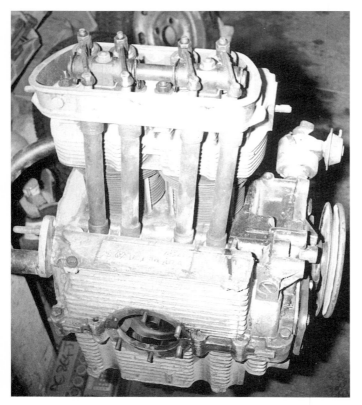

removal requires a special tool or, alternatively, can take place when the crankcase halves are split. Remove the six nuts which secure the oil strainer plate, then remove the oil strainer.

Remove – where applicable – the generator pedestal/oil filler assembly. Remove the oil pressure switch. The crankcase may now be split. Ideally, the crankcase assembly will be held in a special mount of the type already described and photographed; if not, support it so that it leans to the left (viewed from the crank pulley end).

Remove the nuts and washers from the join seam plus, on 1200 cc engines, the two bolts at the flywheel end. There are six large nuts on the right hand side of the casing. Remove these and, if no fastenings remain, the crankcase halves should begin to part when *lightly* tapped with a rubber mallet. Remove the cam followers (tappets) and mark them.

The crankshaft and camshaft simply lift out of the crankcase half. Remove the distributor drive shaft and the fuel pump push rod assembly.

TOP
The beauty of the bench-mounted engine stand is that it allows the engine to be turned through 360 degrees, so that you can manoeuvre it to give the easiest access for any job.

LEFT
When undoing the cylinder head nuts, turn each one a fraction in the advised sequence, then repeat until they are all slack. The bench mounted engine stand again makes stripping the boxermotor a relative breeze.

The rocker shaft can be removed independently of the cylinder head if required; this might prove necessary, for instance, if the rocker adjusting screw slots are damaged, which prevent accurate setting of clearances.

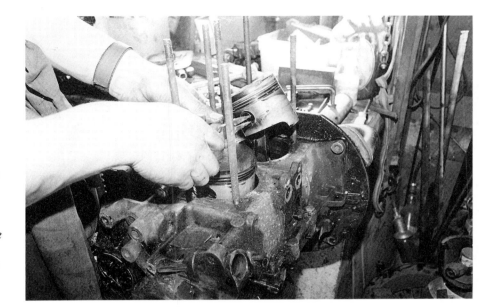

Use circlip pliers to remove the circlips from the piston sides, then push out the gudgeon pins to release the piston from its connecting rod. Don't be tempted to use undue force at this stage if the gudgeon pin is tight; wait until the crank has been removed, dismantle the big end and cushion the piston while you drive out the pin.

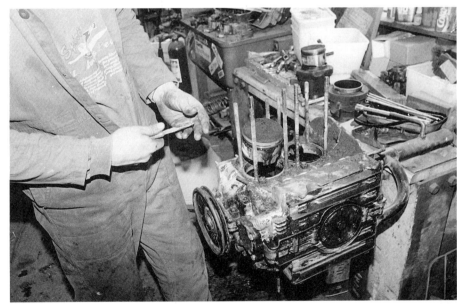

With the push rod tubes and cylinder barrels lifted away (mark everything so that it can be returned to its correct position afterwards), the pistons can now be removed. It pays to store each piston with its respective cylinder to prevent mix-ups.

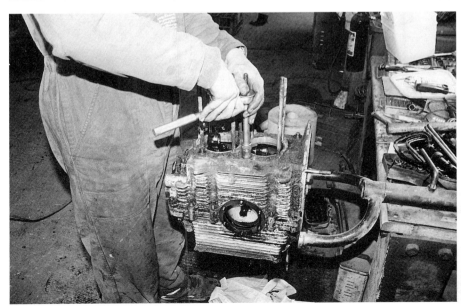

Undoing the nuts from the long crankcase bolts.

Check the marking on the rear of the mains bearings; these should have stamped marks which show whether they have standard external diameter or are enlarged for align bored housings, whether they have standard internal diameter or a tighter one for a reground crankshaft. You can only go so far in enlarging the housings or reducing the crankshaft journals; there comes a point at which both are scrap.

Piston ring breakage left unattended while the loose bits of the rings gouged their way into the cylinder wall and started to smash into the piston. New pistons and cylinders would be the recommended option in this case.

The slightest lapse in concentration during an engine re-build can be disastrous, usually it is merely annoying. DO remember to fit the inlet manifold before the tinware! This sort of thing can happen to even the most seasoned veteran of Beetle engine builds when working against the clock. More haste indeed proving to give less speed!

Inspection

The author would strongly recommend that further stripping (crankshaft) and inspection is carried out professionally. The cylinder barrels and heads, the pistons, crankshaft, camshaft and crankcase should be taken to an automotive engineer for proper inspection and measuring. There is no point in rebuilding an engine with renewed bearings, piston rings and so on if there is excess wear of or unseen damage to any of the retained components, because the life-span of the rebuilt engine would be greatly reduced – perhaps to just a few thousand miles. However, those who feel qualified to attempt the work themselves will find all the necessary details in good workshop manuals – and the best of luck!

Rebuild

Begin by assembling the crankshaft, connecting rods and big end bearings. Remember that rods and caps, rods and crankpin journals must all be rebuilt in the correct locations – don't mix them up. Use new engine oil to lubricate the big end bearing shell halves before pressing them firmly into the connecting rods and caps, then place each rod in turn in position on its crankpin and fit its cap, ensuring that the tongues and notches of the bearing halves align correctly. Torque the nuts to 24 ft lbs and check that the rod turns freely on the crankshaft – if not, dissemble and examine to find the problem – then gently peen the cap nuts with a light hammer to prevent them from working loose.

Fit main bearing three into position (oil hole nearer the flywheel end of crankshaft), and heat the gear assembly gently until it can be located on the crankshaft. Don't use a flame to heat the gear but place it in a hot oven until it has expanded sufficiently. Immersion in hot oil is an alternative, but take care, because of the dangers of fire and also spillage of hot oil!

Spread the snap ring and slide it into position, followed by number four main bearing (oil hole toward crank pulley) and finally the oil thrower. Re-fit number one main bearing on the flywheel end of the crankshaft.

At this stage, set the crankshaft end float before assembling the engine. To do this, fit the rear main bearing then fit two standard end float shims then the flywheel. You will need to hold the crankshaft in a heavily padded vice whilst applying a torque of perhaps 80 ft lbs to the flywheel nut. Using a set of feeler gauges inserted between the bearing and the flywheel, measure the gap then subtract from it 0.0027–0.005 in. (0.07–0.13 mm) to find the thickness of third shim required.

Re-fit the split number two main bearing halves into

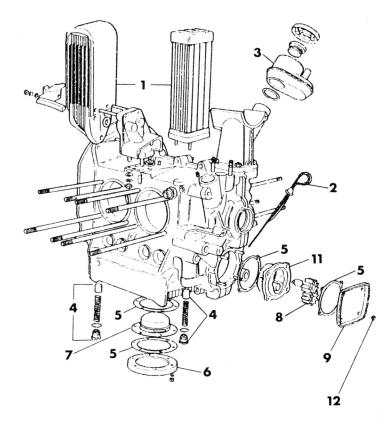

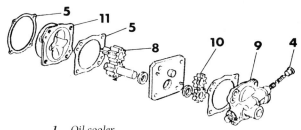

1. Oil cooler
2. Dipstick
3. Oil breather
4. Pressure relief valve
5. Gaskets
6. Strainer plate cover
7. Oil strainer
8. Pump gears
9. Pump cover plate
10. Pump gears (automatic transmission)
11. Pump housing
12. Retaining nut

Oil plays an important role in cooling the engine as well as in lubricating bearing surfaces. If the oil level is allowed to drop then the engine will rapidly overheat, and damage will quickly result. These are the main components of the lubrication system. It is recommended that the oil pump is examined and if necessary exchanged when the opportunity arises. (Courtesy Autodata)

the crankcase halves. Replace the cam followers into the crankcase halves with a little grease to hold them in position and oil to lubricate them.

Fit the crankshaft shims and a new oil seal, and place the crankshaft assembly in the left hand crankcase half, feeding the connecting rods through the appropriate holes. Without disturbing the bearings, turn the crankshaft until the two punch marks on the timing gear coincide with the axis of the camshaft. Fit the camshaft half bearings to the left hand side of the crankcase then the camshaft so that the notch on its tooth is in between the two marks on the crankshaft timing gear. (See illustration.) This ties the opening and closing of the valves to the rise and fall of the pistons.

Fit new rubber seals onto the six crankcase studs. Fit the camshaft half bearings to the right hand side of the crankcase then put a bead of sealing compound on the crankcase half lips and offer the right hand half into position on the left, again feeding the connecting rods through the holes. Replace the lip nuts but do not tighten them until you have replaced the oil pump body. Then progressively tighten the nuts, checking that the crankshaft and camshaft are free to turn until the two lips are pressed tightly together. Using sealing compound, fit the six large crankcase nuts to the threaded studs, again, checking that the crankshaft is free to turn and, on 1200cc engines only, replace the two large bolts near the flywheel end of the crankcase.

The lip nuts should be progressively tightened and torqued to 10 ft lbs; the six large nuts to 20 ft lbs. Re-check the crankshaft then torque the lip nuts to 14 ft lbs and the six large nuts to 25 ft lbs.

PISTON AND CYLINDERS

It is taken as read that you have had the pistons, piston rings and cylinders examined for damage, measured for wear or to ensure they have not become oval, and perhaps the pistons weighed by an automotive engineer and everything machined or renewed as appropriate.

Fit new cylinder gaskets to the crankcase halves. You can fit the pistons alone and the cylinders afterwards, or the pistons with the cylinders already attached as long as the gudgeon pin hole is clearly visible. Lubricate each bore with a little engine oil, then use a ring compressor to fit the pistons into their respective cylinders. Offer the pistons into position on the small ends – ensuring that the arrows stamped into the crown face the flywheel – then gently press home the gudgeon pins and fit the circlips. Use oil to lubricate the cylinder seals before pushing the cylinders fully home.

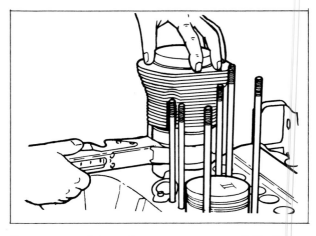

Various types of piston ring compressor are available. Use one if you want to avoid damaging the rings as they re-enter the cylinders. (Courtesy Autodata)

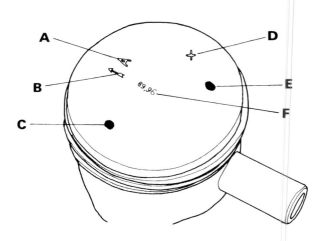

A.	Part number identification	D.	Weight grading mark
B.	Arrow – must face flywheel	E.	Weight grading mark
C.	Paint spot for correct matching	F.	Piston size in mm

All VW pistons have these markings. (Courtesy Autodata)

Cylinder head refit

Pull the push rod tubes to stretch them to a fraction over seven inches, and fit new sealing rings. Slide the cylinder head onto the studs and position the push rod tubes (seam upwards) before pushing the cylinder head fully home. Check that the push rod tubes are correctly located, and torque the cylinder head nuts in the correct progressive sequence. Fit the pushrods then the valve gear.

Cylinder head repairs

The cylinder head is the one part of the engine which commonly requires attention that is within the abilities of most DIY enthusiasts. Although it is still recommended that an automotive engineer inspect them in the course of a full restoration, normal mechanical repairs are another matter, and are covered here.

Clean all carbon from the cylinder head, using the correct tool and *not* an old screwdriver, the sharp edges of which are guaranteed to dig into the head, causing damage. Proprietary cleaning fluids such as Autoline Gasket Remover can help remove stubborn carbon deposits.

Examine the head for cracks between the valve seats or a valve seat and the spark plug hole. Check for signs of exhaust seat/valve burning. If any cracks are found then the author recommends the parts be taken to an automotive engineer or replaced/exchanged. If everything seems in order, it is worth lapping in the valves.

Uneven wear in the valve seats can result in poor sealing qualities and, if the damage is not too bad, the valves may be lapped in. It is worth while doing this as a matter of course whenever the heads have to be removed. You need grinding paste and a tool which is no more than a wooden stick with a sucker on the end – both are widely available and cost very little. Simply, the valve is placed in its guide, its mating edge is coated with grinding paste (coarse first, followed by fine), the rubber sucker attached to the valve and rotated to and fro between the hands. Every few seconds, stop, lift and turn the valve through 60 degrees and start again. Inspect

If the cylinder heads are in good order and free from cracks, always take the opportunity to reseat the valves. (Courtesy Autodata)

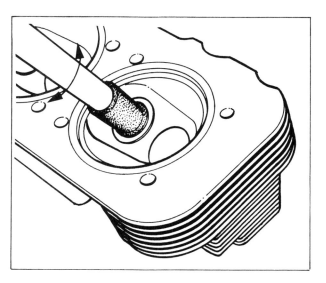

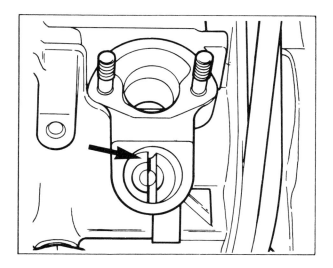

When rebuilding the engine, ensure that the distributor driveshaft slot is as shown. (Courtesy Autodata)

the valve and its seat periodically, and when you can see an unbroken matt line around both switch to the fine paste and repeat the process. When the valve and seat are perfect, the valve will bounce when dropped into its seat from a height of perhaps two inches.

Check for excess wear in the valve stems/guides by inserting a valve into its stem from the outside of the head and feeling for sideways movement. If this is found then new valve guides and valves should be fitted; although this can be undertaken at home it is recommended that the work is entrusted to an experienced professional.

Rebuild continued

Replace the fuel pump push rod assembly and the pump, and refit the distributor drive shaft; when fitting the thrust washers, use grease to hold them together and fit them with a thin length of rod to ensure that they don't drop down into the crankcase! Note the attitude of the drive shaft slot in the illustration.

Refit the oil pressure relief valve (two on cars after 1969) and the oil strainer and its cover plate. Check the flywheel ring gear teeth for damage, replace the gasket and offer the flywheel into position, remembering to line up the dowel and hole which you marked when stripping the assembly. Refit the crankshaft pulley and the flywheel, torquing the former to 33 ft lbs and the latter to 253 ft lbs – OK, let's be honest – we DIY'ers don't usually possess a torque wrench which goes quite as high as that! The sensible solution is to take the engine to a garage for final tightening of the flywheel nut – most people use a long lever on the end of their 36 mm hexagonal socket – the former is recommended.

BELOW

It's another of those useful BSW trolleys; this time disguised as an engine test bed. The flat four can be test run on the floor if you wish, just set it down on its heat exchangers.

ABOVE

Bolt half an early transaxle casing plus a starter motor onto the Beetle, connect up a fuel line and battery, and you can test run it before re-fitting it to the car. Saves the possibility of boxing the car up only to have to then remove the engine if there's a problem with it.

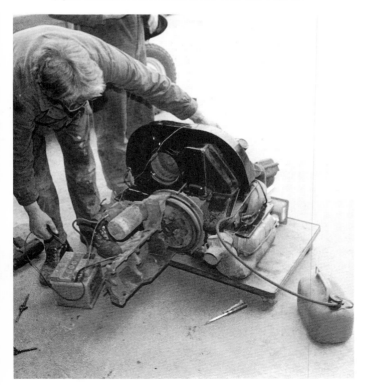

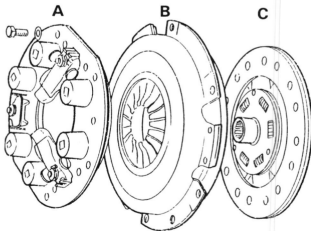

ABOVE

The clutch assembly. 'A' is the spring type cover, 'B' is the diaphragm type and 'C' is the driven plate. (Courtesy Autodata)

Replace the heat exchangers and exhaust system, then the generator pedestal, inlet manifold and carburettor, oil cooler and finally the generator and fan shroud.

You can test run the engine on the floor if desired and if you can obtain an early transaxle half casing complete with starter motor. However, few enthusiasts will possess this, and so they have to refit the engine and hope for the best!

Running in

Before starting up a rebuilt engine, the author strongly recommends that the spark plugs are removed and the engine turned over for perhaps twenty or thirty seconds using the starter motor – it will spin quite quickly without the spark plugs and hence compression. This allows the oil pump to get oil moving in the all-important mains and big end bearings before those components are subjected to the stresses which occur when the engine fires up.

A rebuilt engine does, contrary to popular myth, benefit from being given a 'running-in' period – that is, a period of use on the road when revolutions are restricted to perhaps 3,500 rpm and the engine is not allowed to labour in too high a gear. In other words, drive slowly and be gentle with a rebuilt engine.

The new and the machined engine components in a rebuilt engine will all appear to fit very closely with their neighbouring components, but they still have to be finally 'bedded in' by being run in the assembled engine. During this bedding-in period, wear of components (journals, crankpins, bearings, piston rings and cylinders etc.) is initially very high, but the rate of wear progressively reduces.

Before putting the car on the road the author strongly recommends that you run the engine for perhaps ten minutes at around 1,500 rpm and a further ten minutes at 2,000 rpm – then change the engine oil and clean the filter. These running periods can be increased and indeed many authorities will advise that both the periods and the revolutions are increased. The idea of this is to start bedding the engine components in before the extra stresses of feeding power through the wheels is brought to bear, especially on the mains and big end bearings.

Remember that component wear is also always higher when the engine is cold, so take it very easy on the road for the first few miles each day. If your daily journey begins with a long uphill climb then warm the engine through before tackling this!

The author would personally recommend that for the first 500 miles on a rebuilt engine you limit top

speed to around 50 mph, that you accelerate as slowly as possible and that you tackle steep hills – if at all – in a suitably low gear. He would at that stage be inclined to change the engine oil and clean the filter to get rid of any tiny fragments of metal which the oil should have cleaned from bedding-in new components. During the second 500 miles he would recommend a revolutions limit of perhaps 4,000 rpm, terminating again in an oil change and filter clean. The next two 500 mile intervals should be marked with oil changes if you want your rebuilt engine to enjoy the longest possible life – and, when you've gone to the trouble of restoring your car, who wouldn't?

Remember that during the running-in period, you are effectively 'blueprinting' some of the most important and stressed components in the engine. An engine which is abused during this period will inevitably last less long and will usually give less power and use more fuel than one which is run in correctly. However, don't be so single-minded during the running-in stage that you present a danger to other road users – if you crawl along the motorway at 35 mph then you will present a danger both to other road users and to yourself; avoid such roads until your engine is run in.

CLUTCH/GEARBOX

The clutch is a very simple mechanism. The driven plate has frictional material on its surfaces and is located on the gearbox input shaft splines so that, when it turns, the input shaft also turns. The driven plate is normally gripped tightly in a sandwich between the flywheel and the pressure plate (the latter contained within the clutch cover, and the pressure provided either by diaphragm or coil springs, depending on the type of clutch), so that when the engine turns over, the clutch assembly and hence the driven plate and gearbox input shaft also turn.

When the clutch pedal is pressed downwards, the clutch operating lever moves the release bearing which in turn pulls the pressure plate away from the driven plate, so releasing the driven plate from the sandwich between the pressure plate and flywheel and disengaging drive to the gearbox.

During the course of a restoration it is as well to replace the clutch as a matter of course unless it is in very good condition. If the clutch in daily use develops problems such as a failure to disengage, dragging or slipping then try adjusting it via the large wing nut on the clutch operating lever before removing the engine!

Clutch removal

With the engine removed from the car, lock the flywheel using a large screwdriver wedged against the flywheel teeth and the starter motor aperture. Loosen the clutch bolts evenly in a diagonal pattern to avoid causing distortion of the pressure plate. Release the pressure from the springs slowly until the clutch comes free.

Examine the driven plate frictional material. If this has worn down so that it is close to the rivet heads then replace the plate. If it shows contamination (oil) then replace it and ascertain whether the oil has come from a leaking crankshaft seal or gearbox input shaft seal and replace the leaking seal before reassembling the clutch. If the driven plate shows signs of burning then renew it and ensure that in future the clutch is correctly adjusted and not slipping.

If the driven plate rivets have become exposed then they can severely score the flywheel and pressure plate, in which case the affected components should be replaced, although minor scoring of the flywheel may be turned off; check with an automotive engineer.

Check the condition of the diaphragm or coil springs and replace the pressure plate assembly if wear or damage are apparent.

When re-fitting the clutch, it is important that the driven plate is gripped exactly in line with the gearbox input shaft, otherwise, the plate could be damaged during engine re-fitting. There are many clutch alignment tools available for this purpose; they hold the driven plate in line with the other components whilst the pressure plate is bolted tight. Some people use a spare input shaft to achieve this; others can assemble the clutch accurately by eye.

Gearbox (transaxle) removal and refitting

The gearbox and differential share the same housing, and the complete assembly is called a transaxle. The transaxle cannot be removed until the engine has been taken out, and the swing axle and double jointed drive shaft Beetles each have their own routines, and are covered separately. Because the engine will have been removed before the transaxle, it is assumed that normal safety precautions – especially battery disconnections – have already been taken. It is advisable to clean and

Removing or re-fitting a gearbox has a fun factor on a one to ten scale of nought! There is no real alternative to lying on your back and wrestling with the thing, which makes your arms ache if, as is normal, the gearbox decides to be awkward.

apply penetrating oil to all fixings which will have to be undone some time before starting work, so that the oil has plenty of opportunity to do its job.

Swing axle cars

The transaxle must be removed complete with axle tubes. The job is much more complicated and long-winded than on later cars, and so careful consideration should be given whether to replace the gearbox with a reconditioned unit as a matter of course during a full restoration, when the car will be stripped down completely and the task can be accomplished more easily while the bodyshell is off the chassis.

Chock the front wheels, apply the handbrake and place the car in gear, then remove the hub caps and slacken the hub nuts using preferably a burst-proof hexagonal socket and a very long lever! Slacken the wheel bolts. Disengage the handbrake and select neutral gear. Remove the oval cover plate at the rear top of the spine chassis, and remove the 8 mm square selector rod coupling bolt, which may be wired, then raise the rear of the car and support it on axle stands.

Remove the roadwheels and the hub nuts. Slacken the brake adjusters and remove the drums, then strip the brake components (as detailed in the section headed 'Brakes'), using clamps on the lengths of flexible hose to cut leakage of fluid.

Slacken the clutch cable nut and disconnect it from the clutch operating arm.

Use a sharp chisel or centre punch to make a mark on the trailing arm next to the mark on the hub casing to allow accurate rebuilding, then unbolt the hub from the trailing arm and pull the axle shaft away. Undo the lower damper nut and bolt and pull this away from the hub casing. Support the transaxle and remove the four

The recommended method of slackening the hub nuts; the author made do with a gigantic adjustable spanner and a good kick! (Courtesy Autodata)

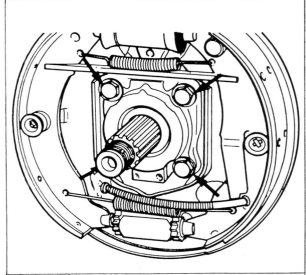

These four bolts hold the bearing cover to the backplate. (Courtesy Autodata)

VAG workshop or Beetle specialist and have the job done properly.

Double-jointed drive axle cars

Check firstly the fixings used on the inner drive shaft CV flanges, and if necessary obtain the correct tool for their removal from a specialist Beetle spares supplier.

Remove the oval cover plate at the rear top of the spine chassis, and remove the 8 mm square selector rod coupling bolt, which may be wired. Chock the front wheels, raise the rear of the car and support on axle stands.

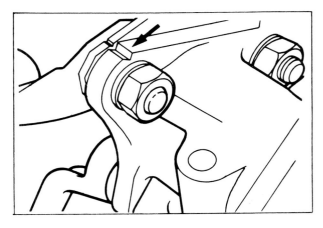

A sharp chisel is the best tool for marking the trailing arm and bearing flange. (Courtesy Autodata)

Pulling the axle shaft away from the trailing arm. (Courtesy Autodata)

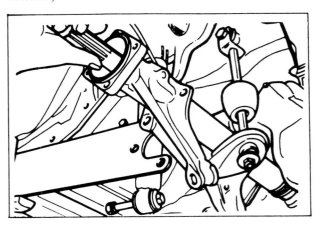

nuts at the front, followed by the two large nuts at the rear. The transaxle, axle shafts and hub assemblies can now be pulled rearwards and lowered.

When re-fitting, offer and bolt the transaxle into position before tackling the axle shafts. Ensure that the mark which you made on the trailing arm aligns with the hub casing mark, otherwise, the rear tracking will be out, causing accelerated tyre wear and adversely affecting road-holding. There is a special tool which clamps to the torsion tube and to the swing axle shaft to correctly position the latter. If you are unsure that the spring plate is correctly positioned, then take the car to a

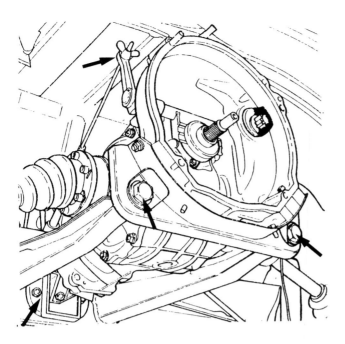

The diagonal arm suspension type transaxle mountings. Don't forget to remove the clutch cable. (Courtesy Autodata)

From underneath the car, undo the drive shaft inner CV joint fixings both sides of the car, using the appropriate tool. It usually pays to clean out Allen heads and splined fixings beforehand. Slacken the clutch lever cable wing nut until it can be unhooked, and remove the two nuts on the transaxle side cover which hold clutch cable clamps to free the cable from the transaxle.

Remove the earth strap from the transaxle casing, then undo the single nut which now holds the starter motor, and remove the starter motor. Check that nothing is left which connects the transaxle to the chassis legs.

Support the transaxle. Slacken the two front mounting bolts (nearest the front of the car) and remove the two main bolts. The gearbox can be withdrawn from the car or lowered onto the chassis legs until you are ready to manoeuvre it out.

Refitting is the reverse of removal: be sure to check the transmission oil level and top up if necessary.

Gearbox

The Beetle gearbox is very long-lived provided that it is not abused. In time, though, even this robust unit can develop annoying noises when under way. Gearbox noises do not necessarily indicate serious problems, and many people learn to live with them as long as they don't become too loud! A noisy gearbox can last for years.

Some gearbox problems, however, are more terminal and, after you have gone to the trouble of restoring your Beetle, it would be heartbreaking to have to remove the engine and transaxle because of some developing fault. Stripping, inspecting and rebuilding a gearbox is no task for a novice, and there are some convincing arguments for opting instead for a complete exchange reconditioned unit.

The individual gears in a gearbox mesh with the laygear cluster, and excess or uneven wear in just one gear in time wears the laygear teeth out of true. If you replace a noisy (damaged) gear, then you should really also replace the laygear cluster because this meshes and has worn with it, which means replacing all of the other gears as well, because the laygear teeth will have worn in concert with the teeth of each of the gears! In short, a complete rebuild using all-new components is required, which is always more expensive (assuming that you can obtain the components) than an exchange reconditioned unit. The lower cost alternative is to fit another gearbox salvaged from a scrap Beetle. Buying such a unit privately from a classified advertisement is risky, buying from a general breaker's gives a guarantee of replacement if the 'box turns out to be faulty; the best option is buy to from a specialist Beetle restorer or breaker.

Whilst replacing the gearbox, consideration should be given to fitting urethane axle gaiters and a urethane gearshift coupling. These are more robust and long-lived than the original rubber items.

The starter motor support bush is located in the transaxle casing and, if worn, the starter can become at first noisy and later it may jam. Offer the starter front spigot into this bush and feel for excess play. It may prove necessary to replace the bush – work best undertaken by an automotive engineer.

The differential shares the transaxle housing with the gear assembly and again it is recommended that any problems be dealt with by a transmission specialist: These businesses can be found in many large towns and, although some will refuse to work on the Beetle transaxle, the better ones will be happy to inspect your transaxle and undertake any necessary repairs.

When you come to box up your Beetle, pay especial attention to the condition of the plate which sits on the spine around the gearshift lever aperture. The two folded protrusions must point upwards and the pressing must be replaced if these are worn. One of the two lugs prevents the driver from shifting into reverse unless the lever is pressed firmly downwards; when the lugs are worn it is all too easy when changing down from third gear to inadvertently go straight across the gate to reverse – not only embarrassing but also hard on the gear teeth!

BRAKES

Beetles manufactured prior to May of 1950 had mechanically operated brakes; all Beetles made from that date have hydraulic braking systems. Because of the comparative rarity of pre-1950s cars, this book covers only hydraulic systems. Owners of Beetles with mechanical brakes will find the details they need in the specialised workshop manuals dealing with early Beetles.

In essence the Beetle, in common with most cars, has two separate brake operating mechanisms. The handbrake is operated mechanically and acts only on the rear wheels whilst the footbrake acts on all four wheels using hydraulic pressure. When the brake pedal is depressed, a piston moves within a cylinder (the master cylinder) which contains non-compressible brake fluid. Because this liquid cannot be compressed, this action pushes it along a series of pipes and hoses to smaller cylinders containing pistons (the wheel cylinders and pistons in the case of drum brakes and the callipers and pistons for disc brakes), so placing pressure against the secondary piston and causing it to move.

The secondary pistons press shoes (drum brakes) or pads (disc brakes) against the drum or disc respectively; these are mechanically fastened to the rotating road wheels. The friction between shoe/drum pad/disc causes the road wheel's speed of rotation to slow, so slowing and stopping the car.

If you are undertaking a bodyshell-off restoration, then unless the brake pipes have obviously been recently replaced (and are not kinked), it is worth renewing them whilst access is good. If you intend keeping the car for any great length of time then consider fitting the more expensive nickel-copper alloy brake pipes, which should last as long as the car. Because it is highly likely that most people who are restoring a Beetle will wish to completely overhaul the braking system, this entire section is devoted to a full brakes overhaul.

It is important to stress that when working with the braking system, cleanliness is vital; keep all lubricants well away from discs, drums, shoes and pads, and do not allow the brake fluid to become contaminated.

Bleeding the brakes

If the brake pedal feels soft and spongy, then there is air within the system. Unlike brake fluid, air can be compressed, and the soft feel of the pedal is due to the fact that pushing it is compressing air rather than pushing non-compressible fluid to operate the brakes. In this case, the brakes have to be bled. The brakes also have to be bled after any part of the hydraulic system has been temporarily disconnected.

Bleeding the brakes entails pumping fluid through the pipes until the fluid which contains air bubbles is removed from the system via one of the bleed valve nipples. The nipple is turned to allow fluid to escape as the pedal is pumped, then tightened before the pedal returns. To prevent air from re-entering the system via the bleed nipple, a short length of transparent plastic pipe is attached to it and the other end is immersed in a container of clean brake fluid.

If you have to bleed the whole system, begin with the wheel furthest from the master cylinder and work forwards (single circuit) or, in the case of dual circuit systems (in which you'll have a tandem master cylinder and front and rear brakes with individual circuits) bleed nearside front, offside front, nearside rear and finally offside rear.

To bleed a brake you will require an assistant to push the brake pedal for you. Attach the pipe to the brake nipple and immerse the other end of this in a small container of clean brake fluid. Open the nipple by turning it and call for the brake pedal to be depressed and held down. When your assistant has done this, tighten the nipple, and then ask your assistant to release the pedal. Repeat the exercise until clear fluid with no air bubbles can be seen coming from the nipple. Ensure throughout this operation that the level of the fluid in the master cylinder is correctly maintained.

Sometimes air can become lodged somewhere in the system and refuse to be bled in the normal manner. If this happens the pedal will feel spongy. The air can usually be dislodged by going through the motions of bleeding the brakes, but ask your assistant to let his or her foot slide off the brake pedal so that it returns sharply.

A cranked screwdriver makes brake adjustment easier. (Courtesy Autodata)

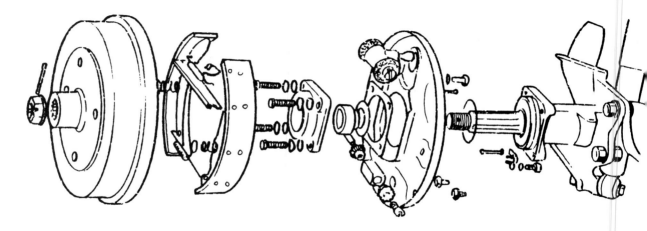

The rear brake assembly. (Courtesy Autodata)

A good brake pedal is nice and solid, and has not too much void travel, so that if one circuit fails (tandem master cylinder) then the other will still operate. If the pedal travel is too great, check firstly that the rear drum brakes are correctly adjusted, then adjust if necessary the master cylinder push rod. If the rear brakes are not correctly adjusted – and even one shoe out of adjustment will cause this – then the pedal will travel some distance as the shoe(s) concerned is moved by the pedal. You can usually hear a sound as the shoe moves and contacts the brake drum when this happens.

You don't necessarily *have* to jack up the rear of the car to adjust the handbrake; it is possible to reach the adjuster holes by lying on the ground at the rear of the car (watch out for the hot exhaust!). (Remember the advice given in Chapter Three about using a nut and bolt to remind you of which way to turn each adjuster.) It is very easy to become confused and to wind an adjuster fully in, and to believe that it is fully out! In addition to the extra brake pedal travel which will highlight the error, the handbrake lever will also possess far too much travel.

Brake bleeding is one of those activities which goes without a hitch nine times out of ten – on the tenth occasion, it can be frustrating when you are unable to obtain a good solid feel to the pedal. The tenth occasion usually follows a full restoration, when you are racing against time to get the car ready for the scheduled MOT test. Don't carry on feeding good brake fluid through the system; it's expensive and should never be re-used. Try using a brake hose clamp (or two on front then rear, in the case of dual-circuit systems) on each flexible hose in turn, and feel whether this makes any difference to the pedal. The chances are that when one particular hose is clamped, the pedal suddenly behaves perfectly, showing you which wheel cylinder or calliper still has air inside.

If, after all your attempts to bleed the system, the pedal is soft, then get a second opinion from an experienced mechanic. The chances are that the master cylinder needs attention in the form of new seals, although dirt in the system, persistent air bubbles,

sticking calliper pistons and other factors could be to blame.

One-man brake bleeding kits, which are fitted with a small non-return valve to prevent air from being sucked back into the system, are available. The author has tried various of these and found that, while some work satisfactorily, some of the cheaper kits give problems with the non-return valve. As ever, you are advised to buy the very best tools which you can afford.

Rear brakes

The rear brakes of all Beetles are drum brakes. The drums are secured to the axle by a large castellated nut torqued to 253 lb ft. This nut should be slackened before the car is raised from the ground. Select first or reverse gear and engage the handbrake, chock the rear wheels, remove the hub caps and the split pin from the castellated nut. Then slacken off the nut, using a large square T drive (preferably a ¾ in. drive), a strong 36 mm socket and a long pipe (the longer the better – a two metre pipe is ideal) to gain the necessary leverage to start the nut. If the nut stays stuck fast and the car moves when you apply pressure, try jacking one side of the car up at a time, removing the roadwheel and chaining a (spare) wheelnut to the chassis. If all else fails, soak the nut in freeing solution or try applying gentle heat to make the nut expand.

When both axle nuts have been loosened, slacken the rear wheel nuts, engage the steering lock (wheels dead ahead), chock the front wheels, raise the rear of the car and support it on axle stands. Disengage the hand brake. Remove the axle nuts. Slacken off the brake adjusters until the drum turns freely (see Chapter 3), and pull the drums from the splined axle shafts, tapping the drums with a rawhide mallet to centre the shoes or even using a puller if necessary.

ABOVE
A 36 mm hexagonal socket and a six foot long extension are recommended for removal of the rear hub nuts; the author possessed neither, but found that a very large adjustable spanner and a good kick did the trick.

BELOW
Adjusting the brakes. This has to be done both to relieve pressure from the shoes on the brake drum prior to the removal of the latter, and to adjust the brakes up.

Some brake shoes contain dangerous asbestos, so don a dust mask and gently wipe the drum and the shoes clean out of doors. If there is less than 0.1 in. of frictional material left on the brake shoes then they will have to be renewed. If a brake drum is scored internally then it should be replaced.

To strip the brakes, use a pair of pliers to remove the shoe retaining springs and their clips. Ease the lower ends of each shoe out from the slot in the adjuster tappet, and then ease the top ends out of the wheel cylinder tappets. Ease out the handbrake cable end and remove the shoe/spring assembly.

Examine the wheel cylinder boots and brake backplate for signs of brake fluid leakage; if this is suspected, then a wheel cylinder kit, comprising new piston (tappet) seals and boots should be obtained and fitted. Clamp off the length of flexible brake hose before removing the wheel cylinder, and bleed the system afterwards. Check that both tappets are free to move and, if they are seized, try using a large screwdriver through the jaws to turn and free them – don't force too hard or you will spread the jaws. On really stubborn wheel cylinders which are completely seized the last resort is to remove them from the car, drain *all* brake fluid from them and then use heat to free the tappets; the heat destroys the tappet seals, which must be renewed. Examine the wheel cylinder bore for damage, and renew if necessary.

The hub oil seal can also leak with the result that the brake backplate becomes covered with fluid, but in this case, the fluid will obviously be oil. Because you will normally discover a leaking hub oil seal when you are working on the brakes, a brief description of the necessary work is included here.

Either drain the transaxle of oil, or jack up the side of the car being worked on so that the hub is at a higher level than the transaxle. Unbolt the four hub cover bolts, then pull the cover from the backplate, having placed a suitable receptacle underneath the catch any escaping oil. Remove the old oil seal, the spacer, the 'O' rings from the casing and axle, the gaskets either side of the brake backplate, and clean all components. Use a block of wood to drive the new oil seal into position – not forgetting to replace the washer first. Fit the axle 'O' ring, spacer and the 'O' ring in the cover. Pull the backplate gently forwards until you can gently feed the inner gasket through the hole in the centre of the backplate and into position, fit the front gasket, and carefully reassemble, taking care not to damage either of the gaskets as the bolts are passed back through. Torque the bolts to the recommended level then, with the car back on its wheels or only slightly raised to allow access to the transaxle filler plug on the nearside, top of the transaxle oil.

ABOVE LEFT
Disconnecting the handbrake cable before removal of the shoe.

ABOVE RIGHT
Each brake shoe is held by a pin, washer and spring. To remove these, push the washer inwards as shown, twist through ninety degrees and the washer should come off.

RIGHT
Ease the shoes out from the adjuster tappets before removing them from the wheel cylinder tappets.

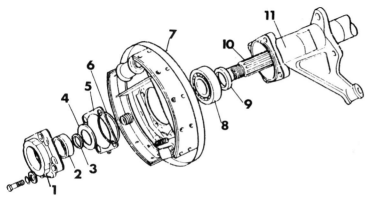

1. Bearing cover
2. Oil seal
3. 'O' ring seal
4. Washer
5. Gasket
6. 'O' ring seal
7. Brake backplate assembly
8. Bearing
9. Inner spacer ring
10. Axle shaft
11. Bearing housing

The hub oil seal (2) should be replaced if oil contaminates the backplate. Also, fit a new gasket (5) and 'O' ring seals (3 & 6). (Courtesy Autodata)

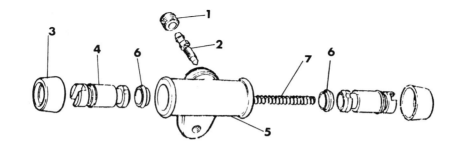

1. Cap	*5.* Cylinder housing		
2. Bleeder screw	*6.* Seal		
3. Boot	*7.* Spring		
4. Piston			

The wheel cylinder components. The cap (1) is normally missing; this keeps dirt out of the bleed nipple (2), and should be replaced if damaged or missing. If the unit leaks fluid, replace the boots (3) and the seals (6). If the pistons or tappets (4) are stuck, remove the cylinder from the car, clean out ALL brake fluid and try using heat as a last resort. (Courtesy Autodata)

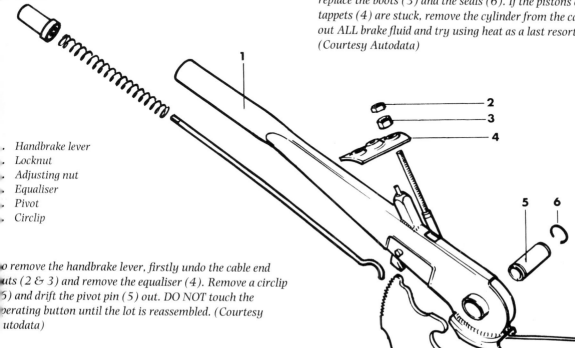

. Handbrake lever
. Locknut
. Adjusting nut
. Equaliser
. Pivot
. Circlip

To remove the handbrake lever, firstly undo the cable end nuts (2 & 3) and remove the equaliser (4). Remove a circlip (5) and drift the pivot pin (5) out. DO NOT touch the operating button until the lot is reassembled. (Courtesy Autodata)

Adjust the cable end nuts after reassembling. Adjust the rear brakes first, then the cable nuts so that the rear wheels lock when the lever is on the fourth 'click'.

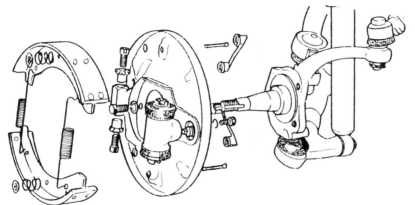

Front drum brakes are the same as the rears, but turned through ninety degrees. Stripping, adjusting and wheel cylinder repair are as per rear drums. (Courtesy Autodata)

On poorly maintained cars, the adjuster star wheels may be seized; if so, try leaving them to soak in freeing lubricant and then gently tapping them. If this fails, try gently heating them – avoid the use of too much force, because the adjusters are easily damaged. Apply plenty of copper grease or preferably Autoline Aluminium Anti-Seize when rebuilding the adjusters, to prevent them from seizing in the future. The adjuster tappet slots are tapered, and should be fitted with the wider end upwards.

During a bodyshell-off restoration, it is a good policy to renew the handbrake cables whilst access is good. Frayed handbrake cables should be renewed as a matter of course, because sooner or later they will either jam in their sleeves or break. To disassemble the system, undo the nuts on the cable ends, remove one circlip from the handbrake pivot, drift this out and pull the handbrake assembly forwards. *Do not* touch the ratchet button until the handbrake has been re-fitted. To remove a cable, remove the drum, free the handbrake cable end from its

lever, remove the return spring clip, undo the sleeve/backplate bolt and pull the cable end through the backplate. Pull the cable from the spine.

To re-assemble, feed the cable end through the backplate along with its return spring and washer, then replace its clip. Feed the other end of the cable through its tube in the spine and ensure that the sleeve is correctly positioned in the end of the tube. The threaded cable end should now be visible under the handbrake aperture in the spine.

Feed the two cable ends through the holes in the lever base, then replace the lever assembly, its pivot and circlip. Replace the equaliser plate and nuts. Adjust the system.

Front brakes (drum)

The front drum brakes can to all intents and purposes be treated in the same manner as rear drum brakes.

86

Front brakes (disc)

Disc brakes work by pressing two friction brake pads onto a steel disc which is attached to and rotating with the road wheel. The friction caused slows the rotation of the disc and hence of the wheel. Disc brake pads are held within a casting called the calliper, within which two pistons are moved under pressure from brake fluid to push the pads against the disc.

Disc brakes are easy to service (as detailed in Chapter Three), but they are not so easy to repair, and most people seem to opt for exchange reconditioned units rather than tangle with the pistons and seals themselves. If the pads have less than 0.08 in. of frictional material then they should be exchanged as a set.

Problems with disc brakes include excessive disc run out and general wear and tear, piston seal failure and piston corrosion. We shall deal with each in turn.

Disc run out refers to a condition where the disc is not rotating properly because it is out of balance, perhaps as a result of uneven wear or a knock. Disc run out can be checked at home by placing a fixed item (with a degree of precision) next to the disc, rotating the wheel and noting whether the disc surface remains a constant distance from the object, but it is far better to have this check carried out professionally at any service centre.

Disc wear and tear includes rusting and thinning of the steel disc through usage, scoring of the disc and colouring of the disc because it has overheated. Scoring is obvious to the eye, but in common with the other faults mentioned above, if you suspect that the discs may possess some fault then have them checked professionally.

Replacing brake pads is very quick and easy. Remove the spring clips from the retaining pins, then drift these out using a long parallel punch. Lift away the spring retainer plate, then the pads.

Corroded calliper pistons must be replaced. As the frictional material on the pads wears down, so more and more of the piston emerges from the calliper to take up the 'slack' (disc brakes are therefore self-adjusting). If the pistons are left sticking out from the body of the calliper for any length of time or in the wrong conditions – such as after driving in salty air – then the exposed portion becomes corroded. This condition is most commonly found on cars which have been standing idle for a long time. Obviously, when new, thicker pads are eventually to be fitted then the pistons have to be firstly pressed back into the callipers; if the piston outer side is corroded then the corrosion destroys the effectiveness of the rubber sealing rings – and the lot has to be replaced.

It is possible to renew calliper pistons and seals using the hydraulic system to push out the pistons, although

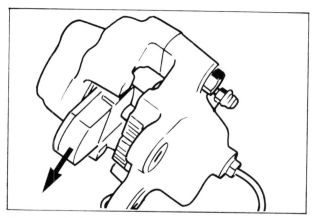

Removing the disc pads; the anti-rattle shims can then also be removed. (Courtesy Autodata)

the job is much easier if the callipers are firstly disconnected from the brake hoses and removed from the car.

Remove the pads as already described, then place a clamp on the length of flexible brake hose to minimise fluid loss. Fold back the locking tabs and remove the two hexagon headed bolts which hold the calliper assembly to the stub axle, then remove the flexible hose.

The calliper pistons may be removed by hand, although normally some assistance will be required from a low-pressure compressed air source. A foot pump will suffice, and if a compressor is to be used then turn down the pressure if possible or alternatively, take most of the air from the cylinder until the pressure is no more than 20 psi. If you try to use higher pressure air, the pistons will fly out at great speed! Whether you use a foot pump or a compressor to push out the pistons,

The components of the calliper. It is advised that you obtain exchange reconditioned calliper assemblies rather than try to strip and rebuild callipers at home. (Courtesy Autodata)

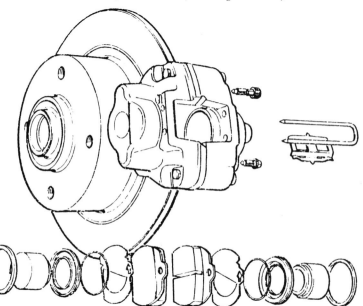

Spring clips hold the brake line/hose union to the suspension.

When refitting brake hoses on the front wheels, ensure that they cannot bend and foul the tyre at full lock.

always wear eye protection, just in case the compressed air sprays brake fluid into the air and, for the same reason, don't work near a naked flame. Fit a clamp (a small G-clamp is ideal) to retain one of the pistons, then use the air to move the other piston forwards but not out of the calliper. Open up the G-clamp to accommodate the freed piston, then use the air to drive the other out of the calliper. The first piston should now be removable by hand.

Examine the pistons and their bores for scoring and replace if necessary. Inspect the dust sealing ring and piston sealing ring for cuts or undue wear, and replace these if necessary. Before reassembly, lubricate the cylinder bores and pistons with clean brake fluid. Fit the piston sealing ring, then the piston, ensuring that the piston does not tilt within the bore. Push the piston in until approximately ⅛ in. remains proud, then finally fit the dust sealing ring and its retaining ring.

Occasionally, a car which has been standing idle for a time will suffer from sticking brake calliper pistons. This greatly reduces braking efficiency, and the extra load it places on the wheels with good brakes will manifest itself by those brakes locking-up under hard braking – this is especially notable when both discs are seized. Remove the pads, then examine the exposed portion of the pistons on the sticking callipers to ensure that they are not badly corroded and hence in need of replacement. If the pistons seem OK, then try replacing one pad and using a small G-clamp or a proper piston pusher to move the other piston back into the calliper. Then fit the pad to the other piston, and repeat. When both pistons are fully home, push them back out by pressing on the brake pedal, and repeat the process until

the pistons are able to move properly. Check the brake fluid level frequently as you work.

One final point; when replacing the brake hoses on the front wheels following a restoration, check that they will not foul the tyres with the steering on full lock – in addition to being an MOT failure point, this causes rapid wear of the brake hose.

SUSPENSION/STEERING

When a moving car hits a bump or hole in the road, a sharp force is imparted to the tyre; some of this force is absorbed by the compressed air contained within the tyre and is apparent as distortion of the tyre wall (the air in the tyre acting as a kind of spring) and the rest is imparted to the suspension system. The object of suspension is to isolate as far as possible the car chassis and body from such forces, and the suspension has two components; springs and dampers.

Like the walls of the tyres, suspension springs distort when subjected to forces and so absorb those forces. Springs which are compressed (or twisted, in the case of torsion bars) contain energy, which they try to release by re-extending. If a spring is compressed and then allowed free movement, it will extend beyond its unstressed length to a certain point (at which it still contains energy), then re-compress under the force of the remaining energy. The spring continues to extend and compress in this way until the initial energy is dissipated. This is called 'resonance'. Resonance is controlled by damping.

The effects of undamped resonance in the suspension springs of a road car would be disastrous, because every time a spring re-compressed, it would reduce the traction of its wheel, perhaps even lifting it from the road. Four wheels all shifting from full to light traction on an undamped car would reduce road-holding severely. To control the resonance of the spring, dampers (often erroneously referred to as 'shock absorbers' or 'shockers') are fitted.

When a correctly damped wheel hits a bump in the road, the spring compresses to absorb the shock (springs and not dampers are in fact shock absorbers), but the damper limits the amount of its deflection and then limits resonance, so that the spring returns to its unstressed length very quickly. This keeps the tyres in the maximum possible contact with the road.

There are essentially two types of suspension fitted to Beetles. The earlier system comprises torsion bars – bars of steel which work in effect as springs when they are twisted. Cars with this suspension are typically known as 'Torsion Bar' or 'Swing Axle' cars.

The later suspension type, fitted to the 1302 and 1303 (and 'S') series cars, comprises McPherson strut (a coil spring with a concentric telescopic damper) suspension at the front and, although there are still torsion bars at the rear, the swing axles are replaced by double-jointed drive shafts, with diagonal arms to locate the hub. Cars fitted with this suspension are commonly referred to as 'McPherson Strut', 'Double-Jointed Drive Shaft' or sometimes 'Diagonal Arm' cars.

Front suspension – torsion bar

This is a very simple suspension, comprising two torsion bars per side, acting on sturdy torsion arms to which the hub assembly is bolted. The damper is attached to a special pressing which is a part of the axle assembly.

Later cars are fitted with an anti-roll bar. This simple device is in effect a 'U' shaped spring which is attached to the lower torsion arms. When one side of the suspension is compressed during cornering, the anti-roll bar flexes and compresses the suspension on the other side to a lesser extent, evening out the forces at work and preventing the car from leaning over too far.

To strip the assembly, firstly chock the rear wheels, slacken the wheel bearing nuts at the front, then raise the front of the car and support it on axle stands. Clamp the flexible brake hose as close to the brake end as possible to prevent fluid loss, then back off the adjusters and remove the brake drums, shoes, wheel bearings and brake backplates (drum brakes) or unbolt the calliper and tie it out of the way so that no strain is placed on the flexible hose (disc brakes).

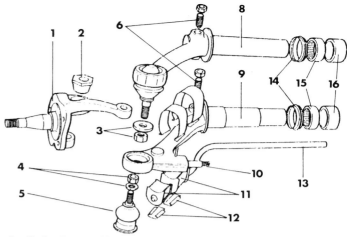

1. Stub axle assembly
2. Eccentric bush
3. Large washer/nut
4. Small washer/nut
5. Ball joint
6. Torsion bar grub screw
7. Pin
8. Upper suspension arm
9. Lower suspension arm
10. Shock absorber pin
11. Stabiliser rubber blocks
12. Metal clips
13. Stabiliser bar
14. Seal
15. Needle roller bearing
16. Metal bush

The front torsion bar suspension components. (Courtesy Autodata)

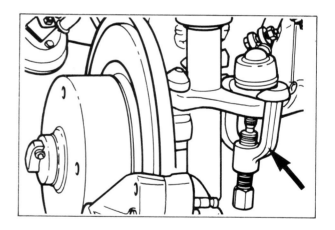

Using a ball joint splitter to disconnect the steering arm. The type of splitter shown exerts a straight pull, and this type or the scissors type is preferable to the wedge type, because the latter can cause damage to the components. (Courtesy Autodata)

Use a ball joint splitter to part the tie rod end from the steering arm and to split the ball joint in the lower suspension arm. Then remove the nut from the upper suspension arm ball joint and raise the arm using a jack and free the eccentric bush. It should now, provided the upper suspension arm is raised high enough (you may

ABOVE
The author using an old jack to raise the upper torsion arm.

BELOW
Jacking up the top torsion arm so that its joint can be removed from the stub axle.

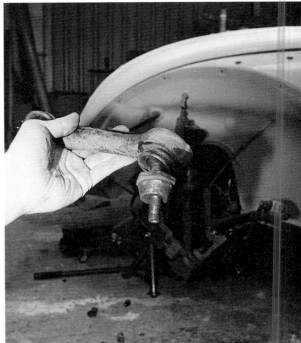

ABOVE
The torsion arm ball joint is pressed into position, and it is unlikely that you will be able to remove and replace it unless you have access to a hydraulic press. Opt for an exchange unit if the ball joint is worn.

BELOW
The notch in the eccentric bush must face forwards when the suspension is reassembled. This bush gives the front wheels positive camber to induce an element of understeer – in other words, the front end of the car runs slightly wide when pushed around a bend. Put simply, this prevents the driver from going around bends at speeds which are sufficient to make the rear end of the car break away – don't mess with camber unless you really know what you're doing!

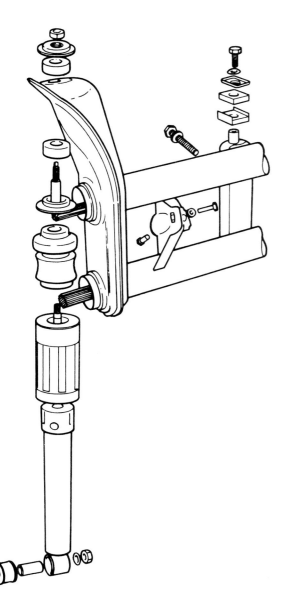

have to press the lower arm downwards slightly), be possible to remove the stub axle.

Check the condition of the ball joints and renew if necessary. The upper ball joint is fitted using a high pressure press, and it may be better to replace the upper arm complete if one can be sourced. At the top of the ball joint there should be a plastic plug which, if removed, gives access to a threaded hole. Fit a grease nipple into this and inject grease using a grease gun, stopping to move the ball joint around to help the grease penetrate properly. Fit a new plastic plug. When replacing the eccentric bush, ensure that the notched face points directly forwards.

During a full restoration, it would be usual to renew the damper units. To remove these, use a spanner on the flats of the damper shaft to hold this still whilst the top fixing nut is undone. The lower end simply unbolts. To test a damper, extend and compress it through its full range of movement; if stiff or weak points are found in the travel, or if there is any sign of fluid leakage, replace the unit.

Wheel bearings

To adjust the wheel bearings, remove the speedometer drive and both bearing caps, slacken the lock screws and torque the clamp nuts to 15 ft lbs then slacken them until the thrust washer can just be moved. Tighten the lock screws. If you wish to replace the bearings, consult a workshop manual for details or, preferably, have the job carried out professionally.

McPherson strut suspension

Unlike torsion bar suspension, McPherson strut suspension feeds great stresses into the body shell – namely the flitch panel tops, where the top ends of the

ABOVE
The damper mounts on torsion bar suspensions. Replace the dampers if they are inefficient or are leaking. To check their condition once removed, pull and push them through their full range of movement; any 'slack' or stiff points in the travel means that they have to be replaced. (Courtesy Autodata)

RIGHT
Wheel bearings must not be squeezed too tightly. The washer behind the hub nut should be able to move when forced with a screwdriver, as shown here. (Courtesy Autodata)

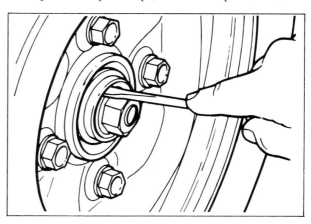

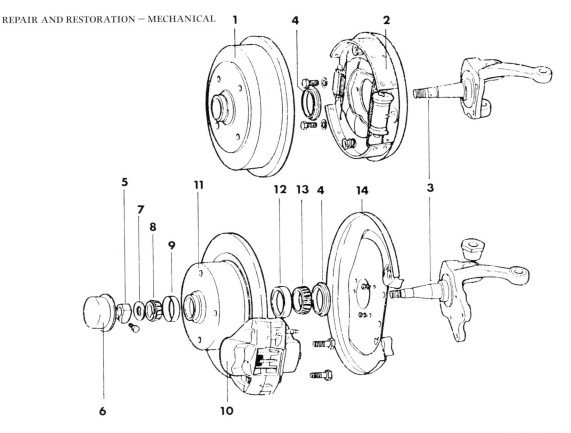

1. Brake drum
2. Brake backplate assembly
3. Stub axle assembly
4. Oil seal
5. Wheel bearing nut
6. Hub cap
7. Thrust washer
8. Taper roller bearing
9. Bearing cup
10. Brake caliper
11. Brake disc assembly
12. Bearing cup
13. Taper roller bearing
14. Splash plate

The differences between the drum and disc (lower) hub assemblies. (Courtesy Autodata)

The scissors type ball joint separator on the stub axle lower ball joint. Note that the nut is slackened, but left in position for the tool to bear against. If you were to remove the nut and allow the tool to bear against the thread, it would distort the thread. (Courtesy Autodata)

You can pull the torsion arm away and leave the torsion bar in place, or pull the two out together as desired. To remove the arm alone, firstly remove the bolt on the top of the torsion arm end, which locks it to the bar. (Courtesy Autodata)

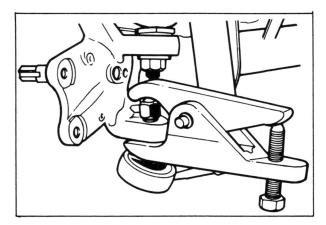

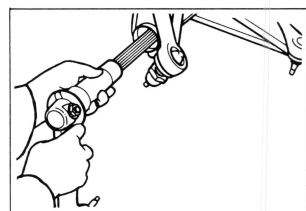

struts are located. On such cars, the panelwork around the strut top mounting must be very sound.

The McPherson strut comprises a concentric coil spring and damper, combining both springing and damping roles in a simple unit, which is connected to the stub axle via a ball joint. The lower stub axle ball joint connects it to the track control arm which, in turn, is mounted on a bracket just aft of the frame head and the movement of which is controlled by the anti-roll (stabiliser) bar.

To remove the strut, chock the rear wheels, jack up the front of the car and support it on axle stands then remove the road wheels. Undo the stabiliser bar end nut on the track control arm, then remove the stabiliser bar mounting clamp nuts and detach the bar. Split the ball joint at the track control arm/stub axle, and the steering arm/stub axle. Clamp the brake hose and remove the brake pipe from the bracket on the strut.

The strut is held at the top in the flitch panel by three lock nuts; remove these – *don't* touch the large central nut, because this is keeping the spring compressed – and lower the strut downwards.

Don't even contemplate stripping a McPherson strut unless you have spring clamps as shown in the illustration. The coil spring is under considerable pressure and can do great damage if this pressure is not release slowly and safely. Broken or tired springs and ineffectual dampers may be replaced, but unless you have a spring compressor this work is best entrusted to a professional who, because he will not have to remove and refit the strut to the car, should not charge too much in labour.

Rear suspension

The two types of rear suspension fitted to Beetles are not vastly different from each other – both have torsion bar springing – but their effect on the road-holding of the cars is! Earlier swing axle cars can, when pushed to the limit, be very difficult for anyone other than the most accomplished competition driver to control. Later cars with diagonal arm suspension are far better behaved.

Swing arm suspension

Torsion bars with splined ends are attached to spring plates which in turn are connected to the axle hubs. A damper connects an extension of the torsion bar housing and the axle hub. The drive shafts have universal joints (UJs) only at their inboard ends, and their angle in relation to that of the road wheel is thus constant.

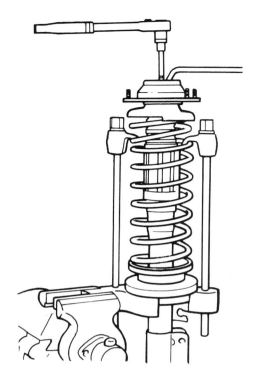

The coil springs of McPherson Struts are always under great compression, even when the unit has been removed from the car. NEVER contemplate stripping the unit unless ALL spring tension can be removed from the top plate by using spring compressors as shown. At least two compressors of the type shown must be used. Alternatively, larger tools which grip two coils in 'C' shaped brackets are available, and arguably safer. It would only take a service centre mechanic a few minutes to strip and rebuild a McPherson strut, so unless you possess suitable facilities at home, have the job done professionally – it won't cost a lot! (Courtesy Autodata)

To strip the suspension, chock the front wheels, slacken the hub nuts (use a six foot long lever for this) and the rear wheel nuts, raise the rear of the car and support it on axle stands placed under the rear ends of the heater channels (with wood packing). Remove the rear wheels.

Slacken off the brake adjusters and remove the hub nut, then remove the brake drum. If it sticks, try tapping it with a leather-faced mallet to free off the brake shoes. Dismantle the brakes (see appropriate section of this chapter).

Use a sharp chisel to make a mark across the trailing arm and the axle housing flange, so that they can be re-assembled in the same positions. Disconnect the damper lower end, and either swing it out of the way or undo the top fastening.

The axle tube is secured to the swing plate by three bolts; undo these, and pull the axle tube away from the

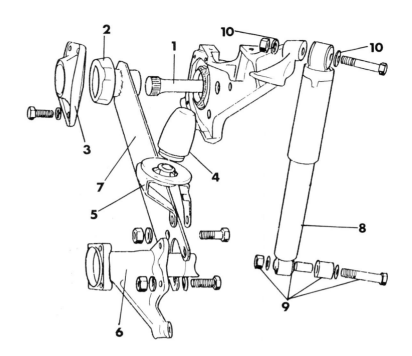

1. Torsion bar
2. Outer rubber bush
3. Torsion bar cover
4. Rubber bump stop
5. Bracket – bump stop
6. Axle hub assembly
7. Trailing arm
8. Shock absorber unit
9. Shock absorber lower mounting
10. Shock absorber upper mounting

The swing arm rear suspension components. The trailing arm (7) fits on the splined end of the torsion bar (1) and, as the arm moves up and down with suspension travel, it twists the torsion bar – the 'spring'. The other end of the trailing arm is attached to the axle hub (6), which, in turn, is connected to the lower end of the damper (8). (Courtesy Autodata)

LEFT
Swing axle rear suspension and associated components. With the bodyshell off, take the opportunity to carry out any and all mechanical work on the engine, transaxle and suspension, in addition to renewing brake and lines. If the restoration is being carried out by a professional, you might be fortunate and have chosen a restorer who is prepared to stop work on the project temporarily whilst you trailer away the chassis and carry out mechanical repairs at this stage – most professionals, however, cannot afford to work in this manner.

ABOVE
Other components which should be renewed as a matter of course whilst access is easy include the swing axle boots – the one in this photograph is leaking oil from the transaxle, which is an MOT failure point. The entire rear suspension is best attended to after the engine and starter motor have been removed, when access is at its best. Wire brush and paint anything which is not being replaced!

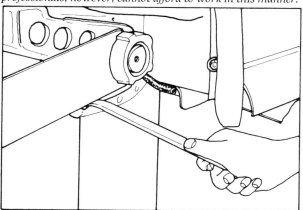

Levering the trailing arm off its stop – a longer lever with the end cranked upwards would be preferable. (Courtesy Autodata)

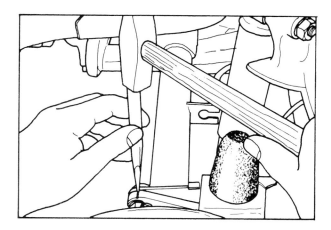

The trailing arm must be reassembled in the correct position relative to the axle hub assembly, and so make a mark across both using a cold chisel, as shown. (Courtesy Autodata)

plate. Remove the torsion bar end cover plate bolts and the cover. Now for the interesting bit. The spring plate is under considerable tension when on its ledge and, when it comes free from the ledge it would fly in a downwards arc with considerably force if you were to choose to remove it by tapping it from behind. Alternatively, you could use a long lever with a cranked end to get the plate off the stop ledge and slowly release the pressure.

When the spring plate is off its ledge note its position carefully, because you'll have to get it back in exactly the same spot if you don't fancy having a lop-sided car! To raise the rear suspension ride height, incidentally, you re-fit the plate one spline further and vice-versa to lower the car. Re-fitting involves using a trolley jack under the plate to 'wind up' the torsion bar until the plate can be slipped onto its ledge. Replace the two large rubber bushes as a matter of course.

To remove the torsion bars, remove the rear wings then pull the torsion bars out of their casing, noting their positioning so that they can be replaced accurately. The splines on either end of the torsion bars are of differing size, so that by moving either the inner splines one notch or the spring plate one notch, a wide variety of ride heights can be accommodated for those who like to experiment with that sort of thing.

When reassembling, coat the torsion bar rubber bushes with talcum power before re-fitting. Use a trolley jack to raise the spring plate over its stop ledge, then use

long bolts to pull the torsion bar cover plate down and so force the spring plate fully home onto the torsion bar end.

Diagonal arm suspension

Raise and support the car as already described, remove the road wheels and hub nut, remove the brake drum, clamp the flexible brake hose and disconnect the hose from the backplate. Disassemble the brakes, the handbrake cable end and remove the backplate. Remove the six Allen headed screws which fasten the outer end of the drive shaft to the hub assembly. Remove the damper.

Mark the spring plate and trailing arm for correct reassembly, then remove the three bolts securing the hub assembly to the spring plate. Lever the spring plate from its ledge stop as already described for swing axle suspension, and note the attitude of the spring plate at rest, so that it can be replaced in the same position.

Note the positions of the washers on the diagonal arm pivoting end; these must go back in exactly the same position, otherwise the suspension geometry will be altered. Remove the diagonal arm socket screw and washers. Undo the four bolts to release the torsion bar end cover plate, then pull the plate end from the torsion bar splines.

LEFT
*The diagonal arm rear suspension. During a body-off
restoration, carry out all repairs to the suspension while the
bodyshell is off the car and access is good. The car shown is a
competitions trials car – hence the longer concentric spring
dampers and modified damper brackets.*

RIGHT
*To disconnect the drive shafts, you'll need a suitable allen-
head drive, available from most motor accessory shops or
VW Tools (address at end of book). (Courtesy Autodata)*

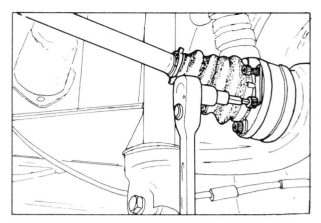

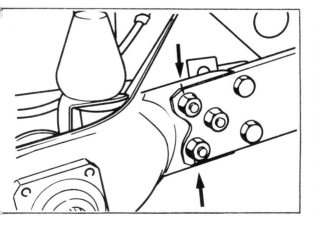

1.   Torsion bar
2.   Trailing arm inner/outer bushes
3.   Torsion bar cover
4.   Trailing arm
5.   Diagonal arm assembly
6.   Drive shaft
7.   Shock absorber
8.   Diagonal arm inner mounting bushes
9.   Shock absorber upper mounting

*The components of the diagonal arm rear suspension.
(Courtesy Autodata)*

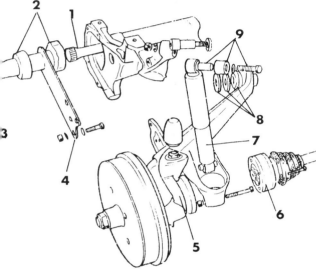

*Before undoing the trailing arm bolts, mark the relative
positions of the trailing arm and the diagonal arm pressing.
(Courtesy Autodata)*

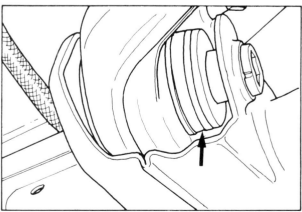

*The washers (which should be renewed) must go back in the
same location and orientation, so make a note of where and
how they fit before removing the inner arm bolt. (Courtesy
Autodata)*

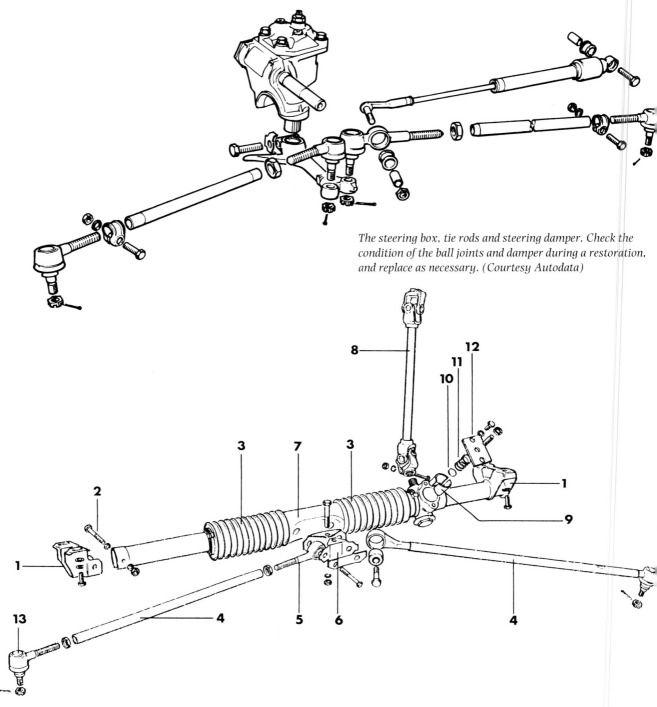

The steering box, tie rods and steering damper. Check the condition of the ball joints and damper during a restoration, and replace as necessary. (Courtesy Autodata)

The later steering rack and associated components. This is the left hand drive version, though the components are the same as for the RHD version. (Courtesy Autodata)

1. Rack support bracket
2. Rack to bracket bolt
3. Rack pinion boot
4. Tie rod
5. Inner tie rod joint
6. Tie rod bracket
7. Steering rack box
8. Universal joint shaft
9. Thrust pad
10. Thrust washer
11. Spring
12. Cover plate
13. Track rod end joint

ABOVE
Torsion bar front suspension. When carrying out a body-off restoration take the opportunity to carry out all mechanical work while access is this good. Before carrying out work on the suspension, study this photograph so that you form a clear picture in your mind of how everything fits together. Note that the original engine capacity is stencilled on the spine – useful if you want to confirm that you have an original or an up-engined car.

LEFT
With the fuel tank stored safely out of the way, the steering column can be disconnected from the steering box by removing the nuts and bolts which hold the two flanges together. It helps if you raise the front wheels from the ground so that the column can be turned more easily to allow you to get at the fittings.

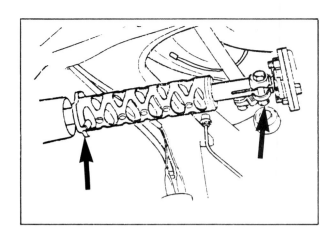

Disconnecting the column from the flange coupling on earlier cars. Note the collapsible section at the bottom of the column. (Courtesy Autodata)

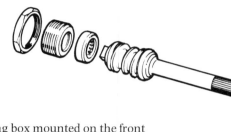

Steering

Earlier cars have a steering box mounted on the front axle, 1302 (and 1302S) have the box mounted on the bodywork and the 1303 is fitted with rack and pinion steering again, mounted on the bodywork.

During a restoration, check the condition of the steering damper by pulling and pushing its arm in and out; if extra or less resistance is felt at any point in the travel, replace the damper. Also, feel for lost steering wheel movement; that is, movement of the perimeter of the steering wheel in excess of 1 in. which does not also turn the front wheels. If this is discovered, check whether there is play in any of the joints, including the track rod ends, before turning your attention to the steering box or rack.

In the case of the steering box, play between the worm and spindle axle can be dealt with by adjusting the screw (turn the steering to full lock and slacken the locknut first) on the front of the unit whilst the spindle is moved from side to side. If this fails to reduce void movement to the recommended level, the roller/worm play will have to be reduced.

Steering boxes can be adjusted to take up this void movement by slackening off the lock nut on the top of the unit, adjusting the screw (don't tighten it right up, but screw it in just until slight resistance is felt), then hold it in that position and tighten the locknut. Check that the steering is not tight before using the car on the road and, if it is, re-adjust the screw. If there is still too much void steering wheel travel, it is best to exchange the steering box.

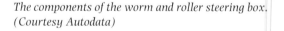

The components of the worm and roller steering box. (Courtesy Autodata)

With steering racks, adjust the bolt situated under the rubber bung in the spare wheel well until it can just be felt to contact the thrust bearing – slackening then re-tightening the locknut accordingly.

ELECTRICS

When the car is being driven, electricity is generated by either a dynamo (early cars) or an alternator (later models) driven by the crank pulley belt, and is used to provide energy to create a spark at the spark plugs, to

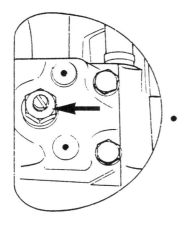

The steering box adjuster screw and locknut. (LHD shown – on RHD cars access is under the removable plate on the offside of the spare wheel well). (Courtesy Autodata)

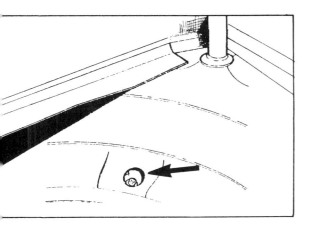

Steering rack adjustment is via the hole in the luggage compartment, which should be fitted with a rubber bung. (Courtesy Autodata)

operate the electrical equipment such as lights and wipers, and to keep the battery fully charged.

The battery provides a source of electricity to operate the starter motor, and to make up the shortfall in generated electricity when the car is on the move and demand exceeds the available supply.

The battery can provide a great deal of power, despite being 'only' 6 volt (early cars) or 12 volt, because it can provide a high amperage, or current. To help visualise just how much power a battery can generate, remember that it is possible – don't try this except to move the car to safety in an emergency – to move the car by placing it in gear and turning the engine over using the starter motor. In achieving this feat, the battery is supplying not only the energy needed to turn over the engine but also to physically move the car!

One terminal of the battery is connected to earth; that is, to the bodyshell/chassis of the car. This allows every electrical device on the car to also be earthed, so that just one feed wire is needed to complete a circuit to the battery and provide power for the device concerned. Most electrical faults – incidentally – are caused by poor earthing, so always check the earth connection first. If a wire which is live (connected to the live terminal of the battery) touches any part of the car which is earthed, current will flow through the wire to earth.

When the battery is connected to a circuit which has very little resistance (i.e., when it is shorted to earth through a wire) current passes through the wire at the battery's maximum amperage. Not even the meaty wire which connects the battery to the starter motor is capable of passing this current, and as a result the wire which shorts gets hot very quickly, burns off its insulation and an electrical fire ensues.

The ability of a wire to carry electricity safely is determined chiefly by its cross sectional area, and so wires which have to carry more current (starter motor feed, high-tension (spark plug) wires and to a much lesser extent the headlights) are thicker in section than wires which have only a small current to carry. The smaller the diameter of a wire, the more easily it catches fire if too high a current is passed through it.

To prevent wires carrying dangerously high currents through shorting to earth or some other electrical fault, most circuits of cars are fitted with fuses. A fuse is a short piece of un-insulated wire of a thickness designed to melt if the current passing through it exceeds a certain level. In the interests of safety, the lights and ignition are not normally fused – though Beetle lighting systems usually are. Whenever a fuse blows, it is not a fault in itself but a symptom of a problem elsewhere in its circuit. Most people simply replace blown fuses – sometimes with fuses of higher rating – but this is a dangerous practice, because it allows too high a current to pass through the wiring which the fuse is intended to protect, and that wire could overheat and start an electrical fire because too highly rated a fuse has been fitted.

If a fuse blows, always trace the fault before fitting a new fuse. *Never* replace the fuse with one of a higher rating or worse with bits of tin foil – unless you enjoy being inside a burning car.

For the same reason, never add extra electrical devices to a fused circuit. Either the demand will outstrip the fuse's safety level causing it to blow or, if a higher rated fuse is foolishly fitted, it can cause a fire in the existing wiring if a fault develops. What is an electrical fire like? The author can answer this one – a minor incident, thankfully – from first-hand experience. Within a few seconds of a wire shorting to earth on a

Wiring Diagram

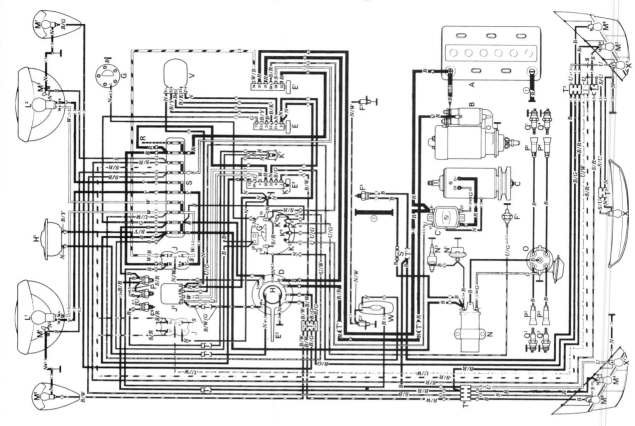

A	Battery	M2	Tail/brake light, right
B	Starter	M3	Parking light, right
C	Generator	M4	Tail/brake light, left
C1	Regulator	M5	Turn signal, front, left
D	Ignition/starter lock	M6	Turn signal, rear, left
E	Windshield wiper switch	M7	Turn signal, front, right
E1	Lighting switch	M8	Turn signal, rear, right
E2	Turn signal switch (switch for hand	N	Ignition coil
	dimmer and headlight flasher)	N1	Automatic choke
E3	Hazard warning light switch	N3	Electro-magnetic cut-off valve
F	Brake light switch	O	Distributor
F1	Oil pressure switch	P1	Spark plug connector, No. 1 cylinder
F2	Door contact switch, left	P2	Spark plug connector, No. 2 cylinder
F3	Door contact switch, right	P3	Spark plug connector, No. 3 cylinder
F4	Back-up light switch	P4	Spark plug connector, No. 4 cylinder
F6	Brake system warning light switch	Q1	Spark plug. No. 1 cylinder
G	Fuel tank sender unit	Q2	Spark plug. No. 2 cylinder
G1	Fuel gauge	Q3	Spark plug. No. 3 cylinder
H	Horn half ring	Q4	Spark plug. No. 4 cylinder
H1	Horn	R	Radio
J	Hand dimmer and headlight flasher relay	S	Fuse box
J2	Turn signal/hazard warning light relay	S1	Single fuse for back-up lights
J3	Parking light relay (for Austria only)	T	Cable adaptor
	these cables are interchanged on	T1	Cable connector, single
	Austrian vehicles	T2	Cable connector, double
J6	Vibrator fuel gauge	T3	Cable connector, triple
K1	High beam warning lamp	T4	Cable connector, quadruple
K2	Generator charging warning lamp	V	Windshield wiper motor
K3	Oil pressure warning lamp	W	Interior light
K5	Turn signal warning lamp	X	License plate light
K6	Hazard warning light	X1	Back-up light, left
	warning lamp	X2	Back-up light, right
K7	Dual brake circuit warning lamp		
L1	Twin-filament bulb, left headlight	①	Ground strap from battery to frame
L2	Twin-filament bulb, right headlight		
L10	Instrument panel light	②	Ground strap from transmission to frame
M1	Parking light, left		

Wiring Diagram 1500 models - August 1968 on

Wiring Diagram

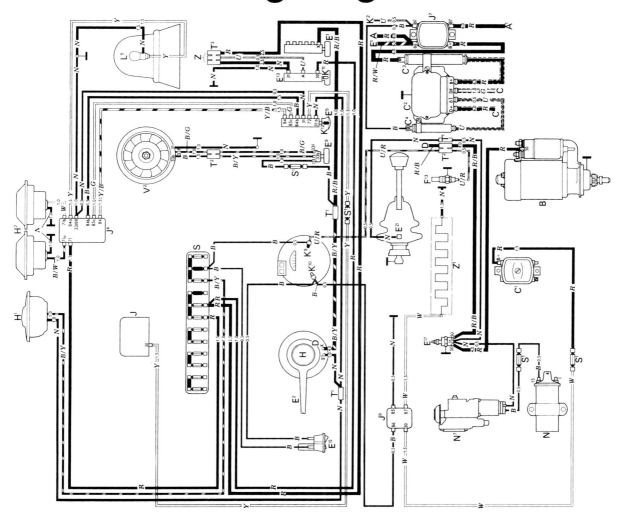

		F13	Switch for ATF temperature warning device
		H	Horn half ring
		H1	Horn
		H2	Dual horns
		J	Relay for headlight **dimmer** and flasher
		J4	Relay for emergency horns
		J7	Battery cut-out relay
A	To vehicle battery	J9	Relay for heated rear window
A1	To radio battery	K2	Generator charging warning lamp
B	Starter	K9	ATF temperature warning lamp
C	To generator	K10	Heated rear window warning lamp
C1	Regulator	K11	Heater warning lamp
C2	Regulator (**suppressed**)	K12	Emergency horn warning lamp
C3	Suppressor, terminal B+	L5	Emergency light
C4	Suppressor, terminal 61	N	Coil
D	Ignition/starter switch	N7	Control valve
E1	Lighting switch	S	Fuse box
E2	Turn signal switch (switch for headlight	S1	Fuses (8 amp) for rear window, control
	dimmer and flasher)		valve, emergency horns and fan
E3	Emergency horn switch	T1	Cable connector, single
E9	Fan switch	T2	Cable connector, double
E15	Heated rear window switch	T3	Cable connector, 3 pin
E13	Heater switch	V2	Fan motor
E17	Starter cut-out switch	Z	To heater
E21	Selector lever contact	Z1	Heated rear window

WIRING COLOUR CODE

R	Red	W	White
P	Pink	S	Slate
G	Green	B	Black
U	Blue	K	Purple
N	Brown	Y	Yellow

Note; Where a wire has a tracer stripe, the
main wire colour code letter is shown **first**,
followed by the trace code. Example U/W
is a Blue wire with a White tracer.

Wiring Diagram 1302 'Stickshift' models - August 1970-71

Wiring Diagram

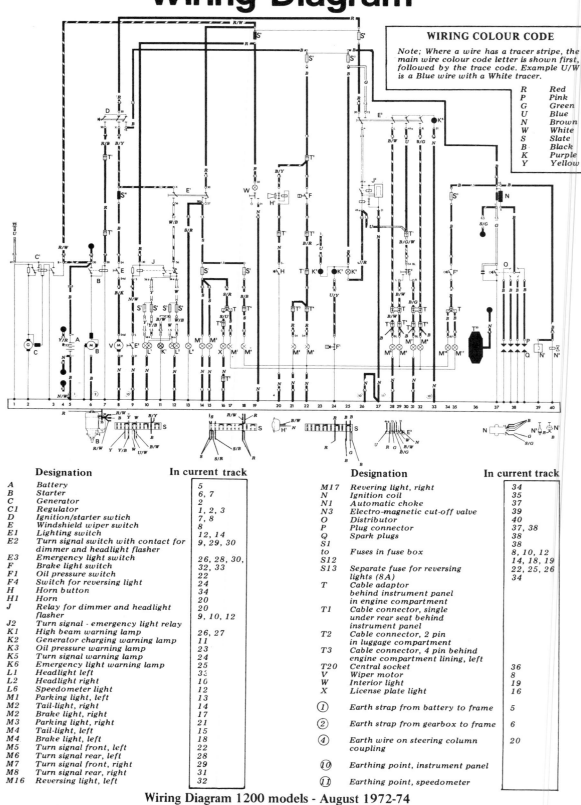

WIRING COLOUR CODE

Note; Where a wire has a tracer stripe, the main wire colour code letter is shown first, followed by the trace code. Example U/W is a Blue wire with a White tracer.

R	Red
P	Pink
G	Green
U	Blue
N	Brown
W	White
S	Slate
B	Black
K	Purple
Y	Yellow

Designation		In current track
A	Battery	5
B	Starter	6, 7
C	Generator	2
C1	Regulator	1, 2, 3
D	Ignition/starter swtich	7, 8
E	Windshield wiper switch	8
E1	Lighting switch	12, 14
E2	Turn signal switch with contact for dimmer and headlight flasher	9, 29, 30
E3	Emergency light switch	26, 28, 30,
F	Brake light switch	32, 33
F1	Oil pressure switch	22
F4	Switch for reversing light	24
H	Horn button	34
H1	Horn	20
J	Relay for dimmer and headlight flasher	20
		9, 10, 12
J2	Turn signal - emergency light relay	
K1	High beam warning lamp	26, 27
K2	Generator charging warning lamp	11
K3	Oil pressure warning lamp	23
K5	Turn signal warning lamp	24
K6	Emergency light warning lamp	25
L1	Headlight left	33
L2	Headlight right	10
L6	Speedometer light	12
M1	Parking light, left	13
M2	Tail-light, right	14
M2	Brake light, right	17
M3	Parking light, right	21
M4	Tail-light, left	15
M4	Brake light, left	18
M5	Turn signal front, left	22
M6	Turn signal rear, left	28
M7	Turn signal front, right	29
M8	Turn signal rear, right	31
M16	Reversing light, left	32

Designation		In current track
M17	Revering light, right	34
N	Ignition coil	35
N1	Automatic choke	37
N3	Electro-magnetic cut-off valve	39
O	Distributor	40
P	Plug connector	37, 38
Q	Spark plugs	38
S1		38
to	Fuses in fuse box	8, 10, 12
S12		14, 18, 19
S13	Separate fuse for reversing lights (8A)	22, 25, 26
T	Cable adaptor behind instrument panel in engine compartment	34
T1	Cable connector, single under rear seat behind instrument panel	
T2	Cable connector, 2 pin in luggage compartment	
T3	Cable connector, 4 pin behind engine compartment lining, left	
T20	Central socket	36
V	Wiper motor	8
W	Interior light	19
X	License plate light	16
①	Earth strap from battery to frame	5
②	Earth strap from gearbox to frame	6
④	Earth wire on steering column coupling	20
⑩	Earthing point, instrument panel	
⑪	Earthing point, speedometer	

Wiring Diagram 1200 models - August 1972-74

Wiring Diagram

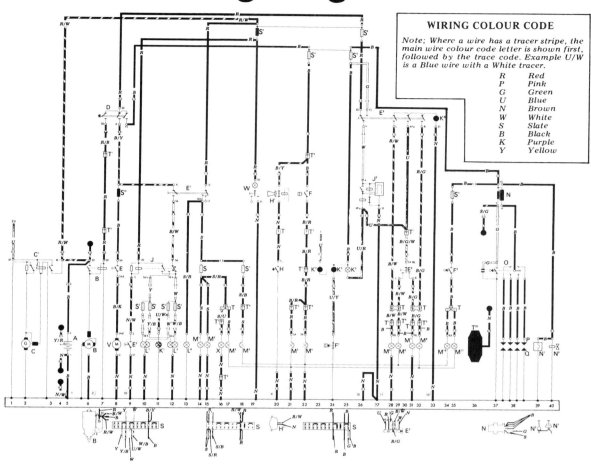

WIRING COLOUR CODE

Note; Where a wire has a tracer stripe, the main wire colour code letter is shown first, followed by the trace code. Example U/W is a Blue wire with a White tracer.

R	Red
P	Pink
G	Green
U	Blue
N	Brown
W	White
S	Slate
B	Black
K	Purple
Y	Yellow

Designation		In current track
A	Battery	5
B	Starter	6, 7
C	Generator	2
C1	Regulator	1, 2 , 3
D	Ignition/starter switch	7, 8
E	Windshield wiper switch	8
E1	Lighting switch	12, 14
E2	Turn signal switch with contact for dimmer and headlight flasher	9, 29, 30
E3	Emergency light switch	26, 28, 30, 32, 33
F	Brake light switch	22
F1	Oil pressure switch	24
F4	Switch for reversing light	34
H	Horn button	20
H1	Horn	20
J	Relay for dimmer and headlight, flasher	9, 10, 12
J2	Turn signal - Emergency light relay	26, 27
K1	High beam warning lamp	11
K2	Generator charging warning lamp	23
K3	Oil pressure warning lamp	24
K5	Turn signal warning lamp	25
K6	Emergency light warning lamp	33
L1	Headlight, left	10
L2	Headlight, right	12
L6	Speedometer light	13
M1	Parking light, left	14
M2	Tail light, right	17
M2	Brake light, right	21
M3	Parking light, right	15
M4	Tail light, right	18

Designation		In current track
M4	Brake light, left	22
M5	Turn signal, front, left	28
M6	Turn signal, rear, left	29
M7	Turn signal, front, right	31
M8	Turn signal, rear, right	32
M16	Reversing light, left	34
M17	Reversing light, right	35
N	Ignition coil	37
N1	Automatic choke	39
N3	Electro-magnetic cut-off valve	40
O	Distributor	37, 38
P	Plug connector	38
Q	Spark plugs	38
S1 to S12	Fuses in fuse box	8, 10, 12, 14, 18, 19, 22, 25, 26
S13	Separate fuse for reversing lights (8A)	34
T	Cable adaptor behind instrument panel in engine compartment	
T1	Cable connector, single under rear seat behind instrument panel	
T2	Cable connector, 2 pin in luggage compartment	
T3	Cable connector, 4 pin behind engine compartment lining, left	
T20	Central socket	36
V	Wiper motor	8
W	Interior light	19
X	License plate light	16

Wiring Diagram 1200 models - August 1974-75

Wiring Diagram

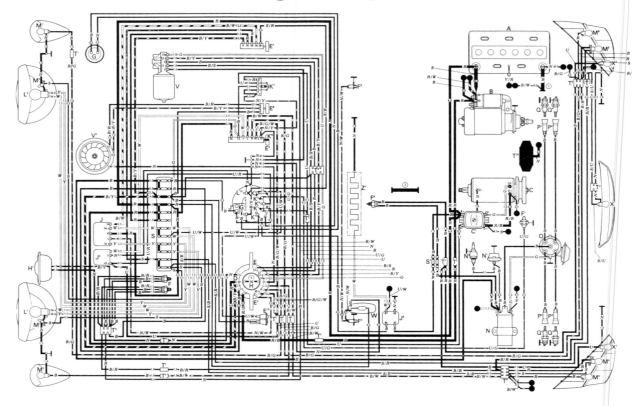

A	Battery	M5	Turn signal, front, left
B	Starter	M6	Turn signal, rear, left
C	Generator	M7	Turn signal, front, right
C1	Regulator	M8	Turn signal, rear, right
D	Ignition/starter switch	N	Ignition coil
E	Windshield wiper switch	N1	Automatic choke
E1	Lighting switch	N3	Electro-magnetic cut-off valve
E2	Turn signal switch (switch for dimmer and headlight flasher)	O	Distributor
		P1	Spark plug connector, No. 1 cylinder
E3	Emergency flasher switch	P2	Spark plug connector, No. 2 cylinder
E9	Fan switch (only 1302)	P3	Spark plug connector, No. 3 cylinder
E15	Heated rear window switch	P4	Spark plug connector, No. 4 cylinder
F	Brake light switch	Q1	Spark plug, No. 1 cylinder
F1	Oil pressure switch	Q2	Spark plug, No. 2 cylinder
F2	Door contact switch left	Q3	Spark plug, No. 3 cylinder
F3	Door contact switch right	Q4	Spark plug, No. 4 cylinder
F4	Back-up light switch	S	Fuse box
G	Fuel gauge sender unit	S1	Single fuse for back-up light (8 amp)
G1	Fuel gauge		heated rear window (8 amp)
H	Horn half ring	T	Cable adaptor
H1	Horn	T1	Cable connector, single
J	Relay for headlight dimmer and flasher	T3	Cable connector, 3 pin
J2	Emergency flasher relay	T4	Cable connector, 4 pin
J6	Fuel gauge vibrator	T20	Central socket connection
J9	Relay for heated rear window	V	Windshield wiper motor
K1	High beam warning lamp	V2	Fan motor (only 1302)
K2	Generator charging warning lamp	W	Interior light
K3	Oil pressure warning lamp	X	License plate light
K5	Turn signal warning lamp	X1	Back-up light left
K6	Emergency flasher warning lamp	X2	Back-up light right
K7	Dual circuit brake warning lamp	Z1	Heated rear window
L1	Twin-filament bulb, left headlight		
L2	Twin-filament bulb, right headlight	①	Ground strap from battery to frame
L10	Instrument panel light		
M1	Parking light, left	②	Ground strap from transmission to frame
M2	Tail/brake light, right		
M3	Parking light, right	④	Horn is grounded through the column tube
M4	Tail/brake light, left		

WIRING COLOUR CODE

R	Red	W	White
P	Pink	S	Slate
G	Green	B	Black
U	Blue	K	Purple
N	Brown	Y	Yellow

Note; Where a wire has a tracer stripe, the main wire colour code letter is shown first, followed by the trace code. Example U/W is a Blue wire with a White tracer.

Wiring Diagram 1300/1302 models - August 1971-72

Wiring Diagram

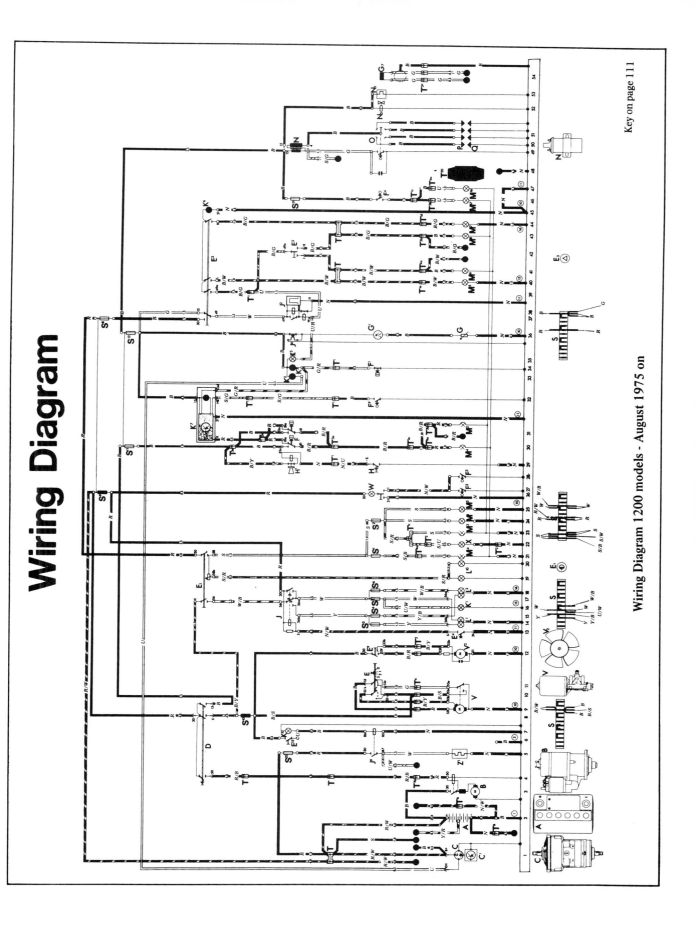

Wiring Diagram 1200 models - August 1975 on

Key on page 111

Wiring Diagram

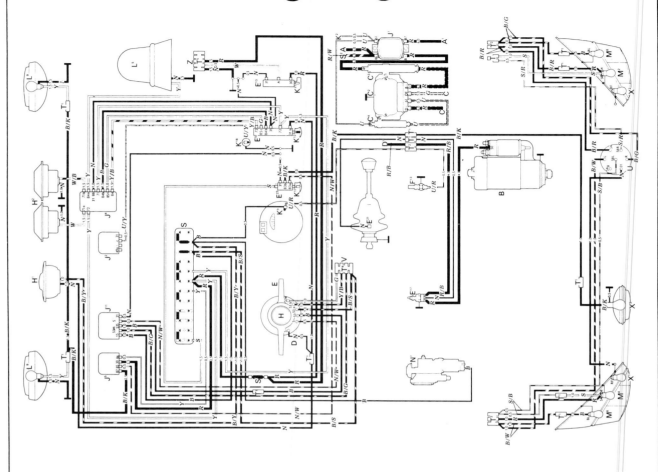

A	To vehicle battery	K11	Fuel/electric heater warning lamp	
A1	To second battery	K12	Dualtone horn warning lamp	
B	Starter	K17	Front and rear fog lights, warning lamp	
C	To generator	K18	Trailer towing warning lamp	
C2	Regulator, suppressed	L5	Rotating emergency light	
C3	Suppressor terminal B+	L9	Fog light bulb	
C4	Suppressor terminal 61	M2	R/H tail and brake light bulb	
D	Ignition/starter switch	M4	L/H tail and brake light bulb	
D1	To ignition/starter terminal 50	M6	L/rear turn signal bulb	
E	Windshield wiper switch	M8	R/rear turn signal bulb	
E5	Dual tone horn switch	N7	Control valve (stick shift)	
E13	Fuel/electric heater switch	S	Fuse box	
E17	Starter cut-out switch	S1	Single fuse for heater	
E21	Selector lever contact	S2	To fuse box terminal 30	
E23	Foglights front and rear, switch	T	Cable adaptor	
F13	ATF temperature warning switch	T1	Cable connector single	
H	Horn half ring	T2	Cable connector double	
H1	Horn	T3	Cable connector three point	
H2	Dual tone horns	T4	Cable connector four point	
J2	Emergency flasher relay for trailer towing	T5	Cable connector five point	
J4	Dual tone horn relay	U	Trailer towing socket	
J5	Foglights front and rear, relay	V	To windshield wiper motor	
J7	Battery separating relay	X1	L/H back up light	
J11	Interval switch relay	X2	R/H back up light	
K2	To generator warning lamp	X3	Rear fog light	
K9	ATF temperature warning lamp	Z	To fuel/electric heater	

This wiring diagram supplements the wiring diagram VW 1300 and 1302 from August 1971.

It contains: Emergency flasher system for trailer towing, automatic Stickshift, suppression (preparation for radio), dual tone horn system, connection for fuel/electric heater, foglights and rear foglight, interval switch for windshield wiper system.

WIRING COLOUR CODE

R	Red	W	White
P	Pink	S	Slate
G	Green	B	Black
U	Blue	K	Purple
N	Brown	Y	Yellow

Note; Where a wire has a tracer stripe, the main wire colour code letter is shown first, followed by the trace code. Example U/W is a Blue wire with a White tracer.

Wiring Diagram 1300/1302 'Stickshift' models - August 1971 on

Wiring Diagram

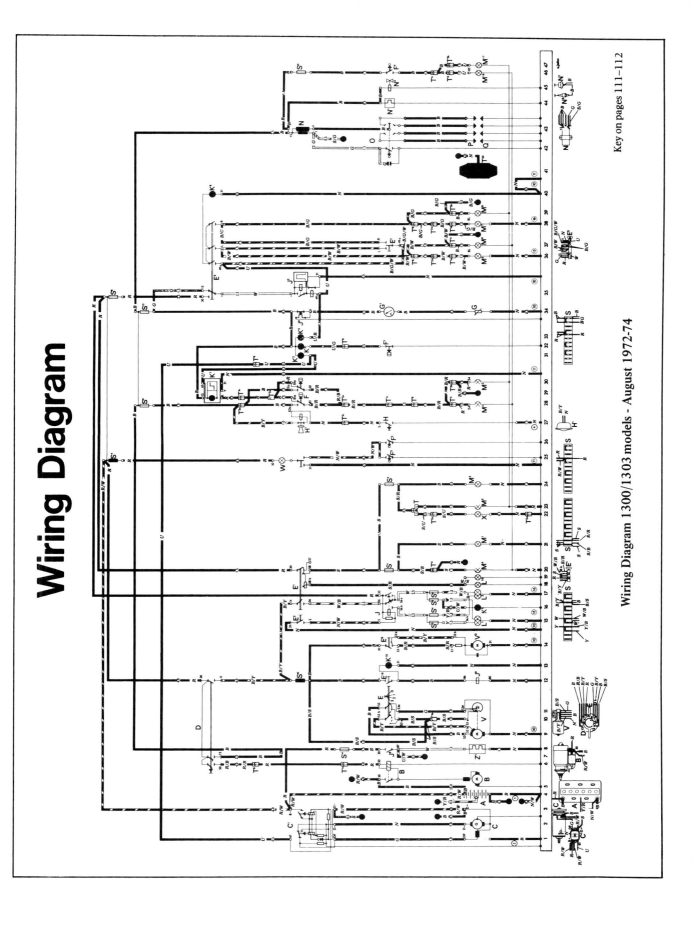

Wiring Diagram 1300/1303 models - August 1972-74

Key on pages 111–112

Wiring Diagram

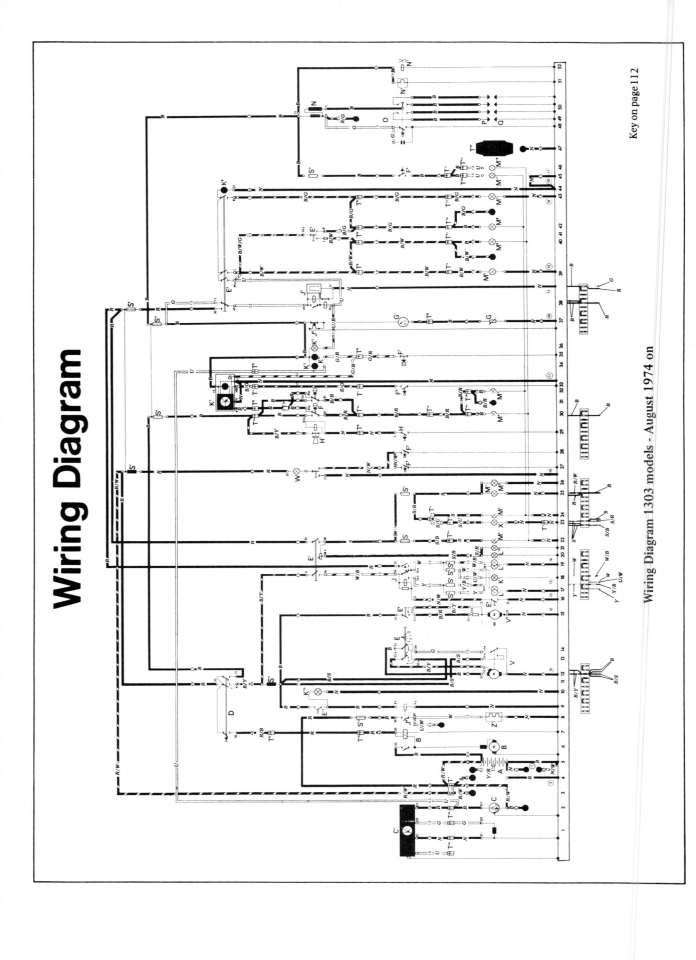

Key on page 112

Wiring Diagram 1303 models - August 1974 on

Wiring Diagram Key

Key for Diagram on page 107

	Designation	In current track
A	Battery	2
B	Starter	3, 4
C	Alternator	1
C1	Regulator	1
D	Ignition/starter switch	4, 8, 9
E	Windscreen wiper switch	9, 10, 11
E1	Lighting switch	17, 19, 20
E2	Turn signal switch	42
E3	Emergency light switch	37, 39, 40, 44, 45
E4	Headlight dimmer and flasher switch	13
E9	Fresh air fan switch	12
E15	Heated rear window switch	7
F	Brake light switch	30, 31
F1	Oil pressure switch	34
F2	Door contact switch left*	27
F3	Door contact switch right*	28
F4	Switch for reversing lights	46
F9	Handbrake warning lamp switch	32
G	Fuel gauge sender unit	36
G1	Fuel gauge	36
G7	Sender for TDC marker	54
H	Horn button	29
H1	Horn	29
J	Headlight dimmer and flasher relay	13, 15, 17
J2	Turn signal - Emergency light relay	38
J6	Voltage stablizer	36
J9	Heated rear window relay	5, 7
K1	High beam warning lamp	16
K2	Generator or warning lamp	33
K3	Oil pressure warning lamp	34
K5	Turn signal warning lamp	35
K6	Emergency light warning lamp	45
K7	Dual circuit brake system and handbrake warning lamp	32
K10	Heated rear window warning lamp	7
L1	Headlight bulb, left	14
L2	Headlight bulb, right	18
L10	Speedometer light	19, 20
M1	Parking light bulb, left	24
M2	Tail-light bulb, right	23
M2	Brake light bulb, right	31
M3	Parking light bulb, right	25
M4	Tail-light bulb, left	22
M4	Brake light bulb, left	30
M5	Turn signal front, left	40
M6	Turn signal rear, left	41
M7	Turn signal front, right	44
M8	Turn signal rear, right	43
M16	Reversing light bulb, left*	47
M17	Reversing light bulb, right*	46
N	Ignition coil	49, 50
N1	Automatic choke	53
N3	Electro-magnetic cut-off valve	52
O	Distributor	49, 50, 51
P	Plug connector	49, 50, 51
Q	Spark plugs	49, 50, 51
S1 to S12	Fuses in fuse box	
S21	Separate fuse for reversing lights (8 amp)	
S22	Separate fuse for rear window (8 amp)	46
T	Cable connector	5
b	Behind engine compartment damping	
T1	Flat connector, single	
a	Behind instrument panel	
b	Under rear seat	
c	Behind engine compartment damping	
d	In front luggage compartment on right	
e	In front luggage compartment on left	
T2	Flat connector, 2 pin	
T3	Flat connector, 3 pin	
a	In luggage compartment on left	
b	Behind engine compartment damping on right	
c	3 pin connector in engine compartment	
T4a	Flat connector, 4 pin	
T20	Central socket	48
V	Wiper motor - single stage on (VW 1200)	9, 10
V2	Fan motor - (only on VW 1200L)	12
W	Interior light	26
X	License plate light	22

	Designation	In current track
Z1	Heated rear window	5
①	Earthing strap from battery to frame	2
②	Earthing strap from transmission to frame	6
⑩	Earthing point, instrument panel	
⑪	Earthing point, speedometer	
⑮	Earthing point, front luggage compartment left	
⑯	Earthing point, front luggage compartment right	

Key for Diagram on page 109

	Designation	In current track
A	Battery	4
B	Starter	5, 6
C	Generator	1, 2, 3
C1	Regulator	1, 2, 3
D	Ignition/starter switch	6, 7, 12
E	Windshield wiper switch	10, 11
E1	Lighting switch	16, 18, 20
E2	Turn signal switch (switch for dimmer and headlight flasher)	15, 37
E3	Emergency flasher switch	35, 36, 37, 38, 40,
E9	Fan switch	
E15	Heated rear window switch	14
F	Brake light switch	12
F1	Oil pressure switch	28, 29, 30
F2	Door contact switch left	32
F3	Door contact switch right	26
F4	Reversing light switch	25
G	Fuel gauge sender unit	46
G1	Fuel gauge	34
H	Horn button	34
H1	Horn	27
J	Relay for headlight dimmer and flasher	27
J2	Turn signal - emergency flasher relay	15, 16, 17
J6	Fuel gauge vibrator	35
J9	Relay for heated rear window	34
K1	High beam warning lamp	12
K2	Generator charging warning lamp	16
K3	Oil pressure warning lamp	31
K5	Turn signal warning lamp	32
K6	Emergency flasher warning lamp	33
K7	Dual circuit brake warning lamp	40
K10	Heated rear window warning lamp	28, 29
L1	Twin-filament bulb, left headlight	13
L2	Twin-filament bulb, right headlight	15
L10	Instrument panel light	17
M1	Parking light, left	18, 19
M2	Tail/braking, right	21
M3	Parking light, right	23, 30
M4	Tail/braking, left	24
M5	Turn signal, front, left	20, 28
M6	Turn signal, rear, left	36
M7	Turn signal, front, right	37
M8	Turn signal, rear, right	38
M16	Reversing light, left	39
M17	Reversing light, right	46
N	Ignition coil	47
N1	Automatic choke	43
N3	Electro-magnetic cut-off valve	44
O	Distributor	45
P	Spark plug connector	42, 43
Q	Spark plug	43
S1 to S12	Fuses in fuse box	43 / 12, 15, 17, 20, 24, 25, 28, 34, 35,
S13	Separate fuse for reversing lights (8A)	46
S14	Separate fuse for rear window (8A)	8

	Designation	In current track
T	Cable adaptor on right behind engine compartment lining	
T1	Cable connector, single	
a	Under rear seat	
b	Near fuse box	
c	Behind engine compartment lining	
d	In front luggage compartment on right	
e	In front luggage compartment on left	
T2	Cable connector 2 pin	
a	on engine compartment lid	
b	Modified to: 8 pin connector behind instrument panel	36, 38
c	Modified to: 8 pin connector behind instrument panel	27
	modified to: single connector near fuse box	28
T3	Cable connector, 3 pin	
a	In front luggage compartment on left	
b	Behind engine compartment lining on right	
T4	Cable connector, 4 pin behind engine compartment lining on left	
T6	Cable connector, 8 pin behind instrument panel (not on VW 1300)	
T20	Central socket	41
V	Wiper motor	9, 10, 11
V2	Fan motor	14
W	Interior light	25
X	License plate light	22
Z1	Heated rear window	8
(1)	Earth strap from battery to frame	4
(2)	Earth strap from transmission to frame	1
(4)	Earth wire on steering column coupling	27
(10)	Earthing point, instrument panel	
(11)	Earthing point, speedometer	
(15)	Earthing point in front luggage compartment, on left	
(16)	Earthing point in front luggage compartment, on right	

Key for Diagram on page 110

	Designation	In current track
A	Battery	5
B	Starter	6, 7
C	Alternator	1, 2
C1	Regulator	1,2
D	Ignition/starter switch	7, 11, 12
E	Windscreen wiper switch	13, 14
E1	Lighting switch	18, 20, 22
E2	Turn signal switch	41
E3	Emergency light switch	38, 39 43
E4	Headlight dimmer and flasher switch	16
E9	Fresh air fan switch	15
E15	Heated rear window switch	9
F	Brake light switch	30, 31, 32
F1	Oil pressure switch	35
F2	Door contact switch left	28
F3	Door contact switch right	27
F4	Switch for reversing lights	45
F9	Handbrake warning lamp switch	33
G	Fuel gauge sender unit	37
G1	Fuel gauge	37
H	Horn button	29
H1	Horn	29
J	Headlight dimmer and flasher relay	16, 17, 18
		19
J2	Turn signal - emergency light relay	38
J6	Voltage stabilizer	37
J9	Heated rear window relay	8, 9
K1	High beam warning lamp	18
K2	Generator warning lamp	34
K3	Oil pressure warning lamp	35
K5	Turn signal warning lamp	36

	Designation	In current track
K6	Emergency light warning lamp	44
K7	Dual circuit brake system and handbrake warning lamp	31, 32, 33
K10	Heated rear window warning lamp	10
L1	Headlight bulb, left	17
L2	Headlight bulb, right	19
L10	Instrument light	20, 21
M1	Parking light bulb, left	25
M2	Tail-light bulb, right	24
M2	Brake light bulb, right	32
M3	Parking light bulb, right	26
M4	Tail-light bulb, left	22
M4	Brake light bulb, left	30
M5	Turn signal front, left	39
M6	Turn signal rear, left	40
M7	Turn signal front, right	43
M8	Turn signal rear, right	42
M16	Reversing light bulb, left	46
M17	Reversing light bulb, right	47
N	Ignition coil	49, 50
N1	Automatic choke	51
N3	Electro-magnetic cut-off valve	52
O	Distributor	48, 49, 50
P	Plug connector	49, 50
Q	Spark plugs	49, 50
S1 to S12	Fuses in fuse box	11, 17, 19, 22, 25, 27, 30, 37, 38
S21	Separate fuse for reversing lights (8 amp)	45
S22	Separate fuse for rear window (8 amp)	8
T	Cable connector	
a	Under rear seat	
b	Behind engine compartment damping	
T1	Flat connector, single on tunnel	
a	Behind dash	
b	Under rear seat	
c	Behind engine compartment damping	
d	In front luggage compartment or right	
e	In front luggage compartment or left	
T2	Flat connector, 2 pin	
T3	Flat connector, 3 pin	
a	In luggage compartment on left	
b	Behind engine compartment damping on right	
c	3 pin connector in engine compartment	
T4	Flat connector, 4 pin	
a	Behind engine compartment damping on left	
b	Connector 4 pin, under rear seat	
T8	Connector 8 pin, behind dash	47
T20	Central socket	12, 13, 14
V	Wiper motor	15
V2	Fan motor	27
W	Interior light	23
X	License plate light	8
Z1	Heated rear window	
(1)	Earthing strap from battery to frame	5
(2)	Earthing strap from transmission to frame	4
(10)	Earthing point, instrument panel	
(11)	Earthing point, speedometer	
(15)	Earthing point, front luggage compartment left	
(16)	Earthing point, front luggage compartment right	

WIRING COLOUR CODE

R	Red	W	White
P	Pink	S	Slate
G	Green	B	Black
U	Blue	K	Purple
N	Brown	Y	Yellow

Note; Where a wire has a tracer stripe, the main wire colour code letter is shown first, followed by the trace code. Example U/W is a Blue wire with a White tracer.

non-fused circuit, the insulation melts and begins to give off choking fumes which can fill the interior of a Beetle to the extent that you literally cannot see your hand in front of your face within maybe thirty seconds. If there are any combustible materials in the vicinity of the fire, these too will ignite from the heat and within a minute or two of the short to earth occurring the car could be full of flames in addition to smoke, which would by now have rendered any occupants of the car unconscious. If the fire includes brake fluid or fuel lines, the car will be a burnt-out shell in minutes.

What this is all leading to is the advice that, unless you are a qualified and experienced electrician, it is best to leave electrical problems and the fitting of extra electrical devices to an auto-electrician.

Restoration and electrics

Car wires are carried tightly bound in the loom. In order that you can, with the aid of a wiring diagram, trace which wires go where, the wires are colour coded. Many elderly cars have at some time been fitted with extra lengths of wire, either to replace damaged lengths or to power an extra device. Sometimes, the wires are of an appropriate colour and rating, but often they are not.

A damaged loom (frequently caused by welding too close to the loom and melting off the insulation, often caused by shorting to earth which also burns off the insulation) is best replaced – even though looms are far from cheap to buy and anything but easy to install. Damaged individual lengths of wire outside the loom may be replaced with others of the same colour and diameter, except in cases where the damage is melted insulation and the wire runs into the loom, because the wire (and adjacent wires) in the loom could also have melted insulation.

Wire damage includes anything which bares the copper core or anything which reduces its effective internal cross sectional area, such as being pinched so that some of the strands of wire break but others survive. Check all visible wiring in the car for damage, and also check that spade and bullet connectors are insulated – it is not unknown for an un-insulated connector to drop off its terminal and start a fire.

Starter motor

The starter motor needs a huge current because of the amount of energy required to turn the engine over. In the interests of safety, the ignition key does not have to handle this high power, but instead actuates a current which operates the starter solenoid. A solenoid is simply a switch which is operated by a small electrical current, but which switches a circuit capable of carrying much higher currents.

The starter motor is a powerful electric motor which drives a gear which meshes with the teeth on the flywheel, turning the flywheel and hence the crankshaft. Competent electricians can carry out repairs to the motor, although exchange reconditioned units are recommended for the rest of us not so bright sparks. If the drive pinion teeth are damaged then the unit is also best replaced (in which case, the flywheel teeth will also be damaged).

The solenoid is mounted on the starter motor. Most problems with the unit occur because it sticks (which can often be cured with a sharp tap from the handle of a screwdriver), although other faults can occur. During the course of a full restoration it would be advisable to replace the starter motor and solenoid complete with professionally reconditioned alternatives.

Generator

A dynamo is far less efficient and generates less electricity (perhaps as much as 60 per cent) than an alternator. If either is faulty, the author recommends that they are either taken to a specialist for renovation or exchanged, and that one of these courses of action is taken during a restoration.

When fitting a new generator, it is advisable to also fit a new drive belt. (See Chapter Three for details of adjusting the belt tension.)

Heat exchangers and exhaust

Heat exchangers comprise a finned core which is contained within the body. Hot exhaust gasses passing through the core heat the fins which in turn heat the air which is forced through by the engine cooling fan. The heated air then passes through the heater channels to the interior of the car.

When replacing heat exchangers, as usual you have a choice between expensive original equipment components and spurious versions. Some of the latter may not have a large enough fin surface area, which reduces their efficiency at heating air considerably, so do bear this in mind when considering economies.

The exhaust is a low-cost item which is not really worth welded repair once it begins to blow (exhaust gasses escaping through a hole in the exhaust), because patches will be welded onto adjacent metal which will have thinned through rusting, and severe corrosion of these areas will usually occur very rapidly.

5 · REPAIR AND RESTORATION – BODYWORK

It is best to begin this chapter by stating that a full DIY car restoration is incredibly hard work and that very few people really appreciate just how much work is involved until they've either finished one or given up part-way through the job. Obviously, the amount of work needed in a restoration will depend on the original condition of the car and on the desired result; concourse cars can take many times as long as 'usable' cars. It is also dependant on the quality of the restoration; cut corners and you can bring the time requirement down – if you can live with second-class workmanship.

Whenever asked how long it takes to restore a car, the author's friend Em Fryer simply replies 'A year'. The best restorations can take thousands of hours; many run into years of part-time work. Many are never completed at all. Before embarking on a full restoration, therefore, you should consider very carefully whether your motivation (and funds) will be sufficient to last throughout the project. On the finance side, make as comprehensive as possible a list of necessary panels, mechanical components and consumables (paint, MiG wire etc.), and see whether the total is so high that you could obtain a better deal by simply selling your own car and buying one in better condition; the costs of even a DIY restoration often exceed the resultant value of the car!

You can cut costs by plating expensive pressings rather than replacing them, i.e.. building up a floor edge from sheet steel rather than spending a lot of money on a proper repair panel or a full floor. The drawback with plating is that the car normally rusts through along the edges of welded seams and a car which is extensively plated can be expected to require more body repair work sooner than one which is largely re-panelled, if for no other reason than because the former has more seams!

You also need to honestly consider whether your own skills are sufficient for the job, because if you subsequently have to pay a professional restorer to put right your mistakes then his bill will probably be greater than that for a straight restoration. Many people appear to prefer to have bodywork and painting carried out by a professional, and then to undertake the mechanical build-up themselves.

One alternative to doing the whole job yourself is in effect to manage the restoration and to bring in a skilled mobile welder and perhaps a competent mechanic as and when required. This means that you undertake the donkey work such as the strip down, cutting out rotten metal, cleaning and so on, but that you can have confidence in the quality of the welding and of the mechanical build-up.

The author finds that decorating the workplace with photographs of the car being restored and of really nice examples of the same model can often provide that little extra inspiration needed to carry on working when every fibre of his body is screaming to get out of the workshop! Whilst on the subject of photographs, it is worth keeping the fullest photographic record of any restoration; not only does this serve to prove that the car has in fact been restored should you ever wish to sell it, but it also shows the depth of the restoration.

Classic car restoration is often depicted in the many books and magazines on the subject to consist largely of cutting away rotten old panels and grafting in new, like a great surgeon heroically performing a life-saving operation. This is actually an important but nevertheless relatively small part of the work encountered in car restoration. In fact, the bulk of the work of restoration is concerned with the far more humdrum business of cleaning. For every minute spent welding, there will usually be an hour or more of cleaning, ranging from scraping away old underseal, accumulated mud and rust from the underside of the car to cleaning burnt oil deposits and sundry dirt and gunge from engine and transmission components.

A large percentage of the restorer's time will also be spent in trying to establish and maintain a coherent and workable 'filing system' for the various components of the car. This is essential if you are not later to waste countless hours during the build-up in trying to find the

ABOVE
A full bodyshell-off restoration. Before starting work on a DIY restoration ask yourself whether your workshop, tools, skills and most importantly your commitment are up to the task ahead. Note: heater channels cut out of shell (internally braced), new channels bolted to floorpans – Terry and Craig size up the task of lifting the shell onto the chassis.

BELOW
With the bodyshell off, the first job is to thoroughly clean the chassis assembly, and a powerful vacuum cleaner is the best tool for the job of removing loose material. Cleaning off loose surface rust, paint and underseal can take forever for the DIY restorer and, coupled with the cleaning of mechanical and electrical components, you'll probably spend more time cleaning than welding! Unlike McPherson strut cars, Beetles with torsion bar front suspension can be wheeled around with the bodyshell off.

right nut, bracket or set screw for a particular component.

Even more so than during mechanical repair work, a good workshop is highly recommended for body repair, restoration or customising work. Ideally, the workplace should allow you a bare minimum of one metre working area all around the car and, if you intend to separate the chassis and bodyshell (which is probable), you will need twice this area. If you have to carry out a full mechanical and trim strip down then do not under-estimate the amount of dry storage which will be required for the components.

A damp workplace will be a constant source of frustration, because new steel panels will begin to rust

as soon as (if not before) they are fitted, tools will quickly become rusted and new paintwork will suffer bloom. Good all-round lighting which illuminates the sides and underside of the car is essential, and a solid, level, crumble-proof concrete floor is absolutely vital. You will require plenty of dry storage for components. If you merely pile them up in a corner then rebuilding the car will be a nightmare because you will waste hours finding parts and many more hours cleaning rust from them if the area in which they have been stored is damp.

Some specialised tools and equipment are essential for restoration. Some form of welding equipment, if only a cheap MiG, is recommended – even if you intend to bring in an outside welder to carry out the bulk of the work, in order to allow you to tack panels into position for final welding up by the professional.

WELDING EQUIPMENT

There are four types of welding equipment which the DIY restorer might typically consider. These are Arc (often called 'Stick'), MiG, Gas and Spot welding equipment. Arc welding equipment is comparatively cheap to buy but has severe limitations regarding the thickness of metal it can be successfully used on. If the metal is less than ⅛ in. thick (i.e. all body panels) the fierce arc welder will quickly burn right through the metal which it is supposed to be joining! Arc welders are best suited to use on heavy section agricultural vehicle metal and are useless for the vast majority of car restoration work. An accessory called the Kel Arc Body Welder is available, however, which is claimed to cut the hot amps from the arc welder and to have a stitching motion which lifts the rod on and off the metal, allowing it to cool and preventing the rod from either sticking to or burning through the metal. The author has not had the opportunity to test this equipment. The costs of the Kel Arc attachment and an arc welder will still be slightly under the purchase price of a MiG welder.

The MiG (Metal Inert Gas) welder is the type normally used by the DIY restorer, and by the majority of professionals as well. It surrounds its electrode (in wire form) in an inert gas, so preventing the metal from burning through. It may therefore be used on the thin metal of car body panels. Two types are available. The more traditional MiG welder uses gas from either a small cylinder strapped to the unit or from a larger, remote cylinder, and different gasses are required for welding different metals. The newer type of MiG (the 'gasless' MiG which can only be used on steel) substitutes a substance contained as a core within the wire for the gas. Because large gas cylinders are expensive to buy,

hire and fill and because small gas cylinders have to be replaced frequently at relatively high cost, this newer type of welder appears to offer advantages. The main advantage of the gasless MiG is that it possesses only one consumable (the cored wire) to run out of! The MiG welder is probably the best type for a beginner.

The author uses a SIP 'Handymig' Gasless MiG welder; a unit which proved quite easy to use and which is capable of first-class results. The cored wire needed for a gasless welder is more expensive than that for a gas MiG, although because no gas need be purchased for the former, the running costs of the two will not differ greatly. As already stated, the fact that there is only the one consumable (the cored wire) to run out is very much in the gasless MiGs' favour, although the author has on occasions experienced difficulties in obtaining the specialised cored wire locally, whilst plain MiG wire is widely available. The cored wire is often (the author believes erroneously) referred to as 'flux cored'. It is essential that you are not inadvertently supplied with standard non-cored MiG wire for use with a gasless MiG, because without shielding gas, this will burn through body panels.

Gas welding is arguably the most versatile of all, and can produce excellent results in the hands of a skilled person. Arc, MiG and spot welders all use electricity to heat a very small area, whereas in gas welding a torch is used to heat both metal and welding rod, and a larger area of metal tends to become very hot as a result. The greatest drawback is that the heat which is necessary tends to warp body panels and can easily give a new panel a corrugated finish! Gas welding equipment can also be used for brazing and for heating stubborn nuts and bolts which refuse to move otherwise.

Spot welders are the easiest to use, although they are limited insofar as they can only be used (unless a range of quite expensive special arms are also available) for joining together the edges of two metal 'lips'. For such joins they give an unbeatable combination of ease of use, strength and neatness. No wire nor welding rod is required, because the spot welder uses electricity to heat and fuse two panels together. Few DIY restorers would go to the expense of buying a spot welder because of their limited applications, and most opt to hire them as and when necessary from a DIY store or tool hire business.

When using a spot welder two conditions are necessary for good results. Firstly, the two pieces of steel being joined must be tightly held together. Secondly, the surfaces must be spotlessly clean. It is nowadays normal practice to spray special zinc-based paints onto the metal before performing the weld, in order to reduce the chances of corrosion occurring.

Yet another accessory which has been available for

the Arc welder for some time is claimed to allow users to spot weld two sheets of steel with access from one side alone, whereas the spot welder requires that one electrode is placed either side of the join. The Arc welder accessories have not been tested by the author, and while he cannot personally vouch for them he cannot see any reason why they should not work. It would be vital that the panels being joined were firmly clamped together in some way immediately either side of the single electrode, because the top layer would expand more rapidly due to heat than the underlying layer, so that the two would tend to move apart. Still on the subject of Arc welder accessories, kits are available which enable it to be used for brazing. Whilst the author has heard no comment detrimental to any of these Arc welder accessories, he has yet to find an experienced professional restorer who champions them.

Most welding equipment can only produce neat and strong results if the operator possesses the appropriate skills. The quickest way to acquire such skills is to enrol in a short welding course, perhaps an evening class at a college. Whilst it is true to say that you can teach yourself to weld, it is not recommended that you do so (especially using your own car as a guinea pig).

Because the MiG seems to be the type of welding equipment most commonly owned by the DIY restorer, an introduction to its use follows. If you wish to find out more then there are several excellent books available on the subject.

Using a MiG welder

The MiG is (apart from the spot welder) arguably the easiest of welding devices for the beginner to use for general bodywork repairs. This does not, however, mean that it is an easy matter to produce clean and strong welds on typically thin body panels for, unless conditions and the user's skills are both excellent, there are many obstacles to good welding.

The worst problem to beset the novice is that of 'burning through', when the electric current melts straight through the metal which it is supposed to be joining. This can occur if the wire feed speed is too slow (or intermittent, which indicates a fault in the welder – usually either the wire jamming in the liner or the driving wheels slipping), if the gun is moved across the metal too slowly, if the current is set too high or if the shielding gas/core fails to do its job.

When the metal to be welded has become thin through rusting then the chances of burning through are greatly increased, and hence the advice to always cut back to not only clean but also to strong and thick metal before attempting to weld.

The correct preparation of the metal which is to be welded is vital. All traces of rust, of paint, oil, grease and any other contaminant must be cleaned from the surface to avoid poor adhesion and spiting. *Any* impurities which find their way into the welded joint will substantially weaken it.

When a joint is being welded, both surfaces should be thoroughly cleaned; if paint or any other contaminant is present on the underside of the panel then it will mix with the molten weld/steel and weaken

This MiG is the gasless 'Handymig' from SIP, and has lasted the author many years. He does now use a wrap-around head mask rather than the lollipop type mask shown here, and has swapped the leather gloves for gauntlets which give better protection against molten weld!

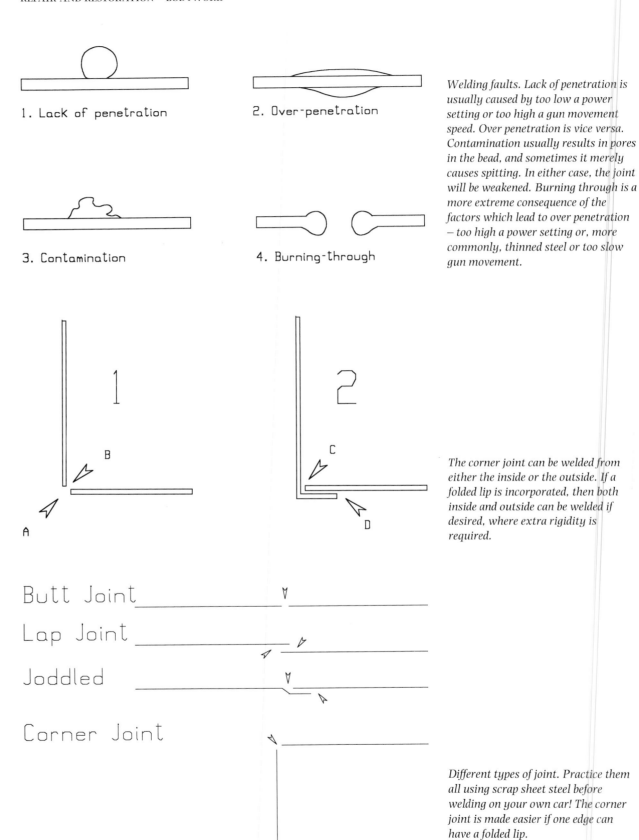

1. Lack of penetration

2. Over-penetration

3. Contamination

4. Burning-through

Welding faults. Lack of penetration is usually caused by too low a power setting or too high a gun movement speed. Over penetration is vice versa. Contamination usually results in pores in the bead, and sometimes it merely causes spitting. In either case, the joint will be weakened. Burning through is a more extreme consequence of the factors which lead to over penetration – too high a power setting or, more commonly, thinned steel or too slow gun movement.

The corner joint can be welded from either the inside or the outside. If a folded lip is incorporated, then both inside and outside can be welded if desired, where extra rigidity is required.

Butt Joint

Lap Joint

Joddled

Corner Joint

Different types of joint. Practice them all using scrap sheet steel before welding on your own car! The corner joint is made easier if one edge can have a folded lip.

the joint. Recently, special paints have become available which can be used on surfaces which are to be spot or MiG welded. The use of these products – such as 'Autoline' weldable zinc primer, will ensure that the welded joint does not – as is normal – become the first part of the repair to rust through again. The metal panels must then be clamped in some way so firmly that the heat of the welding process does not distort either of them and allow them to move apart. Small sections may be clamped using mole grips, although longer runs are usually affixed using self-tapping screws or alternatively pop rivets at regular intervals.

First steps with a MiG

Always practice on scrap metal and do not attempt any welding to the bodywork of your car until you are capable of producing consistently good results.

Safety is the most important consideration. If your workshop does not already possess one, then buy a fire extinguisher. Never weld in the vicinity of a petrol tank nor any other container which holds or has held combustible fluids, especially if the container is now empty or near-empty (an empty petrol tank contains more explosive fumes than a full one). Remember that paint, underseal and certain other materials to be found in a car (such as some sound-deadening material) can be flammable, and that many can be ignited by heat moving along a panel which is being welded. Keep a fire extinguisher handy for blowing out small welding fires.

Always use a proper welding mask. If you view the electric arc with the naked eye then you will later suffer an immensely painful phenomenon called arc eye. Arc eye is painful enough to drive most sufferers to seek hospital attention. The radiation given off by the MiG is not just harmful to eyes, but to skin as well, so always ensure that you are well protected.

Always wear protective clothing, especially strong leather gloves, and a hat (to prevent your hair from catching fire as the sparks shower) is a good idea. It is as well to wear old, thick items of clothing and stout leather shoes (red-hot weld splatter will burn through flimsy shoes and your sock – and when it reaches your foot it hurts like hell), as you will inevitably burn holes in most of them.

Never take liberties with the electric current, which is of a low voltage but quite powerful enough to kill you. Ensure that you weld only in dry conditions, and keep trailing leads off damp floors.

In MiG welding, an electric current passes down the MiG wire, melting both the end of the wire and the metal underneath it, so that the two fuse together. If the surface of the metal has any contaminants on it,

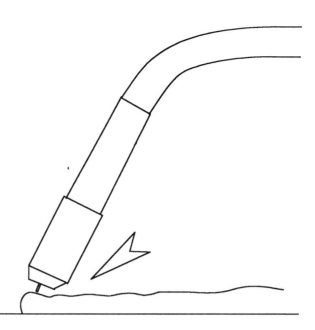

By keeping the gun at a constant angle of seventy degrees, the molten weld is pushed as a 'wave' of sorts as the gun moves across the steel. This gives a more even bead.

including paint, rust or oil, then this will mix with the molten metal and weaken the joint. When welding typically thin car body steel, the steel panels become molten right through, and paint or other contaminants on the underside can be drawn up into the molten metal, again weakening the joint.

When first attempting to weld, try to run a bead onto a flat sheet of 18g or preferably 20g steel rather than attempting a joint between two pieces. Begin by cleaning the metal top and bottom thoroughly of all rust, paint and grease. Trim the wire protruding from the MiG nozzle to around 10 mm. Place the earth clamp on the steel, put on all protective clothing then switch on the machine. Place the wire against the steel, pull the face visor in front of your eyes then press the trigger and begin to push or drag the gun along the surface of the steel, keeping the gun at an angle of around 70 degrees from the horizontal. Do not allow the mask to get too close to the weld, because sparks will quickly ruin it. Wrap-around face masks, particularly those which attach to the user's head, are recommended, because the alternative lollipop-type flat masks can allow in extraneous light from the top and sides which contract the pupils and make the viewed image of the welding process appear very dim.

When you first attempt to weld it will appear that everything happens at once – sometimes too quickly for you to establish gun movement before burning through

ABOVE
Plug welding. A hole is punched or drilled (in the later case, clean off any swarf on the underside) in one sheet, which is clamped or pop riveted to another. The hole is then filled with weld.

BELOW
The completed joint (ground down) is neat and strong. Don't use plug welds on panels which you may at some point in the future remove, because they cannot be drilled out like spot welds.

begins. The solution is to keep on practising and adjusting the settings on the MiG to suit the steel you are welding until you master the art. The author is not possessed of particularly steady hands, and he has never found achieving good welds with the MiG an easy matter. The greatest problem is that of running the weld away from the intended join. He overcomes this problem to a great extent by resting the side of the MiG pistol grip against a solid object such as a length of scrap box section steel which is arranged so that it is in line with the intended join. Many people use proper head-mounted welding visors rather than the 'lollipop' type of mask typically supplied with cheaper welders, and this allows them to use their 'spare' (and heavily gloved) hand to help guide the MiG. Basically, the visor is tilted upwards so that the wearer can place the pistol grip onto the metal and support it using both hands (do not allow your hand too close to the 'business' end), then a flick of the head moves the visor downwards over the eyes, and welding can begin. Do not blame the author if you crick your neck trying this, though! The alternative is to wear MiG-proof goggles, but the author does not personally like these because radiation given off during a MiG welding session will tan your skin.

MiG 'plug' welding is an easy method of producing neat and strong joints. This simulates a spot weld, and is achieved by drilling holes in the uppermost of two panels which are to be joined, then clamping the panels tightly together and filling the holes with weld. The weld fuses to the bottom panel and to the side of the hole in the top panel. After surplus weld has been ground down, the results can be very neat and strong. However, do not use plug welds if you envisage ever having to remove the panel thus welded because, unlike spot welds, plug welds can turn out to be irregularly shaped and they cannot simply be drilled or cut out like spot welds. If you do elect to plug weld, the welds should be as frequent as the original spot welds which they are replacing.

Please check with your local vehicle testing authorities that plug welds are still acceptable for roadworthiness test purposes (MOT in the UK) before rebuilding your car using this technique. Although plug welds are perfectly acceptable at the time of writing, legislation does change and the author and publishers cannot be held accountable for future laws!

There are various types of joint which you will have to deal with. The butt joint is, as the name suggests, a join between two sheets of metal which butt against each other. A small gap should be left in between the two so that the weld can properly penetrate the joint, and the ideal tool for achieving this is the 'Inter-Grip'. This small device (sold in packs of five) can hold flat or curved panels tightly together for butt welding equally well. They are available from Frost Auto Restoration

Techniques (see address in rear of book). The author always tacks the two pieces of metal before continuously welding them, because if you start continuous welding at one end of the join and weld the whole lot in one go, distortion is very likely to occur.

Other joints include right angles (which can be difficult) and stepped joints (detailed in the following paragraph). Practice all types of joint because they will all be needed during a typical restoration.

A joddler (variously referred to as a 'joggler' 'jodder' and, more properly, as an edge setter) is a great aid. This tool places a step into the edge of a panel to allow it to overlap yet remain at the same level as the panel to which it is to be joined. The better joddlers incorporate a ⅛ in. punch, for punching holes in steel through which you can produce neat plug welds.

Two types of commercially manufactured joddler are commonly available. The less expensive is the scissors type, which can incorporate a plug weld hole punch. The more expensive alternative works rather like a can opener and utilises two stepped wheels which are pressed either side of the steel and then turned using a ½ in. ratchet drive as a winder. The author uses the scissors type, but found that the effort needed to step an edge into steel of greater thickness than 20g was too high. He made up a cheap alternative using a large mole wrench, with two stepped blocks welded into the jaws (see photograph and illustration). The adjustable mole wrench allows pressure to be progressively built up as two or more passes are made over thick steel with the tool.

The joddled joint has a great advantage over the butt joint. Because the two halves of a joddled joint can be pulled tightly together and because the stepped edge of the joddled panel is parallel with the rest of the panel, the two panels naturally tend to lie flat when they have been welded together. With the butt joint, it is easy to inadvertently weld the panels up so that they are not quite in line with each other. This becomes important when one of the two panels being joined is under any sort of stress. One instance which springs readily to mind is when a lower side (quarter) repair panel is being welded into position. The cutting process which removed the unwanted metal can easily have distorted the remaining metal. A joddled repair panel pulls this back into correct alignment when the panels are temporarily clamped with pop rivets or self tapping screws prior to welding.

If you have access to a spot welder, then you can utilise a useful alternative to joddled joints. By spot welding a strip of steel behind one edge so that it overlaps the other, you have a nice, flush joint to weld.

The alternative to doing the welding yourself is to bring in a skilled welder as and when required. There

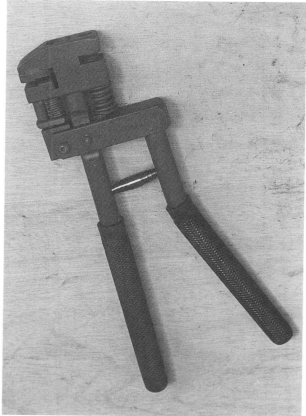

ABOVE LEFT
Frost Intergrips in use on a small curved section. In practice, you would not place the intergrips so closely together.

LEFT
This shows how the intergrips work. They cannot be used on enclosed sections, however, because there would be no way to retrieve the locking bars!

TOP
When the pieces are tacked together, the intergrips may be removed and the tacks joined by continuous beads of weld. Don't place the tacks so closely to the intergrips as shown in this photograph, because as the weld cools it shrinks, and makes removal if the intergrips difficult if the tack is too close.

RIGHT
This commercially made joddler incorporates a punch for making plug welding holes.

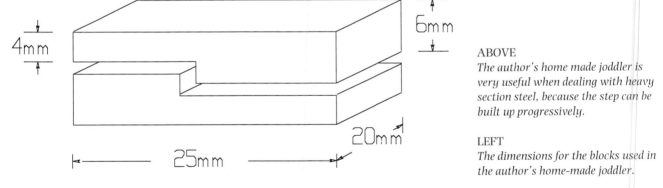

ABOVE
The author's home made joddler is very useful when dealing with heavy section steel, because the step can be built up progressively.

LEFT
The dimensions for the blocks used in the author's home-made joddler.

are many self-employed and mobile MiG and gas welders who may be hired by the hour, and they can usually be found listed in any commercial telephone directory.

When hiring a skilled welder it is as well to prepare as much work per visit as possible, otherwise the travelling expenses could eclipse the actual welding charges! For most DIY restorers who will only ever restore the one car, hiring a skilled welder is probably a better solution than learning to weld, because you will get better results and be able to drive your car safe in the knowledge that the welds will not spring open the first time you drive over a pot-hole!

OTHER TOOLS AND EQUIPMENT

If you intend to carry out a full body-off strip down prior to welding, a means of holding the chassis/floorpan at a comfortable working height is very useful. Strong steel trestles can easily be welded-up (good practice for the novice welder) and if two steel box sections are laid across these, you will have a solid and level platform onto which a few strong adults should easily be able to man-handle the assembly.

An angle grinder with cutting and grinding wheels plus a sanding/linishing wheel and perhaps a cup brush

This small compressor provides enough compressed air to power an air chisel and other useful tools. It is a boon for the Beetle owner if only for its use in pressurising the windscreen washer bottle! It is useful for small paint spraying jobs, but for a full car respray you really need a compressor with a tank capacity ten or twenty times the 25 litres of the author's compressor, and a much more powerful motor.

will save hours of very hard work when you have to clean old paint, underseal or rust from metal. You will need a selection of tools for cutting sheet metal, such as tin snips, aviation shears (straight and curved), a Monodex cutter, hacksaw, sharp bolster chisel and lump hammer. Pneumatic chisels and air hacksaws which are powered by compressors are marvellous if your pocket runs to a large enough compressor to power them, because they allow you to cut body panels without the distortions which a bolster chisel produces. The twin problems with the air chisel are its noise level (guaranteed to annoy neighbours) and its appetite for air, which can easily outstrip the capacity of smaller compressors.

Another very useful but incredibly noisy air tool is the descaler. This tools uses air power to hammer a number of pins down onto a rusted surface, and can quickly remove all traces of rust and leave a surface

ready for de-greasing prior to welding or spraying. The noise level generated when working on a large, resonant panel with either this tool or the air chisel, however, is so great that the user must wear some form of hearing protection. In some countries, laws will allow neighbours the legal means to curtail such noisy activities. In the UK, noise is now treated as a form of pollution, and the authorities could be brought in by a neighbour if you were to make too much noise.

Speaking of compressors, these are incredibly useful, not merely for spraying, but for blowing rust and dust out of nooks and crannies. They are also useful to have to hand for blowing out minor welding fires which can start when paint, underseal or trim in the vicinity of the area being welded suddenly catches fire. Buy the largest compressor which you can afford, because very small units are quickly drained of air by certain attachments, and the motors have a short 'duty cycle' which causes them to shut off automatically to prevent them from overheating. This sometimes happens just as you really *need* them!

The author has also found that an old cylinder-type vacuum cleaner is one of the most useful tools in the workshop. Cleaning off an old bodyshell generates a tremendous amount of dust which, if you try to clear it with a broom, will mainly escape into the atmosphere only to re-settle elsewhere. If you are intending to spray paint in the near future then such dust will ruin the finish; if you are rebuilding a mechanical component then the dust will enter the 'works' and cause accelerated wear. The vacuum cleaner deals with this problem and is also useful for cleaning loose paint and rust flakes off the bodyshell, and for clearing filler dust from nooks and crannies before painting.

A pop-riveter is essential for fixing some items of trim but also very useful for positioning some panels prior to welding. Hand-powered pop rivet pliers are cheap to buy, and you should always look for a set which has long handles, because using them for any length of time can really make your hand ache! Air-powered alternatives are available, but it is up to the individual to decide whether the amount of pop riveting to be done justifies the extra cost of these.

The more ambitious restorer who wishes to fabricate some of the repair panels will benefit from a good set of panel beater's tools, although these can be very expensive and a rubber faced mallet plus a small selection of hammers and dollies can be substituted with some success. The author found a useful set of three planishing hammers and four dollies at VW Tools (address at the back of this book).

Use and abuse of bodyfiller

Whilst the appearance of panels which will ultimately be hidden underneath carpets or underseal is not important, it is obviously vital that external panels are not only strongly fitted but also that they look good. Unfortunately, some of the operations during a restoration create welded seams which will show up through paintwork and which consequently need to be hidden before painting. Shallow dents in external panels, which can easily be accidentally caused during the mechanical build-up, also have to be hidden. The materials for achieving a smooth surface and the correct lines in such cases are either bodyfiller or lead (or a combination of these).

Many classic enthusiasts abhor bodyfiller despite the fact that, if properly used, this material can give perfectly acceptable results. Unfortunately, bodyfiller has suffered from a 'bad press' because the number of cases of filler

misuse easily outnumber cases of proper use.

Bodyfiller is intended and perfectly acceptable for filling shallow dents in external and non-structural car body panels. It is not intended to be used to bridge holes, nor to fill deep dents or cover up areas of bodyrot. Yet those looking for a car (even '70s cars) like the Beetle will doubtless encounter many examples in which quite large holes and deep dents have been filled with a lump of bodyfiller or a mixture of GRP and bodyfiller.

Bodyfiller should only be used to obtain a smooth surface on metal which has shallow dents, such as might result from heat distortion during welding operations, from minor parking bumps, or on a seam produced following the fitting of a repair part-panel. Deep dents should be beaten out so that a minimum of filler is needed. Bodyfiller is the modern equivalent of lead, because bodyshops and car manufacturers for many years treated small undulations in external car body panels by firstly painting on a lead 'paint', melting this to 'tin' (coat) the area in question and to form a strongly-bonded layer to which the lead could adhere, then melting on and spreading with a spatula further lead to build up to the required height. This process is known as 'lead loading' or 'body soldering'. Bodyfiller is far easier to use than near-molten lead, as well as being inherently safer! Lead loading kits and associated equipment are available and widely advertised.

Lead loading offers one great advantage over body-filler because the lead actually seals the surface over which it is applied, and in doing so it prevents future rusting (as long as the metal underneath is bright when coated with lead). In the author's experience, many professional restorers use lead loading for this reason, although obtaining a final smooth finish with lead is not easy, and you could use a very thin layer of bodyfiller on top of the lead to obtain the best of both worlds!

A combination of lead loading and the use of body-filler is especially useful when dealing with welded seams. Clean then de-grease all the area in question (the metal must be perfectly clean), then paint on solder paint, which is obtainable from companies such as Frost Auto Restoration Techniques (address at the back of the book). Apply heat to the solder paint until it melts and wipe it so that it coats the metal, then wipe away any flux from the surface using a damp rag. The metal is now sealed, and may be built up using either lead or bodyfiller.

It must be pointed out that lead is highly toxic, so if you do decide to work with it, treat it with the caution you would if dealing with any other toxic chemical. Don't attack a leaded joint with a power sander, because this will fill the air with lead particles which you will breathe in – always use a body file to profile lead, and wear a fine dust mask.

Using bodyfiller

In order to use bodyfiller successfully, it is vital that all traces of rusting, paint (including primers), oils and other contaminants are removed from the surface to be treated. Filler cannot adhere strongly to painted metal, because the join can only be as strong as that between the paint and the metal! If you apply filler over the slightest amount of rust then you can expect it to literally drop out at a later date when the rusting spreads sufficiently underneath. If you apply filler over contaminants then you may find that poor adhesion results, or the filler could chemically react with certain contaminants.

If cleaning the metal renders it very thin then you should not use bodyfiller because it will offer little or no strength and furthermore, most types of filler are quite rigid and will be very inclined to loose adhesion to a thin and hence very flexible panel, or even to break up as the panel flexes. The only safe option in this situation is to weld in new metal.

Before using bodyfiller, check the surface carefully for high spots. Whilst you can fill and smooth down low areas, high spots cannot be linished out and must be beaten out before the filling process begins. If there are any deep holes, beat these out as shallow as possible, where access permits. Equipment is available for pulling out dents, and consists of sliding hammer rod to which a number of attachments may be affixed. The attachments can fit through a small hole in the surface of the metal, and the sliding hammer is then used to knock out the dent. If the surface can be made clean and yet remain sound, 'key' the surface with a 36 grit disc, then use spirit wipe to remove any grease or oil contaminants.

Most fillers consist of a thick paste and a separate hardener; a chemical catalyst which accelerates the hardening of the filler. The filler itself usually comprises a polyester resin with a mineral-based powder, which forms a thick paste. Alternatives with tiny metal particles instead of the mineral powder can be obtained today. These offer the advantage of not being porous but might not give such good adhesion as the mineral products, which have far smaller particles. Mineral body fillers are porous.

Mix up the smallest quantity of bodyfiller which you feel you can get away with, and always follow the manufacturer's instructions relating to the relative amounts of filler and hardener. Ensure that the filler and hardener are properly mixed and of a uniform colour. Cleanliness is vital, because any foreign bodies in the filler will simply 'drag' as you try to smooth off the surface.

Apply bodyfiller in very thin layers, allowing each to fully harden before adding the next, and gradually build up the repair to the required level. Do not be tempted to apply one thick layer of filler, because this may have small air bubbles trapped within it which will only become apparent when you begin to sand down the surface. Also, some resins and hardeners generate heat as they cure, and, if you apply too thick a layer, the extra heat generated by the greater mass might over-accelerate the curing process.

Build up the surface until it is slightly proud of the required level and leave it to fully cure before sanding it down. If sanding by hand, then use a sanding block. Electric random orbital sanders and air-powered dual action sanders really come into their own when working with bodyfiller, and can both save much hard work and help to gain better results. The author has found the random orbital electric sander which takes one-third of a sheet of paper gives the best results, because it offers a large contact area and so helps to avoid sanding the filler into a concave section. The best tool for the job – if you can afford or hire one – is the long bed sander, which is powered by a compressor. However you sand down the filler, always wear a dust mask, because the tiny particles of filler in the air can cause respiratory problems if you inhale enough of them. Before you begin sanding down bodyfiller, ensure that no engine or transmission components are lying out in the open workshop, as the filler dust really does manage to get everywhere! Always finish off the sanding process by hand using a block.

Most bodyfiller is porous; that is, it can absorb moisture. If the filler is allowed to become wet before it is primed, then the moisture can remain in contact with the surface of the metal underneath, and all of your hard work will have been to no avail! It pays, therefore, to spray primer over a filled area as soon as the sanding is completed. For the same reason, never use wet 'n dry paper wet when sanding down filler!

Panel beating

A set of panel beaters' hammers and dollies comes close to essential for the serious restorer, both for truing up existing body panels and for carrying out final shaping of bought-in repair panels. With some practice you should find that you become capable of fabricating certain repair panels for yourself, which saves money and also means that there are no delays whilst repair panels are ordered or collected.

Two basic skills have to be learnt; how to stretch metal and how to shrink it. This is because whilst it is easy to form a folded lip on a straight edge, to do the same to a curved edge means that either the lip must be stretched (concave curve) or shrunk (convex curve). To

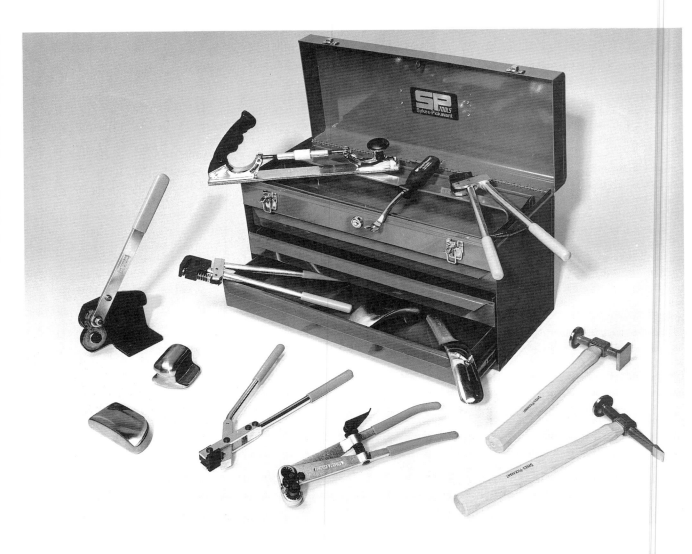

ABOVE
Nearly all body panels are available for all years of Beetle, yet a selection of panel beater's tools not only allows you to make up small repair sections when needed, but also to true up more poorly-shaped bought in panels. Sykes Pickavant have a good reputation and their tools are widely used in the trade.

RIGHT
Panel beating tools also allow you to tailor bought-in repair panels (which often don't fit properly) and to repair small dents in bodywork.

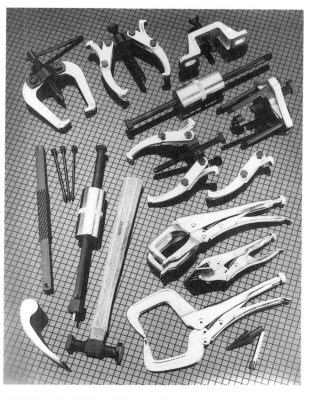

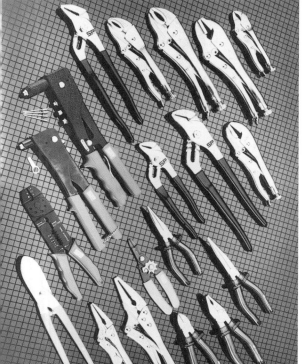

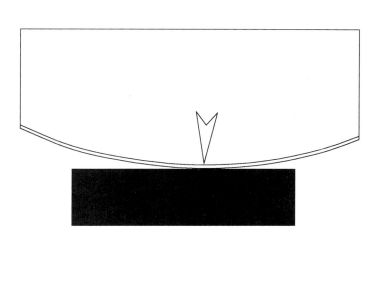

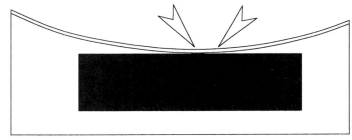

ABOVE

Folding a lip on a straight edge is easy; on curved edges you have to either stretch or shrink the metal. Stretching means beating the steel thin, and shrinking involves hitting it so that it bunches up. The convex lip (below) must be shrunk by heating a small area at a time and striking hammer blows alternately in the directions shown by the arrows – the steel supported by a dolly or an anvil. The concave lip (top) must be stretched by beating as shown by the single arrow.

ABOVE LEFT

When it comes to buying tools, the sky is the limit! Of especial interest in this photograph are the spot weld remover and hole enlarger (bottom right), the welder's clamps, planishing hammer and dolly, and the sliding-hammer type dent puller. (Photo courtesy Sykes Pickavant)

LEFT

Self-locking 'mole' grips can be used to hold panel-edges together for welding; alternatively, pop-rivet guns can be used (though having to fill all the holes afterwards with weld is a pain). (Photo courtesy Sykes Pickavant)

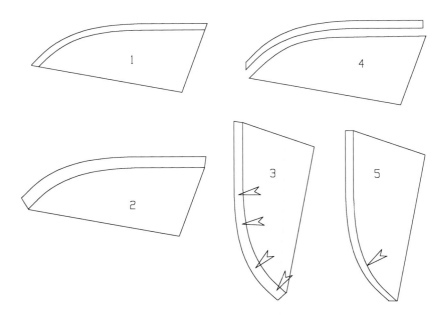

Steps in forming a lip. (1) Firstly, start the bend right along the edge. You can easily manufacture tools with bifurcated ends, or perhaps use an adjustable spanner with the jaws closed tight for this. (2) Then bend the edge more using a hammer and dolly. (3) The main part of the panel will now have started to buckle, so stretch or shrink the edge as

already described until the edge is true – by which time the buckling in the rest of the panel should have vanished (5). It takes a lot of skill to throw an edge in this manner, though with practice you should acquire that skill. Illustration (4) This shows the alternative method of welding a lip onto a piece of flat steel.

shrink metal, you have to make it 'bunch up' by striking it repeatedly as shown in the diagram. In order to stretch metal, you thin it by beating. Heating the metal makes both stretching and shrinking easier.

Repair panels

When you are using a repair panel as opposed to a full replacement panel (for instance during a simple MOT bodywork repair rather than during a full restoration), take time to consider whether fitting the whole panel as supplied is wise, or whether you could usefully cut it down.

If you are able to cut down a repair panel (and still find strong metal to weld it to), then should you ever have to renew that panel – perhaps in five or ten years' time – you can then fit the full repair panel. If you alternatively use the full repair panel as supplied and subsequently have to replace it, then you will discover that when you have cut out the old panel then the resulting hole is too large for its replacement!

Repair panels can vary greatly in quality and fit and, the more complex the panel, the more likely the user is to have to shape them. This also applies to some cheap repair panels, so buy the best you can afford.

Panels as bought have some sort of paint covering; many repair and full panels are often finished in a matt

black paint (probably cellulose). I acquired four new wings for RVH 403J at the excellent Stanford Hall show in 1993 and, before fitting these, I decided to remove the existing paint and apply Tractol anti-corrosion primer in place.

I began by using 80 grit wet and dry (used wet) to remove the bulk of the paint and, after slashing my hand for the second time on the sharp edges of the wheelarch, decided to wear strong welding gauntlets! The areas around the headlamp bowls (which are one of the usual rot spots) needed another paint removal method, and I used cellulose thinners and an old toothbrush to soften then remove the paint. Because this did not, unlike rubbing down with wet and dry, also rub down the metal surface along with the paint, I was able to see exactly what state the surface of the metal was in – and I found light rusting! Surface rusting was also discovered at the wheelarch top, which is the other normal rot-spot on Beetle wings.

When rubbing down the rest of the panel I also discovered quite large areas of contamination – spots where (probably) oil lay on the steel before it was dipped and where the paint had no adhesion. Had the wings been fitted as supplied and merely painted over, then rusting would probably have broken through within three or so years.

It is a real pain to clean paint from new panelwork (it took three full days to clean and prime four wings), and

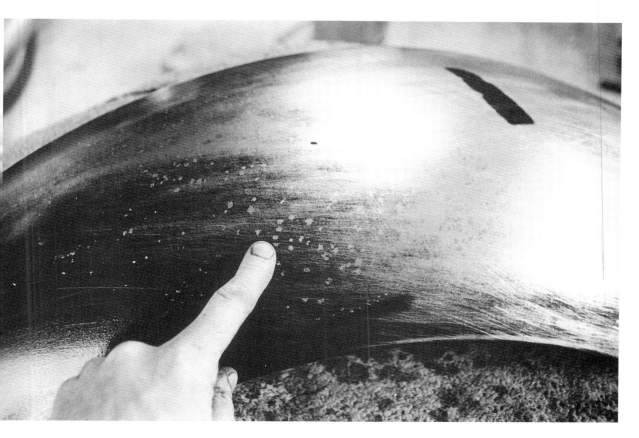

Gentle rubbing with an old toothbrush and cellulose thinners revealed these areas where the black primer had failed completely to adhere to the metal, so that future rusting and before that painting problems would almost be assured. Other parts of the wings were found to possess surface rusting under the black primer paint.

the decision whether the effort is worthwhile must rest with the individual. Acid dipping would remove the hard work from the process, but add cost to the restoration.

Rust proofing

As you fit new and repair panels into position, it pays to give them some rust protection at the earliest opportunity. The author has tried many lotions and potions which are supposed to arrest and/or prevent rusting and, of these, just two primer paints and one rust killer are recommended here. Bonda Glass Bonda Prima is a product which can be sprayed as well as brush painted onto lightly rusted steel, and the author has achieved good long-term results with this product. The second rust resistant primer recommended is for use on clean steel and is called Tractol, which as the name suggests, is an agricultural product available from most

agricultural engineers' supply companies/ agricultural merchants. Tractol is an excellent product and economical as well! It should never be used as a primer for two-pack paints, but works well with other top coats, including cellulose.

The author has never felt able to recommend any of the commercially available products which are claimed to neutralise rust because, of those he has tried, none has proven as satisfactory as the products named. However, in 1993 Practical Classics magazine ran a test of such products, in which Dinitrol RC800 scooped first place by beating all other products whether used alone, with primer or with both primer and topcoat.

Following his own tests, Dinitrol RC800 Rustkiller is the only product of its ilk which the author has ever found to work to his satisfaction – literally, penetrating and converting the rust into a passive organic compound which bonds to the underlying steel. After waiting fifteen minutes for RC 800 to become touch dry, simply primer as normal. This product is available from Autoline in the UK.

It is arguable that the use of any product over rust is not such a good solution as the eradication of the rust through sanding and wire brushing or metal replacement. Any panels which are structurally important must retain their original thickness and hence their full strength. If you wish to extend the life of a non-structural panel, however, the correct use of some products mentioned here can help.

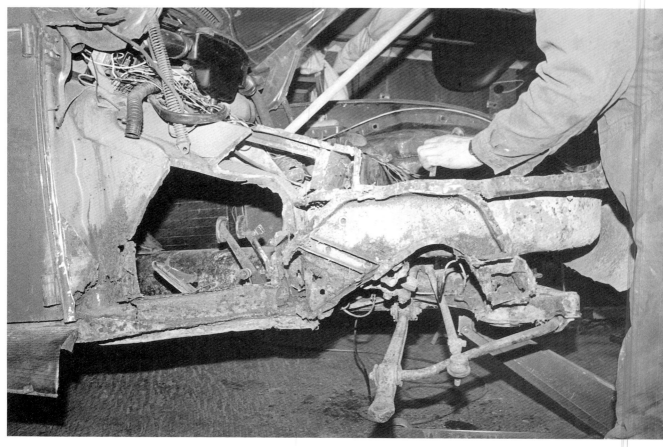

ABOVE
*Look at this mess and ask yourself whether you'd buy a car
in this state. The improbable-sounding answer is actually
'Yes – you would', because the severity of rusting which is
all-too apparent here was not apparent before the flitch panel
had been cut off. If the car had merely been tarted-up rather
than fully restored, it could have been made to appear sound
and presentable. Frightening, isn't it?*

RIGHT
*This luggage compartment had rusting in the spare wheel
well and, predictably, under the brake master cylinder (spilt
fluid is a great paint remover). This rust looks really bad, but
in fact it turned out to be no more than light surface rusting.
Appearances can be deceptive! Both areas cleaned up
satisfactorily and were treated to Bonda-Prima followed by
primer and topcoat.*

A combination of rust-resistant primer, weld-through paints and seam sealant should prevent rust from re-occurring. Don't forget to give the insides of box sections plenty of protection before they are welded up.

Further protection against rust can be achieved after welding has been completed by applying Dinitrol 3125 wax (or a similar product) or old sump oil.

THE RESTORATION PROCESS

There are essentially two ways to tackle bodywork restoration. You can carry out the work on a piecemeal basis – in effect, treating the restoration as a series of separate bodywork repairs – or you can begin by stripping the car down to its last nut and bolt and rebuilding the entire body and chassis.

Before embarking on bodywork repair or restoration, it is necessary to properly establish the full extent of rusted or rotted metal on the car. If you omit this then you could discover part-way through the job that some of your freshly welded repair panels have to come off again in order to allow you access to a newly evident area of rot.

The easiest way to discover all of the rot in a car is to strip it to a bare chassis/bodyshell and send it or take it away for dipping in an acid bath. This process strips all paint, underseal and rotten metal from the shell, leaving some surfaces which can be immediately primed and others clean enough to begin welding to. The problems with acid dipping are that the process can thin some panels slightly and might make some otherwise salvageable panels unusable, and that the shell will be left unprotected against rust until you can get some paint onto it.

Begin by probing every panel of the car vigorously with a sharp metal implement (an old screwdriver is useful and a pointed panel beater's hammer is ideal) to find all rust and rot. What you discover in this way will have a great bearing on how work on the car can subsequently proceed, so build up a list of panels which need attention. Your list of all of the bodywork which needs attention might persuade you that it would be better to entrust the job to a professional, or even to consider re-shelling the car or replacing the chassis/floor assembly. Better to have to make that decision now, rather than part-way through a body restoration!

Underseal presents problems to the restorer. No matter how unblemished the surface of underseal, it can hide serious and spreading rot. It has to come off, and this can be accomplished in a variety of ways.

Underseal clogs abrasive papers and cloths very quickly, rendering them useless. Ordinary wire brushes will have no effect on underseal, and high-speed cup brushes used in angle grinders merely rip away filaments of underseal which stick to whatever they hit. Large flat areas of underseal can be dealt with initially using a blowtorch to soften the material and a wallpaper scraper to remove the bulk of it. Have a fire extinguisher handy before trying this! Alternatively, underseal can be scraped away using an old wood chisel. Both of these methods will remove much of the underseal, but leave enough of it on the surface to still clog abrasive papers. Use paraffin to soften the remaining traces of underseal, then wipe it clean with a rag. Again, beware the fire hazard; have a fire extinguisher handy, and do not smoke or work near any naked flame.

It is not necessary to strip back all of the paint work at this early stage; if you do so then the exposed steel will soon develop surface rusting. Do use a magnet to reveal any patches of filler or GRP, and probe the usual trouble spots (see Chapter Two) vigorously with a sharp metal object to check for rot.

When you examine the car to determine what work needs to be carried out, bear in mind that rotten heater channels almost invariably point to rotten floor edges. It is common practice to replace heater channels but not floor edges, because to replace the latter the bodyshell must be lifted away from the chassis. This is not good practice, because sooner or later (usually sooner) the floor edges will rot to the point at which the job has to be carried out in full and the bodyshell and chassis parted. Replacing a heater channel without lifting the bodyshell off the chassis is also bad practice because the final welding up of the heater channels (particularly the ends) does the belly pan gasket no good at all!

The actual method of working and order of work will depend on the extent of the work. A single task such as replacing the rear bodyshell/damper arm mount may be carried out with the body on the chassis, but for a thorough restoration (which will usually entail floorpan replacement) it is as well to strip the car down to the point of separating the body from the chassis assembly.

The following text describes a complete body-off restoration, with each task approached so that it describes how the individual job can be carried out in isolation where applicable.

Seat removal

It is advisable to remove the front seats if you intend to later lift the bodyshell off the chassis. Have an assistant operate the seat forwards/backwards adjustment lever whilst you sit on the rear seat and push the front seat off the rails using your feet. If the seat won't move far enough forwards, look at the side of the outside runner;

you may find a small catch which, if pressed, will then allow the seat to come free.

Windscreen removal

Although a cheap and cheerful respray can be carried out without removing the windows (provided that they are well masked off), most restorers will opt to remove them. This also becomes necessary if the headlining – which is gripped under some or all of the window surround rubbers depending on the model – is to be removed. Leaking window rubbers can result in rotten surround lips, and surface rusting adjacent to the rubber is a strong indication of this.

If the rubbers are all to be replaced (and actually obtain new rubbers before doing this just in case you have trouble in buying new ones) then the old ones could simply be cut away from the edge of the glass. If the rubbers are to be retained, then the easiest method is to simply push windows and rubbers out together.

Firstly, remove the windscreen wipers and arms and disconnect the rear windscreen heater wire (where fitted). Lift the edge of the rubbers from inside the car in order to break the seal then, with an assistant to catch the windows as they come out, push out one top corner using both feet. It should then be easy to work the rest of the window out.

Window aperture repairs

Underneath the window rubbers, the metal lips can rust away. In the case of the front screen this rust can spread to the top scuttle. The top scuttle also rusts if the drain holes are allowed to become plugged so that water cannot escape. To deal with rusted window lips, simply grind out the rot and butt weld in two thicknesses of

ABOVE LEFT
Fitting the front screen is really a two-man job. One applies pressure on the screen from the outside and prevents it from riding up, whilst the other pulls on the ends of the wire (see text). At this stage, the ends of the wires are being pulled to the point at which they cross over and begin to pull the rubber lip into position.

LEFT
The assistant must be ready to apply extra pressure when the corners are being fitted, whilst still applying pressure to the centre of the screen with his other hand. At this, point, the offside lower corner is in and the upper corner is being fitted; Terry and Craig will then fit the nearside corners.

steel, giving the insides plenty of protection with weldable zinc paint beforehand. Top scuttle repair panels are not, at the time of writing, available, leaving the option of fashioning a repair panel (which can be done with a few basic panel beater's tools) or cutting the section out of a scrap shell. In either case, butt weld the new steel in very carefully to avoid distorting the scuttle.

Windscreen re-fit

You will need sealing compound, strong twine or covered single-core wire which is long enough to fit around the screens, some lubricant and an assistant.

Fit the rubber to the glass, using sealing compound if you wish to avoid leaks! Fit the chrome trim into the rubber, then work plenty of lubricant (some people use washing up liquid, which works well but may contain industrial salts which rot the window aperture lips – Swarfega hand cleanser is better) into the groove in the rubber. Feed the twine or covered wire into this groove, so that the centre of the wire is at the top of the screen and the two ends cross at the bottom.

With your assistant holding the window in position from outside the car, pull on the wire to pull the rubber lip over the steel window aperture lip. Work from the centre bottom (taking care that the window does not ride up), each lower corner in turn, up the front pillars, around each top corner in turn and finally along the top. It is then usually necessary to knock the window edges finally home, using the palm of your hand. If this thought (or the thought of a window popping out the first time you slam the door) worries you, then bring in a mobile windscreen fitter, who should be able to glaze a Beetle in about 30 minutes and who should not, therefore, charge too much!

Headlining removal

Remove the front, rear and the two fixed side windows as already described. To remove the rear view mirror, turn and then pull it. Remove the sun visors; the swivelling end is retained by a stud and a screw. Remove the screw then turn the fixing until it comes free – don't use too much force, because the stud breaks easily.

The passenger side grab handle is affixed by one large and one small Philips headed screw at either end. To expose the screw heads, use a small flat bladed screwdriver to unclip the end trim and work this away from the edge. The grab straps on the B posts are affixed with screws; prise up the cover to reveal. Take care when removing the interior light because it is brittle and easily damaged. At either end there is a spring clip; push

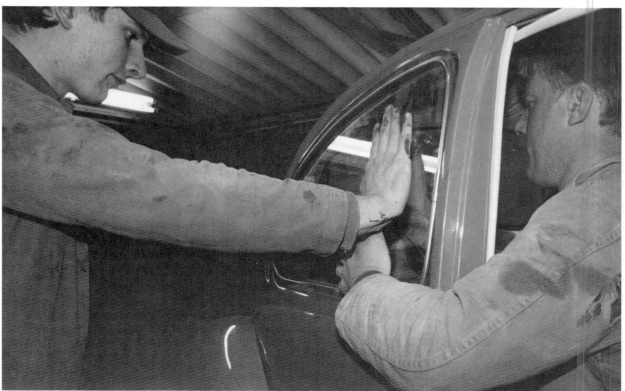

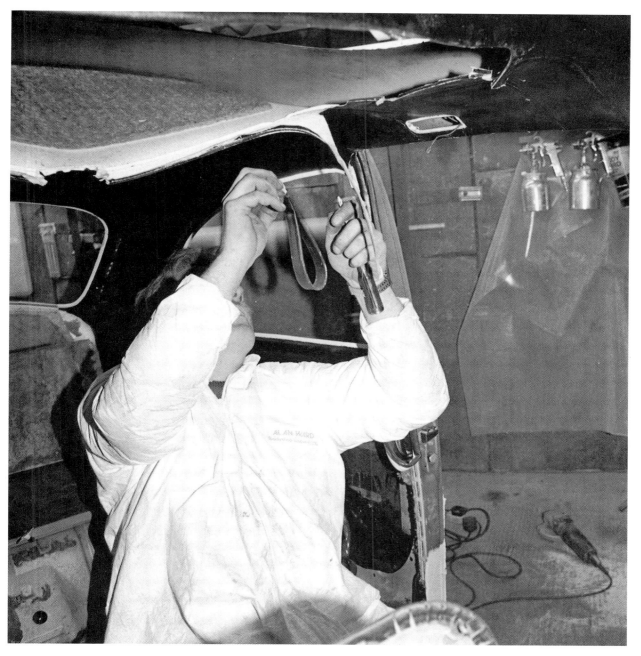

ABOVE LEFT
The rear screen part-way through fitting. Having 'started' the rubber lip, Terry checks from the outside that it is seating correctly in the corners.

LEFT
Fitting the side screens is exactly the same as the front screen, except that their smaller size makes life easier. It is best thought of as a two-man job, although experienced screen fitters can completely glaze a Beetle single-handed.

ABOVE
Working in the interior of a Beetle is never much fun – it's too cramped for comfort! The (painted) headlining in this car is to be replaced, and so Terry is removing the various items of trim which are fastened through it, including the interior mirror (twist and pull), sun visors, interior light and here the grab strap. The number of such fittings varies with the year and model.

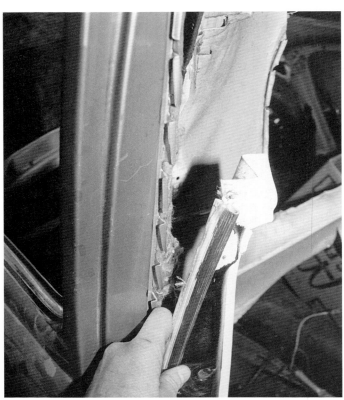

BELOW
The headlining is gripped across the top of the door aperture, by gently prising open the gripper, the lining can be pulled away. If the lining is to be re-fitted, then it obviously pays to take great care during this operation not to tear it.

LEFT
The headlining/door aperture trim grippers up the B post look quite vicious in this photograph, but in reality they don't bite! Prize them open and pull the trim upwards and out.

ABOVE RIGHT
The B post trim pieces are separate and are slid into position – usually with some difficulty. Note the felt wadding on the B post; if this is missing then the trim will never look quite right, so glue a strip on. That quarter panel repair is NOT Terry's work – this particular car was partially restored before being taken to BSW.

BELOW RIGHT
At the top of the B post, Terry folds the material and tensions it before temporarily fastening it to the window aperture edge using the clips shown. It will, of course, be gripped permanently by the window rubber.

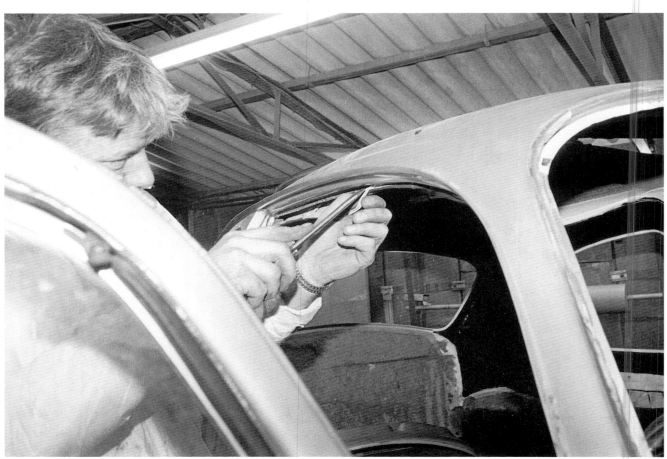

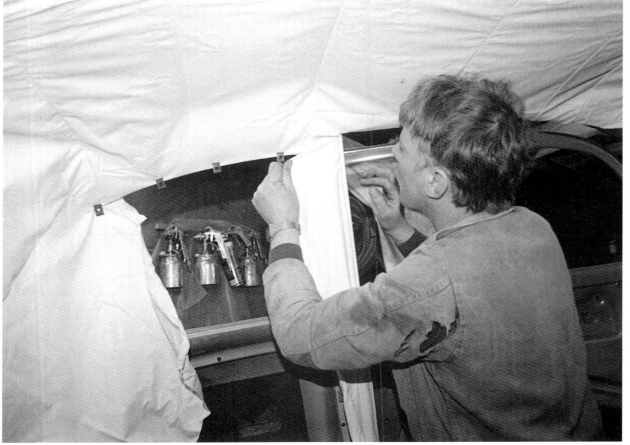

these inwards and the lamp unit should be free to come out.

The headlining will probably be glued to the window surrounds and, if you wish to re-use the lining, be very careful when easing it away from the lips. Within the front and rear window apertures, the lining may also be held in place by spring grips. Remove these.

The headlining is held aloft by either sprung steel rods (there could be four or six depending on year) which run through loops sewn into the material, or it is itself glued to hardboard which is sprung into position. According to the type of headlining fitted, the year and model of Beetle, there may or may not be separate pieces glued or clipped to the pillars. The sequences described here relate to a McPherson strut car, which has everything!

To remove the rods, spring them upwards until one end can be eased from its plastic end piece, then pull the other end free.

At the top of the door aperture, there are a row of clips under which the headlining edge is tucked. Gently prise these down, and the headlining should pull free.

Work from the front window backwards to the B post, then from the rear window forwards to the B post. Where the headlining joins the B post, you remove it by pulling it downwards to free the edge trim from its retaining clips.

Headlining replacement

For this you will need glue (it is best not to use a contact adhesive, but opt for something which allows you to slightly adjust the position of the material before it sets), a Stanley or art knife, a selection of screwdrivers. Also of great help are scissors and (especially) clips to hold the headlining on the window aperture lips whilst the glue sets.

Begin by fitting the rods through the loops in the headlining top, then fit the centre rod into position inside the car, and adjust its position until the headlining reaches both the front and rear screens. Check that the lining is not skewed, then fit the other rod ends and check the positioning again. Bear in mind that you're more likely to run out of material at the rear end, so check that there is enough here to reach down the C posts before you begin fixing it permanently.

Fit the material back into the clips at the top of the door aperture, pulling and smoothing it out as you go. If you are fitting a new headlining then it will probably prove necessary to trim these and other edges.

Spread glue around the front windscreen aperture lip, and attach the headlining to this, using clips to hold it whilst the glue sets and smoothing it out as you go. At the top of the front windscreen pillar and B post, the material folds under to give a neat edge. Glue the headlining to the rear then the side window aperture lips, then stretch it down the C post and glue this.

The B post covering is separate from the headlining and, if you are fitting a new set, you will probably have to trim the material. Open up one of the lower B post retaining clips enough to be able to feed in the edge moulding, and slide this into place. Glue the material to the B post and side window aperture lip. The last two pieces of the headlining kit go underneath the side windows. Glue them to the aperture then stretch and smooth them down and glue the lower edges.

Fit the rear view mirror, sun visors, grab straps and other furniture. You can usually feel their fixing holes through the material. Finally, gentle heat from a hairdryer can be used whilst you smooth out the (hopefully few) wrinkles in the headlining.

Door removal

There are two ways of removing the doors. The simplest (though you'll have to remove the running board first) is to remove the check strap pin and then to drift out the hinge pins from below. This method has the advantage that if the same doors are to later be replaced then the hinges will be correctly aligned. During a full restoration, in which the doors are probably to be repaired or replaced, the answer is to remove the door complete with hinges.

Each hinge is held by three large set screws with a Philips type cross head, best tackled using a large Philips screwdriver or similar. The author uses the bit and ½ in. square drive adaptor from an impact wrench in combination with the speed wrench from a socket set, which gives great purchase on the set screw head. Have an assistant handy to help manoeuvre the door, because a Beetle door with full furniture is rather heavy.

Before you re-hang the door it is as well to remove the striker plate (ignore this if you only removed the hinge pins) first. Fasten the hinge set screws lightly, with just one off each hinge tightened sufficiently to take the weight of the door. Adjust the position of the door until its lines match that of adjacent bodywork, then tighten all hinge screws and refit the striker plate.

Door stripdown

Begin by prising out the inside door pull cover to reveal the fixing screw, and undo this. The window winder fixing screw is situated under either a plastic plug or, on some models, under the one-piece trim cover. Prise out

Refitting headlining is a job best handed over to someone with experience. Begin by fitting the roof rods in the lining and, starting at the windscreen, fit the ends into position as you work back along the car. Then check that the lining is correctly positioned fore and aft by clipping it around the side window apertures.

BELOW
The pieces under the side window are also separate from the main headlining. These are best glued to the window surround. Use an adhesive which allows for adjustment and final smoothing rather than the contact variety. Note that at this stage the rear screen is still to be fitted. There is no harm in leaving the material stretched and held with the clips for a few hours before fitting the rear screen, because it gives you a better chance of finding and dealing with sags and creases before the screen is fitted.

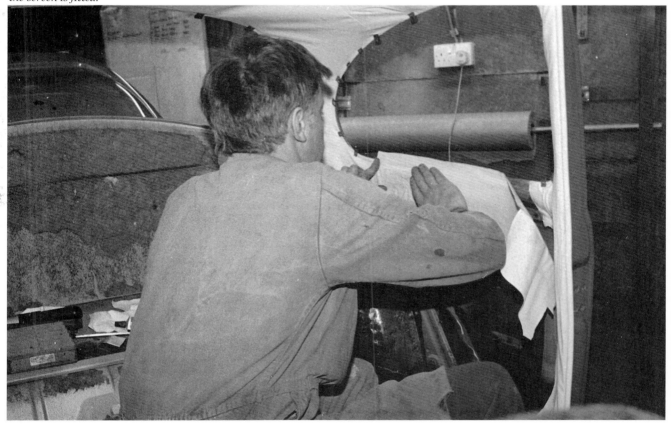

LEFT
This piece is folded at either end to give two neat edges. The loose material at the bottom will of course be covered by the side trim panel.

BELOW LEFT
With the screen fitted, check from the outside that the rubber and chrome filler strip are properly in position. The creases which can be seen will later be smoothed out using the upholsterer's secret weapon – a hair dryer!

RIGHT
Fit the door striker mechanism but don't fully tighten it quite yet, then try closing the door and adjust as necessary. Note that the quarter repair panel (not fitted by BSW) was not prepared too carefully – the manufacturer's sticky label is still in situ!

BELOW
Getting there. The fact that this car had a sun-roof did complicate the fitting of the headlining slightly. Terry is fitting the sun-visors and other trim before final smoothing of the headlining with a hair dryer. The power screwdriver makes life easier.

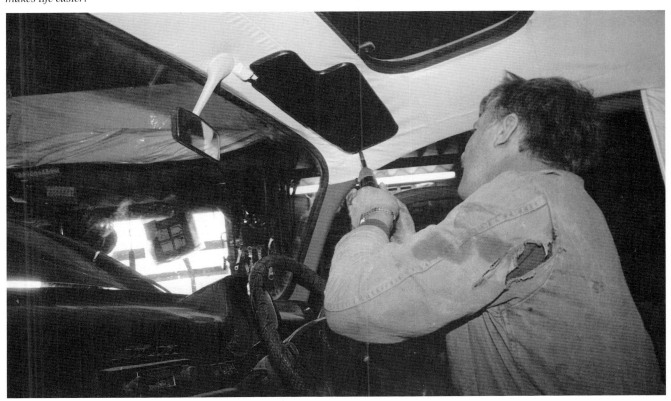

LEFT
On goes the second sun visor. You have to feel through the new headlining material to find the holes for fitting trim like this, and puncture it only when you're confident that you have found the relevant hole!

BELOW
To strip the door, begin by prising out the plastic dish behind the interior door lever. This gives access to the fixing screw. Remove the window winder handle, then gently prise the door trim fittings open. Finally, give the arm rest a sharp tap with the heel of your hand to free the trim panel. Don't loose the spring from behind the winder handle.

RIGHT
If you are working alone, then before removing the winder mechanism, use masking tape to secure the glass — otherwise it will drop down into the door where it can jam and be a pain to free again.

he plug or lift the cover and remove the screw and
andle. On early models, the door pull and winder are
ixed by a pin which should be drifted out.

Remove the armrest (where fitted) by undoing the
wo fixing screws. These screws are angled on some
models, in which case better purchase will be obtained
y angling the screwdriver.

The door trim panel can now be removed. This is
ecured by spring clips which can quite easily be broken,
o work carefully, starting at the bottom of the door and
sing a flat implement to prise the spring clips out. On
ater models, a spring situated behind the window
inder mechanism will come free, so try to catch it
efore it disappears into the dark recesses of the
orkshop! If the door trim won't come away from the
oor, give the grab handle a sharp tap upwards with the
alm of your hand to free it from the bracket.

Before progressing further, it is as well to support the
indow by taping it to the top of the door frame using
ide masking tape. Remove the winder mechanism
xing bolts, then pull the mechanism from the door. The

glass may now be lowered and removed through the
lower door aperture.

Gently ease out the window surround trim, which is
held by spring clips which can easily be damaged. Use a
small flat-bladed screwdriver for this. Undo the screw at
the top rear of the quarter-light pillar and remove the
quarter-light assembly. The chrome door trim can now
be removed.

The external door handle is secured by a single cross-
head screw situated in the door rear edge. Remove this,
then tap the handle assembly free. The internal locking
mechanism is held by one screw in the door frame and
two in the edge. Remove these, then remove the bolts
which hold the remote pull. The assembly can now be
removed from the door.

Make a note of any components which need
replacing, and be sure to obtain the necessary spares
before you begin the rebuild. The spring clips which hold
the window channel are especially prone to breakage
when you try to re-fit them, and it is a good idea to
obtain a few spares.

145

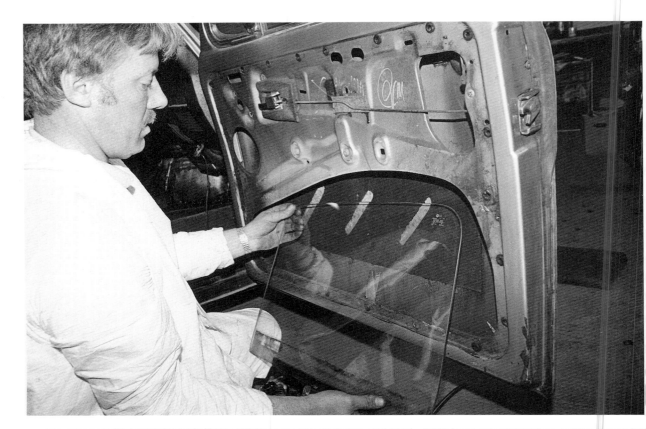

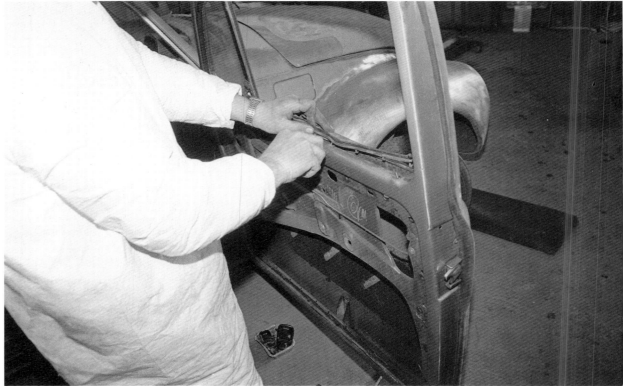

LEFT
The window glass is tough, but handle it with care.

BELOW LEFT
With the window and its mechanism out, the rubber can be removed. In this case it is to be replaced. Perished and/or cracked window rubbers should always be replaced; they allow water down inside the door to rot out the base and skin.

RIGHT
Having pulled the window aperture trim partially out, Terry gets to grips with the quarter-light assembly – held by a small screw at the top and a bolt on its leg.

BELOW
Removing the lock mechanism. Note the hole three inches or so above this; this is the location for the single set screw which holds the outer handle in place. To remove the handle, undo the screw then give the handle a gentle tap, and off it will come.

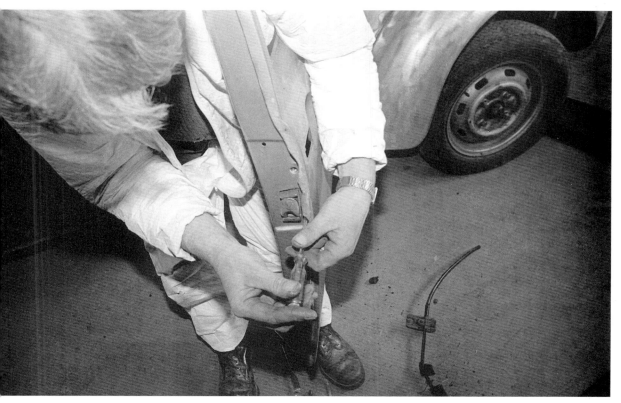

LEFT
Persuading the lock to come out is not the easiest job you'll ever do, but with a little patience it should be possible to manoeuvre it through this hole.

BELOW
If the window winder (regulator) is to be re-fitted, give it a good clean then lubricate it with engine oil. Fit the handle and operate the winder up and down a few times to ensure that the oil is well distributed.

ABOVE RIGHT
The two types of window winder mechanism.

BELOW RIGHT
Cutting the old lower doorskin away, yet another task made much easier with an air hacksaw.

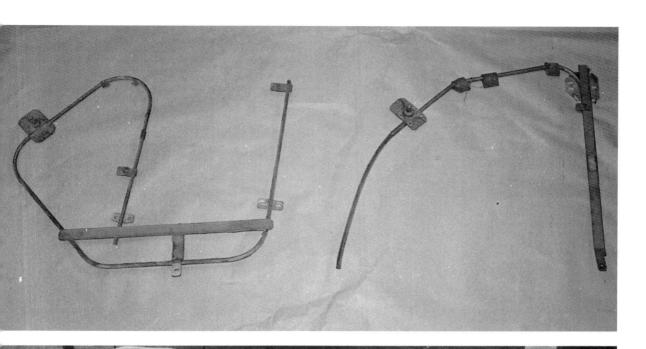

Door panel repairs

The economics of repairing Beetle doors are to a great extent affected by the wide availability and attractive prices of second hand doors – go to any major Beetle show or autojumble and you should be able to acquire a pair of doors in good condition at a reasonably low price. Against this, door skins and repair panels are far from cheap, and far from easy to fit.

Moreover, the main part of the door panel is large and susceptible to denting when being manhandled and fitted and, if a door skin is rusted then it would be very unusual for the base to be good enough to weld to, so that the repair would consist of replacing the base then removing the old skin and fitting the new. The cost of the panels would represent over 60 per cent of the price of a new door and could never be as good – sooner or later other rust would start to bubble through.

However, most doors rust firstly at their base and in the lower portion of the door skin, for which repair panels are available at not too high a cost. The repair sequence is to cut away and replace the base firstly, and to leave the existing skin bottom in situ to help position the repair panel correctly.

In cutting away the door bottom edge, you will also have to cut the skin panel partially; this will still leave the skin attached sufficiently strongly to allow it to be used as a guide for fitting the bottom repair panel, which is best MiG butt jointed.

Because the main outer door panel is so large, it is very prone to buckle if you attempt to gas or MiG weld it, no matter how careful you are. The best method of carrying out the lower door skin repair is to cut away the rotten metal, to clean it and then to spot weld a strip of steel on the back. The repair panel can in turn be spot welded to this, to give a neat butt joint ready for body-filler.

The door panel is also prone to rot out in its centre, because water which gets past perished window seals can lie trapped underneath the patch of material stuck to the inside of the skin. Very few people will have access to the long spot welder arms which would be necessary if a repair patch were to be let in and, from personal experience, the author can vouch that the most careful attempts at MiG welding in a patch will buckle the panel. If a door skin is rotted in the centre, GRP and bodyfiller repair might be a short-term solution – better to obtain a good second-hand door.

Door rebuild

Start by fitting the lock mechanism. Feed the small rod upwards through the aperture in the door top and push

ABOVE
Most people would be well advised to replace the door skin repair panel and the inner door repair panel one at a time to ensure that both go in the right place – Terry relies on measurements and experience to get it right when replacing both in one go. Here, he's welding on the inner repair panel.

OPPOSITE ABOVE LEFT
The door skin repair seen from the inside. A strip of steel has been spot welded on to the existing skin, and the repair panel spot welded in turn to this.

OPPOSITE ABOVE RIGHT
Seen from the outside, this method of joining gives far less distortion than normal MiG welding.

RIGHT
Finally, the two repair panels are fixed with braze, then the flange folded tight.

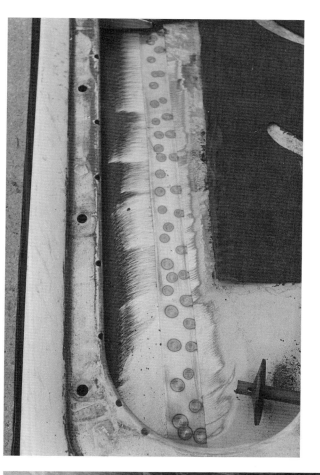

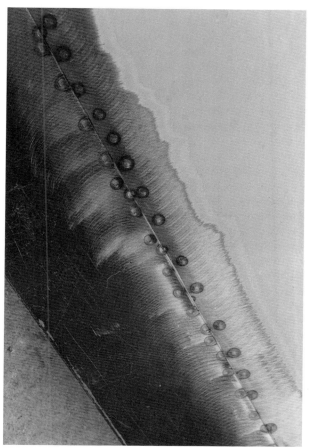

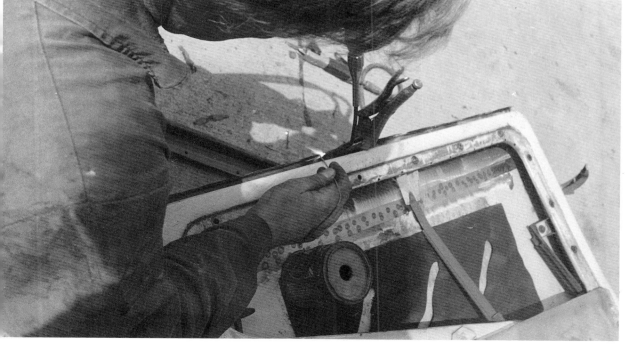

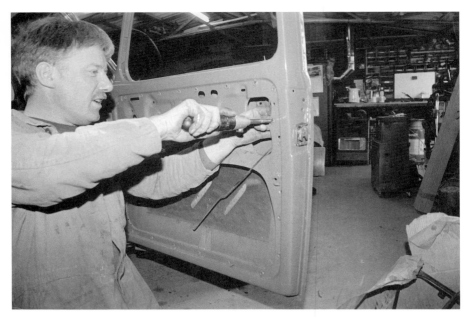

When boxing up the doors, begin by fitting the lock mechanism.

Bolting the winder mechanism to the window base. One hand is needed to hold the two in position – make sure that the bolts are to hand.

Then fit the bolts with your free hand. Whilst you have one hand stuck inside the door, it is as well to have an assistant to pass tools and bolts as and when needed.

the catch into place, which will hold the unit while you secure it with screws. Then fit the winder mechanism, ensuring that it locates under the door top lip. Use the handle to wind the mechanism down and carefully slide the window back into the door before fitting the window aperture trim.

The window trim has a number of spring clips which locate into holes in the door; at the top it is affixed with a small screw, and the side and top are partially held in by the clips which affix the window channel. Fit the clips.

It may prove difficult to get the quarter-light assembly back into position. Offer it at an angle to begin with, then push it downwards whilst and forwards simultaneously into position. If it won't go then use a piece of softwood to spring the window aperture open slightly. Then fit the window channel.

Bolt the window to the winder mechanism. Check that all fastenings are tight, that the window opens and closes and that the quarter-light opens and closes with no sticking before replacing the door trim.

Wing removal

Disconnect the battery. If the existing wing is to be scrapped, then you can make its removal rather easier by cutting the bulk of the wing away with an air chisel or air hacksaw so that you can get a socket onto the bolt heads.

All four wings are bolted into place (yippee!) but the bolts are often seized to the extent that they shear or the captive nuts break free (hiss!). Begin by cleaning the dirt away from the bolt heads then apply penetrating oil and leave this to do its work for as long as possible before attacking the bolts. Also apply oil to the bumper bolts, because these too will have to come out.

While the wing bolts are soaking up the oil, remove the light clusters, taking great care not to break the plastic rear lenses, which become brittle with age. The rear lamp reflectors (which hold the bulbs – remove these now to avoid breakage) can be fastened in a variety of ways: remove the screws and lift off the lips according to type. Disconnect the wiring from the terminals, and feed the wires back through the wing. Put tabs on the wires to remind you where each goes if necessary.

Remove the bumper mounting bolts from both sides of the car and pull the bumper and its brackets away. Remove the wing fixing bolts, starting with the nut and bolt to the running board and the bolt at the rear, then work your way upwards to the centre top bolt. Use brute force sparingly; not only can you shear bolt heads off but you run the risk of losing the captive nuts. If you manage to shear any of the bolts then you can either

Because wings tend to rust in a line nearest the beading, an air hacksaw goes through them like the proverbial hot knife though butter. DIY restorers who are tempted to acquire an air hacksaw, however, should be warned that when it is used on most panels, the din is terrific and guaranteed to annoy neighbours.

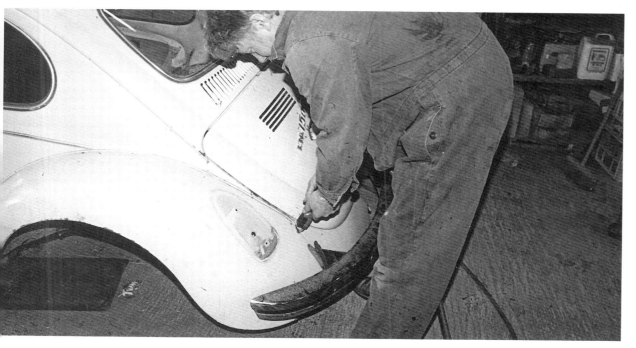

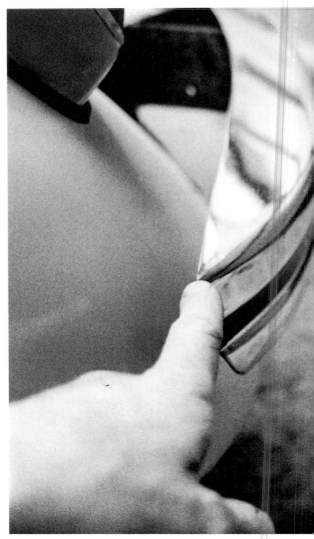

ABOVE LEFT

This car is to have the rear body/damper bracket mounting panel replaced, a very common repair on Beetles – especially at MOT time! First step is to remove the rear bumper and its brackets, then undo the 13mm headed bolts which hold the rear wing on. Note that only spanners can be used because there is not sufficient room for a socket. If the wing is to be scrapped and you have an air saw, however, sawing away the wing gives access for a socket and makes the task much quicker. Expect some of the bolts to be very hard to shift and for some to shear or pull away their captive nuts.

ABOVE RIGHT

It is unfortunately possible for a replacement wing to turn out to be the 'wrong' shape, most apparent if the gaps between the bumper ends and the wings differ each side, check that the problem really does lie with the wing and not the bumper.

drill them out afterwards and re-tap the captive nuts or try using a proprietary screw extractor.

Tip: if you can obtain longer bolts with the same thread as the original wing bolts, use these with spacers to hold the wing away from the bodyshell during the respray.

Wing replacement

If the olf beading is in reasonable condition then it can be re-used. If it has been painted during a general respray then thinners can be used to get the paint off – Beetles look so much sharper with nice black wing beading! If it is damaged, renew the beading and if possible use new wing fixing bolts, with plenty of copper grease or Autoline Aluminium Anti Seize on the threads

to make subsequent removal easier. If you are using new wings then be warned that some cheaper varieties will be of dubious fit and that their holes might not align perfectly!

Begin by fixing the top centre bolt, but fit this and all other bolts loosely until all are in position and you are satisfied that the wing will mate well with the shape of the car. Then begin to tighten to bolt which is adjacent to the 'corner' to ensure that the wings pulls properly into shape. Work down each side of the wing, then fit the beading and tighten the bolts.

Running boards

The running boards are each secured to the sills by four 10 mm bolts, and to the wings by nuts and bolts. To remove the running boards simply undo these.

Brazilian or other third-party running boards are usually made from much lighter gauge steel than the more expensive German ones, and it is worth paying extra for the longevity of the German items if you can afford them. Also in the name of longevity, the author would recommend the use of a good corrosion-resistant paint.

As supplied, the running boards' rubber covers are

Terry has cut off the rotten old front wing, allowing the author to get a socket and ratchet onto the wing nuts. Not only does this make their removal easier, it lessens the chances of breaking free one of the captive nuts. In the event, only one wing captive nut gave problems on this car. When fitting wings, use copper grease or preferably Aluminium Anti Seize on the bolt threads.

not always fitted, so begin by stretching the rubber over the steel and fastening the other edge. Then slide the chrome trim clips into place in the trim strip, and push these through the run of fixing holes in the running board. Grab each tag from the other side with a pair of pliers, pull and twist to secure.

Rear inner wing (bodywork mount reinforcing panel) repair

Within the rear wheelarches, the prime rust spot is the reinforcing panel which contains the rear body mount and (on some cars) the 'Z' or anti-jacking bar. It's the old story; mud (sometimes salt-laden) is kicked up from the wheels and settles in any suitable cranny, such as the

155

ABOVE
If you remove enough gunge, you should be rewarded with a view of the 17 mm headed bolt. Unfortunately, the bolts often seize solid and/or shear – in the latter case, they must be drilled out or, alternatively, try placing a large blob of MiG weld in the exposed bolt shank – the heat sometimes frees the threads and the weld gives you something to grip with a mole wrench.

BELOW
The panel is replaced along with the actual bracket, and here Terry is drilling out the spot welds prior to removal of the old panel. It is not always easy to find the old spot welds, and a practised eye helps.

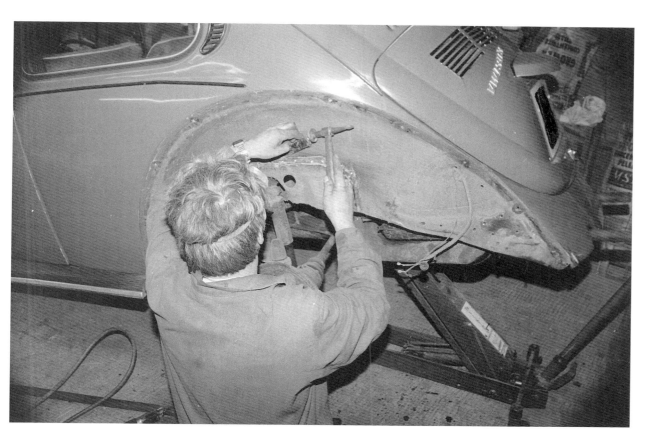

ABOVE
Having drilled out all of the spot welds, Terry uses a multi-purpose tool made from a sharpened 1 in. industrial hacksaw blade. In addition to being a very capable scraper, it is the best tool the author has used for parting spot welds. That panel beating hammer is very old; normally, you would not dream of using such a tool for hitting chisels because you would mark the face so that the hammer would be useless for panel beating!

BELOW
Old panel off. The surrounding area has been taken back to bright metal so that a good weld can be obtained. This is precisely the sort of work where a weld-through zinc paint can be used to help delay the onset of rust.

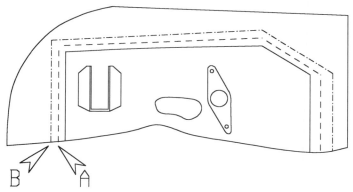

ABOVE
The replacement panel is cut down (see text) and bolted with the body mounting bolt to hold it firm. This one has to come off so that its edges can be cleaned in addition to the inner wing along its rear edge.

LEFT
The full panel could usefully be cut down to dotted line A. When it next has to be replaced, the new panel could be cut down to dotted line B, and so on.

pull the bumper assembly away from the car.

When welding up the nearside rear bodyshell mount repair panel, do remember that the wiring loom runs very close to the line of your weld. It is advisable to remove the rear half of the loom before undertaking this task – new looms are quite expensive.

Remove the rear wing bolts and place the wing and filler strip to one side. This improves access, and it may be wise to double-check the inner wing condition at this stage, including the bumper mounting areas.

Using a hexagonal socket if possible, undo the 17 mm body mounting bolt. This might prove very reluctant to start and, if you resort to brute force you can easily shear off the bolt head, so clean out the recess and then apply more penetrating oil and leave it until later. If you do manage to shear the bolt head then try putting a blob of weld on what remains of it; this can break the seal (by the heat from the welding process)

folded pressed steel body mounting. If this area is not well protected, then it will succumb to rust quite quickly and, in the UK, fail its roadworthiness test.

The first step is to raise the rear of the car and rest it on axle stands, then remove the roadwheel and clean up the area so that you can establish the extent of rusting. Also clean the bumper bracket bolts, the wing bolts, the damper bolts and the body mounting bolt and apply penetrating oil to them in order to make removal easier.

Disconnect the battery and the wires leading to the generator, then remove the tail lamp lens, remove the wires from their terminals (use masking tape tags to remind you which is which) and pull the wires back into the wheelarch. Remove the bumper bracket bolts and

The panel tacked at the corners. Some considerable work has to be done with a hammer and dolly to get the panel into the correct profile. Shape a bit then tack it before moving along to the next bit.

and give you something to grip with a mole wrench. If this fails then you have no alternative to drilling out the bolt. Remove the rear damper, again, if the fittings are too tight, apply penetrating oil and leave this to soak well in.

Locate and drill out the spot welds which hold the reinforcing panel in place then, using if possible a 'chisel' fashioned from a 1 in. hacksaw blade, part the welds. You may discover that the lower trailing edge is MiG or gas welded if this panel has (as is likely) been replaced at an earlier date, and any weld should be ground down.

Clean the newly exposed and surrounding metal bright. As ever, it is not necessary to fit the entire repair panel and, in fact, it may be preferable to cut down the panel provided that you can find sound metal to weld to (see illustration). Any future rusting is likely to occur around the area of the welded joint, and by fitting in effect a smaller panel, you then have the option to fit the full repair panel if rusting occurs. Trimming the repair panel also gives you less welding to do!

Inside the car, remove the rear seat and any combustible material from the parcel shelf, plus any combustible material on or near the inner rear wing. If

you have a fire extinguisher then place it inside the car, and if you have an assistant then ask him to assume the role of fire-fighter! If you are working alone then you will have to check for (and possibly deal with) fires inside the car every few seconds, which will make the welding process a protracted one.

Clean the edges of the panel which are to be welded (then apply weld-through paint to all the newly exposed bright metal if you want the repair to last), then bolt the panel onto the damper top mounting bracket. Use a self-tapping screw to pull it roughly into the shape of the inner wing, then push it further inwards, tack it and beat it until the panel edges touch the inner wing. It is as well to tack weld the repair panel edges perhaps as close as at 1 in. intervals, and to check during the welding that the repair panel is not bucking away, which would increase the chances of burning through. Continuously seam weld the repair panel edges, grind down surplus weld then apply plenty of paint to slow the rusting process.

On the inside, the panel has to be welded to the parcel shelf panel, but all too often this will be found to have rusted away at its edges. If so, make up an 'L' shaped repair panel and continuously seam weld this into place.

Don't forget to use copper-based grease or similar on all bolt threads when you come to reassembly. Remember to test your rear lights before taking the car out onto the road; if there are any problems and the wires are connected to the correct terminals, then clean all of the spade connectors and retest. Any faults remaining will either be due to bulb failure or, more commonly, poor earthing.

Rear bumper mounts

Like the rear body mounts within the rear wheelarch, the rear bumper mounts tend to catch lots of mud and water thrown up by the road wheel and consequently to rust out, resulting in a loose bumper (and an MOT failure even if the bumper doesn't move). Repair patches for this panel are widely available, though rather difficult to fit.

Begin by removing the bumper, then the rear wing, then scrape away the accumulated gunge from the vicinity of the mounting points so that you can see clearly enough to judge the extent of the rot. Then fold back the retaining tabs and remove the sound deadening material from the engine bay side, taking care not to spear yourself on any stray lengths of wire protruding from the material. Also remove the engine bay seal.

If you're not sure how strong the steel in the vicinity of the bumper mounting is then clean it bright and any rust will be all too apparent. Cut the repair panel down to the smallest practicable size, so that, if you ever have to do this job again, you will be able to cut back to sound metal without exceeding the area of the repair panel.

Drill out the spot welds which hold the bumper bracket, and part the seams. Then offer up the repair panel and scribe around its edges before cutting out the rot. The author would recommend that the bumper is temporarily re-fitted to the fixed bracket on the other side of the car and to the repair panel, to ensure that the new bracket is positioned so that the bumper sits level to the rest of the car.

Two points of importance to bear in mind when welding in a rear body mount repair panel assembly. Firstly, the loom passes very close to the line of the weld, so ensure that it is out of harm's way before you start welding. Secondly, expect small fires to begin in the remnants of interior trim; these can be 'batted' out by an assistant using a piece of scrap sheet steel or blown out using a compressor. Keep the fire extinguisher handy.

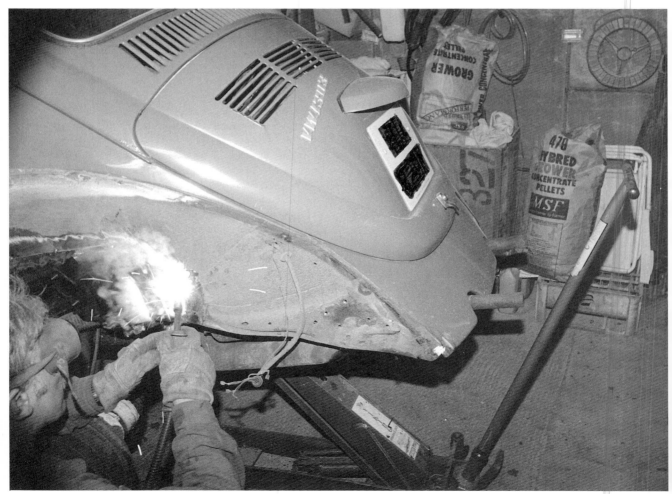

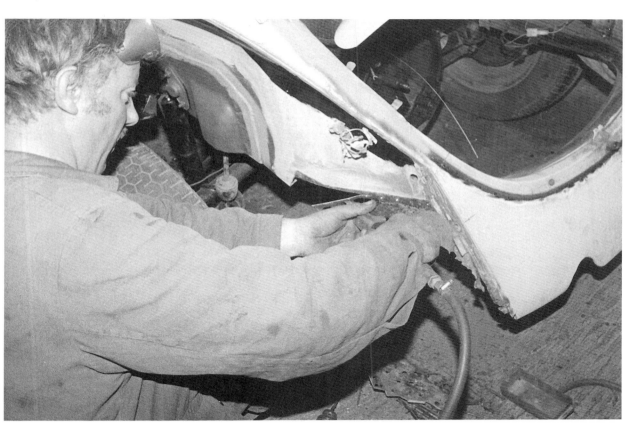

Clean those edges of the new panel which are to be welded, check that the rear lighting and other wires are well out of harm's way and weld the new panel up (keep the fire extinguisher handy), using a continuous seam weld.

Finally, drill a hole for the rearmost wing fixing bolt, then fasten a bolt and nut through the hole and tack weld the nut (on the inside) to provide a new captive nut for the wing bolt.

The front end

The pressings which make up the Beetle front end differ to some extent between the torsion bar and McPherson Strut versions; in practice the two are quite similar, consisting of the dashboard/A post/roof pillar assembly, flitch panels, luggage bay floor, spare wheel well and valance. A complete assembly is available from Autobarn; the author would recommend that this is fitted professionally.

To completely rebuild a front end on a piecemeal basis – flitches, luggage compartment floor, spare wheel well and valance – is approaching the limits of economic and practical DIY restoration; not only is the chance of ending up with a lop-sided car disturbingly high, but there is also a strong possibility that more serious rot will be discovered in various adjacent and underlying panels. When this happens, you should give serious

The rear bumper mounts were not themselves rusted on this car, but the panel underneath was (as is usual), and so Terry cuts out the offending area. Again, the repair panel was cut down to the smallest practicable size before being welded into position.

consideration to using a better or a new bodyshell.

If you do decide to carry out any front-end repairs, don't weld any panel finally into position until you have offered up the wings and bonnet, to check that the lines are all correct. Even after taking this precaution, you could discover that panels are not correctly positioned only after fitting the bumper and getting the car back on its wheels.

Flitch replacement

This is not a job for the faint-hearted; even on a Beetle which has not previously suffered any welded 'repairs' to the footwell side panel area, the heater channel, front panel or in fact any of the panels in the vicinity, the job can be very tricky. On a Beetle which has been bodged in these areas, the job can be soul-destroying. It is advisable for all but the most experienced (and hardened) DIY enthusiasts to hand this particular job over to a professional Beetle restorer.

You will need an air hacksaw, although you might

161

be able to get away with a padsaw if you have several days to spare cutting out the old flitch panel. The use of air chisels and any other brutal devices is ruled out because they'll damage the lips of adjacent panels.

Disconnect the battery. Remove the front bumper. Remove the fuel tank and push the fuel line well out of the way. Disconnect the lower ends of the bonnet springs and use a prop to hold the bonnet up (remove the bonnet if you prefer, although if you do so then it will have to be re-fitted to check flitch alignment at a later stage), remove the front wing(s) and remove the spare wheel. According to the model being worked upon and which side of the car is being attended to, remove any wiring, piping and components from the vicinity.

Strip the front suspension and brakes. On McPherson strut cars, support the frame head from under the car and remove the strut complete. Remove the three large bolts which hold the steering box. Before starting to hack away at the offending flitch panel, make up a measuring device with which you can fix the distance between two suspension strut holes (McPherson strut models) or two fixed points on the flitches, to help later

with correct alignment of the new panel. The ideal measuring device is a length of box section steel with holes drilled to correspond with the McPherson strut holes in the flitch or alternatively, for torsion bar cars, holes which you drill (accurately measuring for the hole placement in the new flitch) and which can later be filled with weld. You can run nuts and bolts through these holes, which not only positively locate the flitch but which also hold it firmly in position whilst welding up is taking place. Alternatively, a series of measurements could be taken.

Flitch replacement on a McPherson strut car. Not a job for the beginner and one which the author would strongly recommend is entrusted to experienced professionals. To avoid damaging the lips of adjacent panels, the flitch is cut away a bit at a time before the spot welds on the assorted lips are drilled out. The first cut Terry makes runs at 45 degrees from the top of the valance to the spare wheel well lip. If you don't possess an air hacksaw, take sandwiches and a camp bed to the workshop!

ABOVE
The first section cut away. Note that Terry has avoided the spare wheel well lip by a fair margin, and is now cutting the rear top of the flitch, avoiding the heavy section steel in the McPherson strut top housing.

BELOW
Having cut around the wheel arch until meeting up with a hidden welded lip, Terry now cuts down the front of the A post.

With the rear of the flitch cut away, access to the spot welds which will have to be drilled out is greatly improved.

Now a cut is made underneath the welded lip. This part of the flitch forms the footwell side panel.

Finally, the air hacksaw is used to cut away the last remnants of the old flitch, revealing some pretty comprehensive rot underneath!

OK, you've got to start somewhere . . . The A post lower repair section is offered into position. The front end will have to be rebuilt from the A post lip forwards.

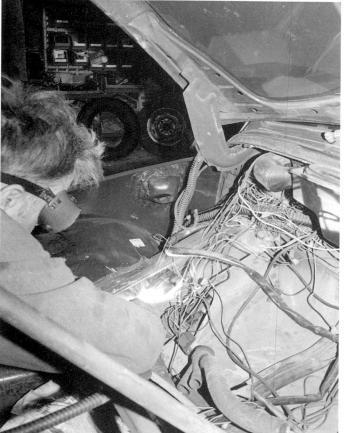

ABOVE
The new flitch being spot welded into position. Note the cross brace which has been re-fitted to precisely place the flitch. Failure to do this could result on the suspension strut being fitted at an angle, ruining the suspension geometry.

LEFT
An experienced restorer knows exactly how close he can weld to wiring and other flammable materials in safety. The DIYer would be better advised to move all wiring and other trim from the vicinity before striking an arc.

The flitch panel should be cut away in stages, starting at the top and working slowly downwards – at all times, taking care not to hack through the various lips of adjoining panels. The photographs illustrate this process. As sections of the old flitch are removed, compare them with the replacement and salvage any fittings which may be absent from the new panels.

The flitch is generally joined to adjacent steel by spot welds, which have to be partially drilled and then split. Try to avoid drilling holes right through any lip which is visible from within the luggage compartment, because the holes will later have to be filled with weld and ground down. Prise open the A post folded seam to remove the flitch rear lip.

The flitch in place. Through the repair, the bonnet was frequently lowered to check its shut lines. Now, a simple trolley with large castor wheels has been fitted with three wood blocks and a long centre bolt which protrudes half an inch proud of the top block. This locates in the drain hole in the frame head and allows a McPherson strut Beetle with no front suspension to be wheeled around easily.

When the panel has been removed, examine all newly exposed metal, particularly enclosed box sections, the A post base, heater channel and front panel. If these show signs of bad rusting then they should be replaced, otherwise, take the opportunity of applying rust-preventative measures and clean the edges to which the flitch will be welded.

Offer the flitch into place and check that it is accurately positioned by using the measuring device you made earlier and by lowering the bonnet to check for any gaps or misalignment. Be prepared to spend some time getting the flitch in the correct position, because even the best repair panels can offer problems. Clamp the flitch tightly into position, lower the bonnet and check that the two align correctly.

When you are satisfied that the flitch is in the correct position, clean the areas which are to be welded and preferably apply weldable zinc paint. Fold the A post seam back over the flitch rear lip with a hammer and dolly, and check that the curvature of the flitch is correct. Then begin welding the flitch panel into place. If you don't have access to a spot welder and the appropriate arms then you could use plug welds in their place – as many and as close together as the originals – or preferably continuous seam welds.

Flitch repair panels

The flitch panels (inner front wings) often rot out at the lower front ends, and repair panels are available for this. Remove the front wings, fuel tank and any wiring in the vicinity. As ever, firstly clean the affected area so that you can determine the extent of the rot in the existing panels before deciding whether to fit the full repair panel or to tailor it. Gently drill out the spot welds holding the luggage lid seal retaining strip and remove this; the chances are that the flitch steel underneath will show some signs of rusting, so clean and later treat this area with weldable zinc paint before fitting a new seal retainer strip.

Drill and part the spot welds to the valance and spare wheel well – the flitch end should now be free and can

ABOVE
Partial flitch repair panels are much easier to fit than complete flitches. Firstly, cut out the rot using if possible an air hacksaw to minimise distortion, then tailor the repair panel to fit.

BELOW
Clamp and/or tack the repair panel into position and check that it IS in the correct position by trial fitting the bumper complete with mounts. When the panel is tacked into position, it is a good idea to also check the wing fit and captive nut alignment.

A partial rear lower flitch/footwell side repair panel being offered into position. If possible, cut the repair panel down in size.

A spot welder with a set of long arms makes life much easier, and results in a far neater job than would a MiG.

Terry welds a strip of steel to the back of the existing flitch lower rear edge, to help the repair panel lie flat.

be cut away. Most people favour an overlapped joint between the flitch and the repair panel: it could be butt welded, but the extra strength of an overlapped joint favours the latter.

Tack the repair panel into position and check the wing and bonnet fit (adjust the position of the repair panel if necessary) before welding up the flitch, using continuous seam MiG welds.

Spare wheel well

The spare wheel well will often be found to be rotten, due to water being allowed to lie in the base for long periods. Small areas of rot in the base may be patch repaired (remove all wiring from the vicinity, plus the fuel tank and line), and a full repair panel is also available for cars with more widespread rot.

However, if a full spare wheel well panel is required, the chances are that one or both flitch panels also require replacement or repair; the author would recommend that these are attended to firstly, and the spare wheel well/front valance left in situ throughout to help locate the flitch or the flitch lower front repair panel. There is a temptation to cut everything away to improve access and then to try and reconstruct the front end using the bonnet and wings to help locate panels;

the author has seen more than one lop-sided Beetle, which should serve as a warning to those so tempted!

Remove the fuel tank and all wiring from the vicinity. Drill out the spot welds from the original spare wheel well panel edge flanges, then part the joints as gently as possible, to avoid distorting the metal to which the new flanges will be welded. Because the original seam spot weld lines are easily visible, locating the new panel should pose no problem. Seam weld the new panel into position, working a short length at a time, then allowing the steel to cool to avoid buckling.

ABOVE RIGHT
Front valance replacement on a McPherson strut car. Note the line of the cut. Before attacking the valance, take a series of measurements to allow you to position the replacement accurately, and check bonnet fit before welding it in.

BELOW RIGHT
A McPherson strut car with the valance cut away. This is a good time to clean and patch or repaint the underside of the spare wheel well.

BELOW
The spot welder is invaluable for this work . It is easier to work with and gives results that are neater and stronger than Mig or gas. Hire one for the day.

ABOVE

An air impact wrench is a useful tool to have around for starting the front body mounting bolts. Note the steel bar which is bolted across the mounting holes for the McPherson struts; one flitch panel complete is to be fitted to this car, and the brace will allow the new flitch to be placed precisely when the time comes.

LEFT

The air wrench (referred to in the workshop as the 'wizzy tool') makes removal of the heater channel bolts much easier. Some will inevitably wrench the captive nuts free so that they turn along with the bolt; grind away the heads if this happens.

RIGHT

It is best to have five people on hand when lifting the bodyshell in this manner; one on each corner, one to slide the steel rods into position while you supervise. If the four lifters complain that you have the easy job, explain that you alone are shouldering the heavy burden of responsibility! Note the flitch panel lower edge repair. With the bodywork supported as shown, the chassis can simply be wheeled out from underneath.

Removal of bodyshell from chassis

This task can be accomplished single-handedly, but it is recommended that four strong adults are on hand to do the lifting, plus an observer to shout out if you forget to remove or disconnect anything during the preparations. The most common reason for parting the body and chassis is floorpan repair or replacement and, if the floorpan is thus rotted then the heater channel/sill assembly is certain to have also rotted – and vice-versa. It is vital that the heater channels are welded to the body shell *only* with the heater channels bolted to the chassis, so that the bolt holes of the two are correctly aligned. Bolt or weld in stiffening braces across the door apertures and between the A posts to prevent the shell from distorting as it is lifted. Leave the rear seat support in position throughout.

Remove the seats, battery, fuel tank and wings, then bleed the entire braking system dry before removing the flexible brake hoses. On McPherson strut models, support the framehead and remove the strut assembly from the wheelarch. Disconnect the wiring in the engine bay, including the oil light, ignition and reversing light wire if fitted, and disconnect the speedometer cable.

Underneath the fuel tank there are two holes in which you'll find 17 mm headed bolts; remove these and also disconnect the brake master cylinder pipes. Remove the nuts and bolts from the steering column bottom flange (early torsion bar cars) or the clamp bolt on later cars.

Remove the 17 mm headed rear body mounting bolts from within the rear wheelarch, the two from the front of the heater channels and the 8 mm headed bolts which run along the heater channels. It is likely that some of the captive threaded plates which the 8 mm bolts run into will break free from their position inside the heater channels; grind off the heads of the bolts concerned. Some bolts will shear; leave these until later, when the bodyshell is off. Even if you are replacing the floorpan and heater channels, be sure to keep the shaped outer washers from the heater channel/floorpan fixing bolts.

From inside the car, remove firstly the rear seat (leave the support in place to help brace the body), then the four bolts from the front end of the spine. Disconnect the heat exchanger ducts. Disconnect the starter solenoid wires and the red/white wire running from the battery to the regulator. Disconnect the earth strap.

On the 1302/3 series cars, remove the steering stabiliser bolt under the spare wheel and also the two adjacent 17 mm headed bolts which run into the frame head and, from inside the car, the two bolts at the top front of the tunnel. Split the track rod end ball joints and tie the track rod ends out of harm's way.

Before attempting to lift the body it is a good idea if you have not already done so to internally brace the bodyshell before lifting it, by welding in lengths of box section steel across the door apertures and between the two A post bases.

The less you have to lift the bodyshell skyward the better, so always remove the front seats and seriously consider also removing the engine. Removing the engine obviously lessens the chances damaging it when the body is lifted away. Rather than moving the bodyshell away from the chassis, you can make up supports (BSW use plastic milk crates) so that the one end of the body at a time can be lifted and beams fitted between the supports. The chassis can then be wheeled out from underneath the bodyshell.

As a matter of course, it pays to renew all brake pipes and the fuel pipe with copper/nickel alternatives while the body is off the car. The steel originals do rust and burst brake pipes or a leaking fuel line present obvious dangers.

Floorpan repair/replacement

You have to determine the extent of rot and so begin by thoroughly cleaning the floorpan/chassis assembly top and bottom. Be quite brutal when probing for rot (use a pointed panel beaters' hammer), because a sound-looking spine can in fact be very weak if it has rotted out from within, and floorpans covered with sound-looking underseal can be heavily rotted underneath that layer of underseal. If rot is found to extend up into the chassis spine then perhaps it is best to scrap the chassis and either use a new one (available from Autobarn) or to take one from another Beetle.

The decision whether to patch repair or replace the floorpans should be taken according to the extent of the rot and, more importantly, according to whether you wish to have to repeat the repair at some time in the future! If you patch it, then sooner or later more patching will be required. Bear in mind that repaired panels usually rot out first along welded seams and, if you elect to turn the floorpans into a kind of welded patchwork quilt then they will rot all over in double-quick time! Replace the lot, properly rust-proof it and the floor should last as long as the car itself.

If the engine has been stripped from the chassis (as it should) it is little problem to turn the chassis onto its side so that you can get at the underside of the floorpans – drain the transaxle oil firstly on swing axle cars. If money is very tight and repair is the only option, begin by cleaning both floorpans back to bare metal so that you can find every trace of rot. If possible, make use of proper repair panels and, for the sake of strength, use an overlapped joint continuously seam welded both top and bottom. Rot most frequently occurs at the floorpan outer edges, for which complete, front or rear half repair panels are available.

Combined floorpan halves/heater channel replacement

The complete floorpan pressing is by far the better option, though fitting it is really too advanced a task for all but the most experienced DIY restorers. If the floorpan has rotted then it follows that the heater channels will also have rotted and need to be replaced, and it is essential that the work is carried out in the correct sequence. This is as follows.

1. Internally brace the bodyshell. 2. Lift the shell off the chassis assembly, then clean off all traces of old belly pan gasket. 3. Cut out and replace the floorpans. 4. Bolt the new heater channels onto the floorpans. 5. Cut away old heater channels from shell. 6. Lift shell back onto chassis. 6. Weld shell to heater channels. 7. Remove shell, fit gasket, re-fit shell.

To begin with, strip the interior of the car. Weld braces across the door apertures and between the two A posts so that the shell will keep its shape after the old heater channels have been cut out. Lift off the shell and clean all traces of the old belly pan gasket from the chassis assembly.

To cut out the floorpans, an air hacksaw is ideal, but an air chisel could also be used if you can stand the noise! Take care not to cut into or distort the flange

ABOVE
The author dismantling the pedal assembly. Spine nearside cover off, cable disconnected, bolts undone and off it comes – easy. Don't, incidentally, expect a restorer to allow you – the customer – to carry out work on his premises, because of insurance problems if you were to injure yourself and sue him!

BELOW
Terry and his faithful air hacksaw cutting off the nearside floorpan. The floorpans were actually in rather good condition and could easily have been dealt with by fitting edge repair sections. However, the author decided that while the bodyshell was off, it was probably better to go the whole hog and fit complete floorpans.

175

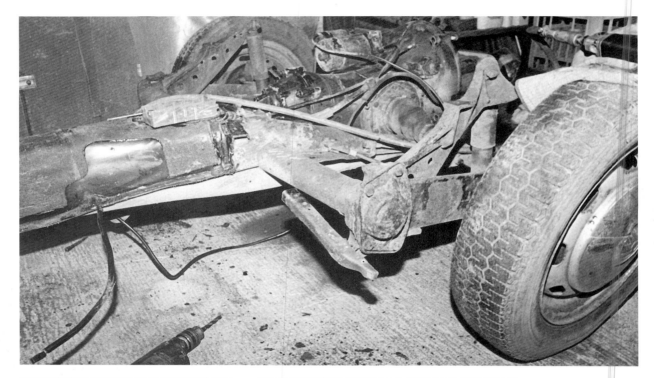

ABOVE LEFT
When the bulk of the floorpans had been cut away, the spot welded joints in the various lips were drilled and parted. Note the heavy section pressing just ahead of the torsion bar; this must be left in situ and unscathed, so take care when cutting in this area. The tube sticking out of the spine to the bottom left of the photograph contains the rear heater control cable; this must be ground from the old floorpans and welded to the new.

BELOW LEFT
This is what you should be left with at the front end. The replacement floorpan more or less positions itself, butting against the spine and the assembly to the rear of the frame head. Those flanges now have to be cleaned to bright steel using a linishing disc.

ABOVE
Even the most experienced and careful restorer will sustain the occasional injury. You should equip your workshop with a first-aid box, plus some clean water just in case you need to wash harmful liquid from your hands in a hurry.

RIGHT
The spine ready for the new floorpans. It is a good idea to wear gloves when you're handling floorpans, as well as the flanges to which they will be welded, because their sharp edges can make a mess of your hands otherwise.

between the spine chassis top and base sections. At the rear of the floorpans, take care not to damage nor distort the bracket from the damper mounting.

Then, using firstly a ⅛ in. followed (if necessary) by a ⅜ in. bit, drill out the spot welds which fasten the old floorpan edges to the spine flange. These occur approximately every ¾ in. on original floorpans. Expect to have to grind out weld at the corners. Clean the flanges.

Prepare the new floorpan by cleaning all edges which are to be welded, then spray a coat or two of weldable zinc-based paint on the internal faces of the joint. Offer the floorpans up, and bolt them only at the rear damper mounting extension bracket, and offer up the heater channels then bolt these into position. The two large bolts which pass through the heater channel into the front of the chassis are then fitted to bring both the floorpans and heater channels into the correct position.

Expect both the floorpans and heater channels to be less than perfect; some tailoring of the floorpan edges might prove necessary, although the most common problem is poor alignment of the bolt holes. On the heater channels fitted to RVJ 403H, the closing (bottom) plate holes did not align with the internal captive nuts, and the metal surrounding three of the holes partially obscured the nuts!

Your typical DIY spot welder will probably not have enough grunt to weld through the two thick spine flanges plus the floorpan edges, so don't go investing large sums of money on very long arms until you have tested the welder on similar thicknesses of steel! The alternative is to continuously MiG weld the joints – not so pretty as spot welds, but no one will ever see the joints anyway! Clean all paint from the parts of the heater channels which are to be welded, and apply weldable zinc paint before welding.

Now cut the old heater channels out from the bodyshell; this is made far easier if the shell is rolled onto its side, with plenty of padding to prevent damage. Check firstly that your internal bracing is still firmly welded so that the shell cannot distort. Cut carefully along the flitch base, around the A and B post base flanges, and below the rear quarter panel. Some 'persuasion' with a lump hammer may be needed to get the heater channels free!

Lift the bodyshell onto the chassis (which now has the new heater channels bolted in place) and carefully manoeuvre it so that the two rear body mounts align with their holes on the damper brackets and the shell sits correctly. Fit the rear body mounting bolts, check again that everything is in line and fit the doors temporarily so that you can see whether the door gaps are right (you may have to remove the cross brace at

The replacement heater channels left a little to be desired in the quality of their assembly; some of the holes in the base plate partially covered the captive bodyshell mount nuts within – sadly, typical of spurious panels not just for the Beetle but throughout the restoration world. It is difficult to enlarge this hole without destroying the thread of the captive nut but, with patience and a large drill bit, it can be done. In an ideal world, the assembly would be rejected; the problem is of course that the restoration will be delayed.

he first floorpan in. We did attempt to spot weld it but found
hat the welder was not man enough for the job – those spine
anges really are thick and a far more powerful welder would
ave been required – and even the impressive set of welder
rms owned by BSW did not include one long enough to
each right over the floorpan. The heater channel is being
olted on – made more difficult by the problems with the
oorly assembled channel base plate. The components as well
s repair sections for heater channel assemblies are available:
hese might be OK for MOT work but they are not
ecommended for a car which is being restored. In practice, if
ne specific area of the heater channel assembly is rotten,
hen other sections will also be on the way out, and it is best
o simply replace the whole unit.

By replacing complete the more rot-prone panels and
assemblies rather than patching or fitting repair panels, you
end up with a car which is structurally as good as new!
Hopefully, with good rust-proofing these expensive
components will last as long as the originals' 23 years.

179

ABOVE LEFT
This is what happens within rotten heater channels. Holes begin to appear in the inner channel, so that the screen demister becomes completely ineffectual. Even though the VISIBLE external panels may show no obvious signs of rot, don't be surprised to discover a similar mess when you lift the body from the chassis.

BELOW LEFT
After a good deal of sawing and chiselling, the heater channel assembly rear end can usually be man-handled out, although a sharp tap with a mallet is sometimes needed.

ABOVE
Rather than lift the bodyshell completely off the chassis (again) for belly pan gasket replacement, with four plastic milk crates and two baulks of timber you can simply raise it out of the way!

RIGHT
By making a 'V' cut in the belly pan gasket, you can keep a continuous bead around the outside edge. Copious amounts of windscreen sealant can be placed in this area to ensure a really good seal.

The clusters of holes in this floorpan edge are the consequence of fitting new heater channels to a body without firstly bolting the channels to the floorpan edges – whoever re-fitted the body had to have three goes at drilling the holes before everything lined up correctly!

this point), then gas or preferably MiG weld the shell to the heater channels.

When all welding is completed, lift the shell from the chassis and then fit the belly pan gasket. Some people glue this in place using impact adhesive, but manoeuvring the shell when re-fitting it can rip the gasket out of position unless it is securely held by the recommended fixing method of pop rivets. (See 'Re-fit Bodyshell to Chassis' later in this chapter for more details.)

Re-fit the shell. The accelerator pedal base has to be welded to the floorpan: it is best to leave this until the engine, clutch/brake pedal assembly and accelerator cable have been attached. This will allow you to check that you have full accelerator lever response to the pedal travel – if you weld the pedal too far away from the lever, then you could end up with only a fraction of the available throttle lever movement!

Heater channels replacement

Heater channels are normally covered with carpeting and the first evidence of rot might be the fact that the windscreen stays permanently misted-up because no hot air is reaching it! It is possible to renew the heater channels without taking the body off the chassis, but this will mean fitting new belly pan gasket strips under the heater channel ends where they would almost certainly be damaged by the heat of welding, and this usually spells water leaks at the end of the strips, which accelerates new rusting. Far better to remove the body and fit a complete belly gasket as already described, but if you cannot lift off the bodyshell, read on.

If the heater channels have rotted badly, then the floorpan edges will usually be found to have also rotted, so attend to these first.

The rear seat brace should be kept in position throughout. Cut through the old heater channel just ahead of the B post and behind the A post (take care not to cut into the floorpan edge), then part the welds to the flitch and the inner quarter panel. If the lower part of the flitch is also rotten, then cut this away, and weld in new steel after the new heater channels are in place. Cut the rear up to the lower inner wing flange.

Depending on whether the channel has been replaced before, you might also find weld between it and the flitch inner surface and bulkhead panels; this must be ground off, though in many such cases you will have to cut away the base of the flitch. Carefully cut around the bases of the A and B post. Remove the remaining sections of heater channel; if no welded joints remain then a (controlled) clout from a hammer will usually do the trick.

Bolt the new channel into position on the chassis assembly; a replacement length of belly pan gasket should have been obtained but not yet be fitted, because welding at the ends of the heater channels would burn it away! You may require an assistant to push the floor edges downwards as you push the heater channels into position. Then re-fit the door and check that the gaps are correct front and rear. Tack weld the bases of the A and B posts into position, remove the door, then knock down the inner quarter panel and seam weld this to the heater channel, and seam weld the flitch.

Undo the heater channel to floorpan bolts, push the floorpan edge downwards and try to work a new length of belly pan gasket into position.

Frame head

The frame head is the primary location for most of the front suspension/steering mounting points and, if this assembly is rotten then the car's handling will be unpredictable and dangerous. The base tends to suffer from rot long before the top section. Because the cost of a replacement frame head assembly is almost as much as that of a new chassis assembly complete with framehead, repair is an attractive alternative. This is far from an easy task and would normally only be undertaken during a full body-off restoration. Access to a spot welder is almost vital.

Strip the car to a bare chassis, then clean off the top of the frame head to check that it is passable before turning the chassis upside down. It is as well to pull the fuel pipe out of the spine before you begin cutting steel.

Clean off the lips of the two halves so that you can see the spot welds, centre punch then drill these out, taking care not to drill through the lip of the top pressing. Split the join as you progress. Cut across both sides of the track control arm pressing, drill out the spot welds holding this to the frame head lower pressing, grind away any MiG or gas weld you find and finally prise off the pressing.

The repair panel should have captive nuts for the anti-roll bar fixings, intended to replace the two internally threaded rods per side of the upper frame head pressing. If possible, clean, re-tap and use the original fixings, and grind off the captive nuts on the repair panel. The original fixings spread the loadings from the anti-roll bar between both pressings of the frame head, whereas the captive nuts on the repair panel place all of the strain on the repair panel itself if they have to be used.

Clean up the inside of the top frame head pressing and apply a good rust-proofing primer, then offer the lower pressing into position and bolt it down as shown in the photographs. It would be possible to plug or seam weld the two panels together, but strength here is so vital that the author would urge the use of a spot welder, even if it has to be hired for the day.

Frame head replacement

This becomes necessary usually on cars which have been left standing in long wet grass for some years, or cars which have suffered heavy front-end collision. In the opinion of the author, it is not a task for the DIY restorer, because the precise positioning of the replacement frame head is critical; if it is a fraction out, then handling and road-holding will suffer.

If you *must* attempt this repair, then the author

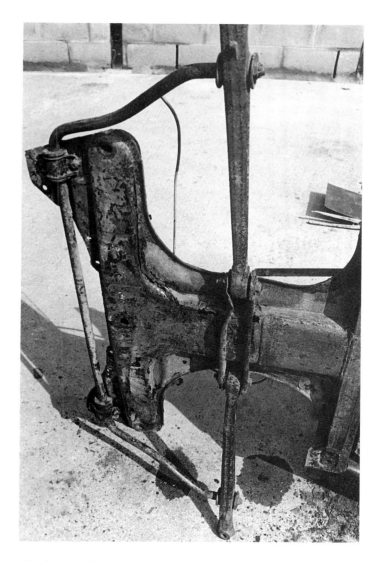

This framehead looks rather sad, and in fact a few stabs with a sharp implement showed that it had extensive rot which substantially weakened it. Normally, this would be cut off and a replacement grafted into place – not a job for the amateur – but the owner decided that it had to be repaired instead.

recommends that you begin by making up a welded steel framework (in effect, a crude but accurate jig) which passes from the floorpan to the framehead and which has holes drilled through it to align with the various holes in the existing frame head. This will allow the new framehead to be bolted firmly into the correct position prior to welding.

Bulkhead panel (toeboard) replacement

For Beetles with torsion bar front suspension a third party bulkhead panel is available, but for cars with

ABOVE LEFT
Removing a frame head base plate is a tiresome affair. First, you have to find all of the spot welds – no easy matter in a rotten surface – and drill them out, then you can begin to part the flanges. There are a lot of spot welds joining the frame head and its base.

BELOW LEFT
The track control rod bracket has its own complement of spot welds to be dealt with.

ABOVE
Other areas are best dealt with using an oxy-acetylene torch.

RIGHT
At the rear, an oxy-acetylene torch is the best tool with which to cut away the old metal.

ABOVE
Finally, with the lips cleaned up, the repair panel can be bolted down to locate it for welding.

LEFT
A spot welder really is essential for this repair; MiG or gas welds along the edge won't have the necessary strength and plug welds are not really up to the mark.

McPherson strut suspension there is only a VAG panel, which is very expensive. The third party panel can be modified to fit McPherson strut cars.

If this is a first-time repair, begin by drilling out the spot welds which hold the old panel in position, then splitting the welds. If the car has been 'got at' and the panel is plated or has been replaced previously and MiG welded into position, grind away the welds until the panel comes free.

Offer the new panel into position and tack weld it, ensuring that the lower line of the panel matches the profile of the chassis front end. When it is correctly positioned, seam weld it in, starting along the top edge, down both sides. When you come to the lower portions, weld a little, let the metal cool, then weld a little more before again letting the metal cool, to prevent heat build-up from destroying the belly pan gasket.

ABOVE

Fact: two people can complete some tasks three times as fast as a person working alone. Terry drills the holes and Craig pop-rivets the belly pan gasket into place.

RIGHT

If it doesn't move, spray chassis black onto it! The rolling chassis now looks very presentable before it is rolled back under the bodyshell for the final reunion.

It is preferable to carry out this work as part of a full body-off restoration and, if this is the case, tack the bulkhead panel securely into position with the body on the chassis for correct alignment, then seam weld with the body raised to improve access.

If you wish to weld the torsion bar version of this panel into a McPherson strut Beetle, then firstly dolly the edge lips so that they lie flat, then position it correctly and measure the gap between the panel edges and the flitches. Cut strips of steel to make up the gap and weld these to the panel before offering it for final welding into position. It is also necessary to weld in plates to cover the gaps from within the front wheelarch.

LEFT
Spot the obvious mistakes! The full quarter panel has been fitted, which not only precludes using another of these repair panels in the future but also means more welding and welding in the centre of a large and prone to buckling panel.

RIGHT
The quarter panel repair section being welded into place whilst the shell is on its side and the spot welder can be used. Simply spot a strip of steel onto the top inner surface, and spot the repair to this. Using a spot welder rather than a MiG lessens heat distortion.

Re-fit of bodyshell to chassis

The first stage is to remove and throw away any of the old sealing strip which may be stuck to the floorpan edges and to clean (and if necessary true up) the edges. Many people seem to try to glue the new seal into position on the floorpan edge, but glue cannot not hold the seal strongly enough once you start to manoeuvre the bodyshell into the correct position, so affix it with pop rivets instead.

Don't make the mistake of cutting the new seal up into pieces, but begin by laying out the seal along one floorpan edge, starting from a front corner, drilling and pop riveting it in place as you go. When you come to the corner at the rear of the floorpan, cut the seal only part-way through. This allows you to fold the seal around the bend and to keep a continuous bead around the outside to keep out water.

Work across the back, then make another cut at the opposite corner, and start drilling and riveting up the other outer edge of the floorpan. Then you can cut off the remaining section of the seal, which will be fitted across the front.

Terry Ball cuts the edges of the front seal strip, then lays one seal partially across the other to give a good seal. The remaining section of the seal is riveted across the front of the floorpan. To improve the sealing qualities, Terry then applies a generous glob of windscreen sealant to the four corners of the seal.

With some lifting gear and a great deal of ingenuity, the bodyshell can be manoeuvred onto the chassis by one person, but it is far better to have two strong adults and preferably three or more (two, three or four to lift and one to check that the mounting bolt holes are aligned). Before lifting on the bodyshell, check that there is nothing lying on the top of the seal and nothing lying on the frame head to prevent the body from seating properly. Align the rearmost holes first (those on the rear damper bracket); fit the spacers into position and bolt the bodyshell loosely (remember to use copper grease on all of these bolt threads) at this stage. Then move to the front of the car and try to align the two long bolts at the front edges of the frame head. Fit the bolts with new M10 washers, then fit the four (two per side) smaller bolts which locate further back in the frame head.

If any of these bolts do not align correctly with their respective holes then running a tap through the threads can help, but do not force anything at this stage, because you will only be rewarded with a crossed thread if you do. If you cannot even get a tap through a hole, then try gently levering the bodyshell in the appropriate direction and try again.

Finally, fit the small bolts which run into the sill/heater channel assemblies and, when all bolts are in position, tighten them all.

many tack welds on the join and then welding only a short length of steel at a time, you reduce the chances of the panels bucking.

'A' and 'B' post repairs

As the heater channels rot, rust spreads up to the bases of the A and B posts. If these have previously been repaired or welded onto new heater channels at some time, rusting will usually be found to have started at the actual weld. Either way, the bases have to be repaired and, as usual, both long and short repair panels are available.

Remove the door. Clean the old paintwork from the post base, so that you can determine the true extent of the rot, then decide whether you will have to fit the larger repair panel (which incorporates the lower hinge

This shot clearly shows the make-up of the A post lower end. You have later, incidentally, to try to juggle the heater down pipe onto the heater channel outlet pipe through the tiny hole in the footwell side panel.

Quarter panel repair

The quarter panel is the panel which runs from the rear of the door to the rear wing, and the lower area is very prone to rot. Both large and small repair panels are available; fit the smaller of the two if possible and, if you have to use the larger panel, cut it down to size rather than fit the entire panel. The author has seen quite a few full large repair panels needlessly welded into position where they could usefully have been cut down, so that the next time the panel rots out, the hapless owners have the option of patch repairing or going to the considerable expense of acquiring and fitting a full side panel.

Furthermore, the full repair panel edge runs right across the centre of the panel where welding-generated heat will almost certainly give corrugations; *always* cut the repair panel down to the smallest practicable size.

To fit the repair panel, either cut it slightly oversize and use a joddler to set an edge which can tuck underneath the edge of the existing panel or, alternatively, spot weld a strip of steel onto the back of the repair panel to give the same effect. In addition to helping cut the chances of buckling from occurring, this also pulls the two panels into line. Fix the two panels together with pop rivets or self-tapping screws, tack weld them at ½ in. intervals then join the tack welds together with continuous seam welds. By placing so

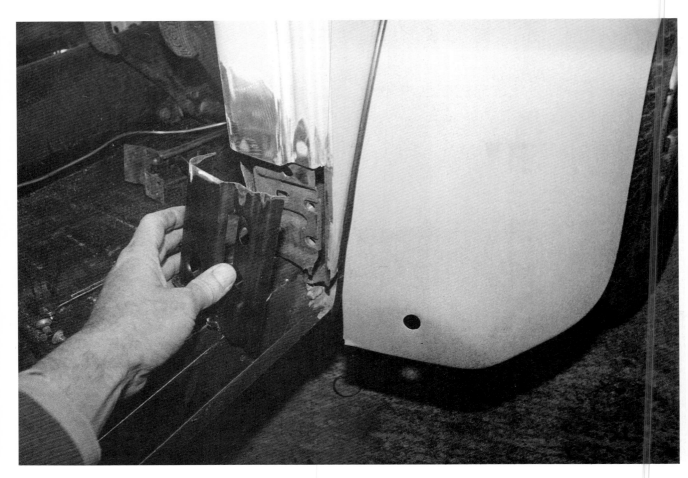

ABOVE
The lower A post repair panel being offered into position. Be aware that some panels don't posses the flange which bends around the flitch rear edge.

LEFT
This is the long A post repair panel; apply full rust-proofing measures because if this repair panel rots, then major surgery will be called for. You would probably have to fabricate your own longer repair panel; these days, the chances of finding a crashed Beetle with a good A post in a scrap yard are virtually nil.

OPPOSITE
With the old heater channel removed, the heater pipe in the A post can be seen. The chances are that this will sustain damage during the rough and tumble of restoration, so it's best to replace it. Getting the end back onto the top of the heater channel assembly calls for some team-work; one person feeds it in from the top and applies pressure whilst the other manipulates it into position through the hole in the inside of the A post.

mounting point), or whether you can get away with the shorter version and still find clean, sound steel to weld to on the post. The hinge mounting point must be sound if you are to use the shorter panel and, in this instance, it is as well to take the opportunity to clean and hand paint the mounting point before covering it with the repair panel.

Prise the folded edge of the old panel from the flitch lip. The rot is best cut out using an air hacksaw, although patience and a junior hacksaw will also do the job – *don't* use a chisel or air chisel, because both will distort the remaining edge and, because the join will have to be butt welded, it will prove difficult to true up the edge sufficiently to get a good result.

Some tailoring may prove necessary to get the repair panel to fit the heater channel properly. If you are fitting the larger panel, have an assistant hold the door whilst you ensure that the mounting built into the repair panels matches the hinge bolt holes, then tack the panel into position and carefully fit the door (supporting the door so that the repair panel does not take any weight) to ensure not only that the hinge holes are aligned but also that the door shut lines are correct.

If all is in order, butt weld the top join, seam weld the bottom join to the heater channel and spot weld (if possible) the outer edge. The inside upright joint can be butt welded or overlapped – the former looks neater. Use weldable zinc paint prior to welding, then clean the outsides of the joints and apply a good rust-retardant primer.

Luggage/engine bay seal retaining strips

It is usual to discover slight rusting of these thin strips, but don't be fooled – more serious rust will be lurking underneath them. The recommended option during a full restoration is to drill out their spot welds and remove them, clean the underlying metal and apply weldable zinc paint, then to spot weld on new strips.

These strips really do need to be spot welded in – they are so thin that a MiG will be very inclined to burn through, and cleaning up surplus weld without damaging the lips will be verging on the impossible.

Flitch top rail repair

When rot under the luggage bay seal retaining strip is left unattended, it results in rot in the underlying flitch tops. Repair panels do not appear to be available for this area so, if practicable, rot can be dealt with by cutting

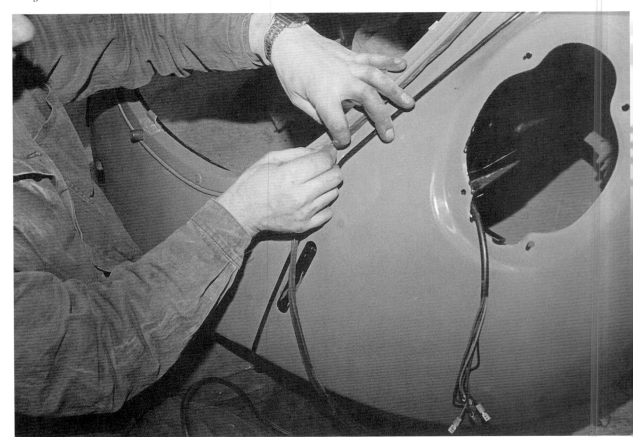

RIGHT
The new luggage bay weather strip retainer is spot welded into position. This is very thin section steel and MiG welding is very likely to result in burning through and an unsightly finish, so hire a spot welder if you don't possess one. Use weldable zinc paint before welding, then clean off any surplus afterwards and treat the lot to Bonda Prima or similar rust-retardent paint.

BELOW
Terry chooses to work the engine bay seal into its retaining strip; alternatively, it can be fed into place, using a lubricant.

away the weak metal and letting in a strip of new steel. If the rot extends very far down the flitch on torsion bar cars, a replacement flitch panel is the best (although very difficult and fairly expensive) option. On McPherson strut cars, the flitch tops are the location for the strut top mounting; the replacement panels are very expensive and *very* difficult to fit.

To work the engine or luggage bay seal into its strip, use a blunt screwdriver – don't use anything with sharp corners, because they'll rip the seal for certain.

Interior

Carpets are generally glued into position along the footwell sides and around the parcel shelf area. The author has tried using non-impact adhesives but found that an impact adhesive was essential.

Before re-fitting the pressing which lies under the pedals, check that the pedals are correctly adjusted; that the throttle pedal has a full range of travel (it won't if the hinged base has been welded into the wrong position on a new floorpan), that the brake and clutch pedals both have reasonable amounts of free travel. The pressing itself hooks into two slots on the toeboard and is held by a single self-tapping screw. This and the edges of the footwell side carpet are then covered with the rubber mat.

Ready for masking up to the topcoats. The dark area at the front of the bonnet is 'stone chip' paint; ideally it would be applied to the lower edges of the front wings, the valance, and to the lower portion of the leading edge of the rear wings.

PAINTWORK

Every person who sprays paint at cars has or has had disasters at one time or another; even the most experienced professionals get it wrong from time to time and, in some cases, there is no alternative to removing the topcoat and primer – and starting off afresh on bare metal. There is greater potential for things to go seriously and expensively wrong during the painting of the car than there is at any other time during the restoration. The whole process involves a considerable investment in paint, and all this outlay can be wasted due to mistakes during preparation, due to there being the tiniest particles of silicon in the atmosphere or dust blowing through a gap in the door, or to the paint being contaminated by water and/or oil from the compressor. There is a thus strong case for having the spraying and paint preparation of your Beetle carried out professionally, and the majority of people who do restore their own cars appear to take this option.

Some people prefer to carry out the preparation work themselves and to have just the topcoats sprayed by professionals. This approach is fine as long as the preparation is of the highest standards, because any shortcomings in the preparation are equally as serious as problems with the application of the topcoats. If you choose to prepare the car for spraying yourself and have the topcoats sprayed at a professional spray shop, it is worth asking the person who will be doing the work to carry out the final preparation for you.

Before starting spray preparation, do stop to consider whether the existing paintwork can be salvaged. If there is a good depth of paint then it is often possible to flat then polish the most unpromising finish and end up with good looking results.

The primary object of painting a car is to prevent the steel of the bodywork from corroding, which paint achieves by insulating the metal surface from the atmosphere. In order for the paint to achieve this result, it must be applied on to corrosion-free, clean, dry and grease free metal. If paint is applied on to metal which has started to corrode, however slightly, then that corrosion will spread under the surface of the paint. If paint is applied on to a contaminated surface, then one of two things can happen. Either the contaminant can react with the chemicals in the paint to cause blistering or one of a dozen different problems, or the paint can fail to adhere properly to the metal. In both cases the paint will sooner or later lift from the surface of the metal and allow corrosion to begin.

The first stage of paint preparation is thus to remove all traces of rust from exposed metal, and to remove any contaminants (including earlier paint of types which are incompatible with the paint which you now wish to spray). In other words, the shell should be taken back to clean, bright metal. This can be achieved using emery paper and much energy, although the modern dual action and orbital sanding devices speed and ease the process so much that there can be few who would nowadays carry out this work by hand.

Previous layers of paint and primer do not necessarily have to be removed, so long as they are sanded down to provide a key for the new paint and to remove totally any traces of silicones or other contaminants which may lie on the surface. Also, the previous paint and primer must be of a type which will not chemically react with the paint which you intend to use. Problems can arise if you attempt to spray cellulose over other types of paint, because the powerful cellulose thinners will soften and possibly lift the underlying paint. Before buying your paint, therefore, ascertain which type of paint has previously been used and ask the paint mixing specialist which paint type can be used over this.

It is best to remove all chrome trim and windscreens from the car, and to thoroughly mask off the interior before you begin to spray paint. Screen removal is described elsewhere in this chapter; to remove the chrome trim, gently prize away one end with a blunt screwdriver or similar, then use the shaft of a small screwdriver to ease the trim off the clips.

Equipment and facilities

There are three types of equipment which could be considered suitable for painting cars. Small electric sprayers have a very low output and although they might prove ideal for re-touching a small area of damaged paint, they will prove inadequate for spraying whole cars or even whole body panels. The recently introduced warm air sprayers offer a high volume of low pressure air, and are claimed to reduce paint wastage (high pressure compressed air wastes a lot of paint in the atmosphere) and give good results. Unfortunately, no example was made available for testing whilst this book was being prepared.

The traditional equipment consists of an air compressor and spray gun. Air compressors for spraying range from tiny units which have so short a duty cycle

(the period of continuous operation) that a roof panel might have to be sprayed in two goes, to giant floor standing units with huge air tanks. In between there are a number of compressors which are popular with DIY restorers. The minimum acceptable compressor for serious work would have a 25 litre air tank, although 50 litres is far better and a 100 litre tank would be by far the best option. Small air tanks rapidly run out of 'puff' when the air pressure drops and this has to be replenished by the air pump. This places warmed air into the tank, which can dry the paint in the air before it ever reaches the panel!

In addition to the compressor, you will need at least one and preferably two water/oil traps for the outlet connection. When air is compressed, water droplets form in the tank and can be blown through the spray gun to mix with your paint and ruin the painted finish. Also, tiny droplets of oil from the pump will contaminate the air within the cylinder, and both this and the water will have to be filtered out before the air reaches the paint gun.

Most spray guns work rather like a carburettor, because as air is forced past a jet of sorts at high velocities (and hence at low pressure) paint is drawn up to mix with the air in exactly the same way that petrol mixes with air in a carburettor. Other guns have a gravity paint feed and are characterised, not unsurprisingly, by the paint container being mounted on top of the gun. You should buy the best spray gun and compressor that you can afford, or alternatively, hire them.

You will also need a mask. Paint which dries in the air forms a fine dust which you should avoid breathing in, and because the fumes from thinners are also to be avoided, a respiratory mask is needed rather than a simple dust mask which cannot provide sufficient protection.

It is possible to spray a car out of doors given favourable conditions. The weather should not be too hot nor too cold, it must not be wet or windy. A still day is essential, and the temperature should be somewhere in the range 10–20 degree C. A warmer day may appear a better prospect, but warmer days see greater activity from winged insects, which appear to be fatally attracted to wet paint! However, it is far better to apply paint indoors if this is possible, because it allows you some control over the conditions.

The paint should be applied in a clean dry atmosphere which has reasonable ventilation. The corner of the workshop in which you recently rubbed down bodyfiller is no place for paint spraying unless it is scrupulously cleaned firstly. The floor should also be lightly damped down with water to prevent dust from being kicked into the atmosphere by your own movements. You will require good, even lighting so that you can see which areas you have covered and which you have not.

The temperature and humidity at the time of spraying are important factors. If the temperature is too high, much of the paint can dry in the air before it ever reaches the panel, giving what is known as 'dry spray'. If the humidity is too high then water contamination will be apparent as 'bloom'. The surface will be very dull. Avoid very windy days if your workshop has a lot of ventilation.

Types of paint

Earlier Beetles were finished in cellulose paint. This is quite a good choice for the novice to use, because it dries fairly rapidly and so lessens the chances of dust falling on to the still wet fresh paint surface and spoiling it. Another advantage is that the thinners used will soften existing paint, so helping blend in any future touching-up.

Another beauty of cellulose is that, as long as there is sufficient depth of paint, the surface can be flatted with 1000 or 1200 grit wet 'n dry then cut and polished to give a superb finish. Even brushed-on cellulose can be cut and polished to give a top-class finish, provided that there is sufficient depth of paint to allow all of the brush marks to be flatted out! Against these advantages, with cellulose there is rather a lot of wastage. The paint has a low pigment content and so a fair thickness of it is required to produce a luxurious finish.

Most body shops today use either synthetic or two-pack paints. Synthetic paints can give an excellent finish but they tend to look at little 'plastic' if used on an older car. Synthetic paints have a fairly long drying time, and so there is a greater chance of air-borne dust being able to settle on the surface before it dries. Only two coats of the paint are necessary to produce a gloss finish.

Two pack paints have a high pigment content and so produce a deep finish. Unfortunately, some of the ingredients of the paints are highly toxic and so they should only be used with proper breathing apparatus, which in practice really means an external air supply. The two pack paints are therefore used in the main by well equipped professional spray shops.

Preparation

The quality of the paint finish is wholly dependent on the quality of the preparation. The entire area which is to be sprayed should be flatted using increasingly fine grades of wet 'n dry, used wet (except on bodyfiller,

which would absorb the water). Begin using a coarse grade of 400 grit then progress through to 1200 grit for the final finish. The surface to be sprayed should be perfectly smooth with no ripples. Use a flexible straight edge to check for unevenness in filled areas. When the finish is acceptable, begin masking off. Masking tape and newspaper is quite acceptable. Avoid using plastic sheeting, because the paint will not adhere strongly to this and will quickly dry to a powdery dust which can be blown around the workshop and on to the painted area before it has dried. Large plastic (dustbin liner) bags are, however, ideal for quickly masking off wheels.

When the masking off is complete, damp down the floor. Clean the metal using a tack cloth, which will remove all traces of paint and filler dust, then finally use spirit wipe to remove any traces of oils or greases.

All types of paint have to be thinned before they can be sprayed. The paint manufacturers produce data sheets which will give the correct concentration for the paint being used. Stir then strain the primer before thinning it, because even 'new' paint can contain stringy lumps which clog the paint spray gun. An old stocking can be used to strain the paint. After adding the appropriate amount of thinner, stir the mixture well before pouring it into the spray gun. You can obtain special cups which you can use to gauge the paint/thinner solution viscosity by allowing a set amount to drain from a hole in the base of the cup and timing it, and one of these could prove worthwhile for checking the paint/thinner mixture, because the viscosity of the mixture will vary according to temperature. More experienced sprayers can judge viscosity by lifting the stirrer out of the paint and gauging how excess paint runs off. In the case of cellulose, aim to get the solution just weak enough for the paint to come off in droplets, rather than in a continuous flow.

You can now set the spray gun controls. There should be one for controlling the air flow and one for the paint needle. Set the output pressure from the compressor tank firstly to 30 psi, then open the paint and air controls fully on the spray gun. Make a rapid pass with the gun over a test surface. If large spots of paint can be seen, increase the air pressure at the tank in 5 psi increments until the rapid pass produces a suitably fine and even spray. Now adjust the spray gun air and paint controls until the correct sized pattern is achieved.

When using the spray gun, the technique is to keep the gun at a constant distance from the surface. Too close and the paint will go on so thickly that runs will develop immediately, too far away, and some of the paint will be air dry before it reaches the surface. Keeping the gun at a constant distance also gives a even spray band width. The gun should have a two-stage 'trigger pull', where stage one allows air to pass through and stage two opens the paint needle and allows paint into the airflow. The two stages can usually be felt through the trigger, and at the end of the first stage of travel there will be a discernible stop. Further movement of the trigger introduces the paint.

The technique which is preferred by the author is as follows. When making a pass over a panel, begin to one side of it and start moving the gun with the trigger at stage one, then press it fully home just before the edge of the panel is reached. Move the gun over the panel in a single, clean movement, and release the trigger back to the first stage when the far end of the panel is reached, to clear paint from the nozzle. Then repeat the exercise until the panel is covered.

Beware the 'dry edge'. This is when a band of sprayed paint is allowed to dry before the next band is applied. It could occur if, for instance, you were to begin in the middle of the roof panel and work your way outwards. By the time you came to spray the other half, the first paint to be applied would be thoroughly dry and a visible edge would result. Always begin spraying the roof at an edge, and do not spend too much time moving around the car when you have reached the middle.

When you have sprayed your first panel, allow it to dry and inspect it. You are looking especially for signs of contamination. Small dark spots surrounded by lighter circles of up to ¼ in. in diameter are caused by oil/water contamination from the compressor, and another oil and water filter will have to be placed in line. If the surface has paint runs then you could be moving the gun too slowly, the air pressure could be too high or the paint could be too thin. If the paint begins to wrinkle before it dries then the underlying surface is contaminated, and the primer will have to be removed completely and the surface properly cleaned.

Look closely for scratches, dents and hollows which are in the underlying surface but which the primer may highlight. The problem with matt primer paints is that they can make a rough surface look quite acceptable, even though the final gloss will make every little blemish stand out like a sore thumb. Filler-primers are high-build primers which can be used over areas with small scratches, and they place such a depth of paint on the surface that flatting off afterwards can remove many scratches.

The majority of people spray on primer, flat it off and then immediately spray on the topcoats. A friend of the author, Em Fryer, questions the wisdom of being in too much of a hurry to get the topcoats onto the primer. Like all paints, primer does not harden fully for some considerable time after it has been sprayed on and, in the case of cellulose, this usually takes two weeks. If you spray the topcoats onto the primer whilst it is still 'soft',

then the thinners will have a much more marked effect on the underlying primer than they do after the primer has hardened. This manifests itself as marks in the topcoat which show the outline of any bodyfiller used.

The author would recommend that primer is left to harden for two weeks before being flatted and covered by topcoats.

When it has hardened, the primer may be flatted down with very fine wet 'n dry. Small scratches in the surface which now become apparent may be filled using body stopper, which should be allowed to cure then primed. Not even the tiniest scratch should remain if the car is to be painted in cellulose, because this paint shrinks, and the final gloss will show every little flaw – however tiny – in the preparation. The author prefers to remove all masking materials and re-mask the car at this stage, because over-spray on the masking materials can enter the air as a fine dust which will contaminate the final finish. Before final masking-up, go over the primer with 1000 or 1200 grit to get the primer surface really smooth, then examine it minutely – this is the last chance you get to put any tiny defects right!

Clean the entire surface again, using a tack cloth to pick up any paint and filler dust which lies on the surface. The topcoat paint should be strained and thinned, then the surface should be given a last wipe over with spirit wipe before the first of the topcoats is applied, ensuring that there is enough thinner in the paint to allow it to flow by test spraying a piece of scrap hardboard or similar. The number of topcoats will vary according to the type of paint being used. With synthetic paint, two coats will be sufficient to give a good gloss. With cellulose, you could almost add as many coats as you wish although three coats should give sufficient depth. Each extra coat should be applied around twenty minutes after the preceding one with cellulose, to allow the thinners to evaporate. You can obtain slow or fast thinners for use in warmer or cooler conditions.

Remove the masking materials as soon as the paint has dried. If you remove them too soon then dry paint dust which is unsettled will land on the still wet surface of the paint. If you remove them too late then the paint could have cured to the point at which the paint which has settled on the masking material rips at the paint on the car.

The preferred order for spraying the car is to do the roof first, followed by the roof pillars on one side of the car, then the bonnet, followed by the other roof pillars and finally the sides, engine bay lid and valances. If the interior, engine bay and luggage compartment are also being sprayed, then it is best to complete these before starting on the outside of the car.

Car spraying is too vast a subject to be covered comprehensively in a book like this, and so the reader is

advised to seek out further reading material such as 'How To Restore Paintwork', published by Osprey Automotive. It is also worth seeking specialised advice from your paint supplier when you buy the paint.

The best advice for the person who is restoring just the one Beetle and who does not intend to make restoration into an on-going hobby is to have at least the final stages of preparation and the application of the topcoats carried out professionally. The costs of purchasing paint and reasonably competent equipment can by a wide margin exceed that of a reasonable quality professional respray, and the potential for things to go badly wrong for the first-time DIY car sprayer is immense. Even if you cut the overall outlay by hiring good equipment, you could still spend almost as much as a reasonable professional respray would cost, but with all the attendant risks of DIY.

Under the wings

The areas underneath the wings are subjected to flying mud and stones when the car is on the move, and so tougher coverings are usually favoured. Underseal can be applied by spray or brush, along with 'stone chip' and other tough paints which absorb some of the knocks and help keep rust at bay.

Still with the wings, the author favours primering these off the car and applying stone chip or similar protection to the inside before bolting them up, using small spacers to hold the wings just off the body. The primer is then flatted and the topcoats applied.

When the spraying has ended, careful examination of the car will usually reveal many small areas which have been missed, or perhaps small blemishes in areas which were not sprayed. These can be dealt with by brushing on paint. On the author's car, the bottoms of the A and B posts, the visible section of heater channel within the door step and various blemished areas on the doors were all hand-painted in this way.

Steel wheels may be stripped (usually they will have plenty of rusting which needs to be laboriously removed) and painted, using a variety of paints. Because the author was building a car to be used rather than for

ABOVE
The areas under the wings of Project were given several coats of paint – each in a different colour from the underlying one, so that complete coverage could be assured.

BELOW
The author busy flatting high-build primer. The sunglasses are a cunning disguise to stop anyone from recognising that it is him flatting without using a rubbing block.

show, he chose to remove loose rust and apply Smoothrite paint – white first as an 'undercoat' followed six weeks later (after this had fully cured) with silver. For show and custom cars, the wheels are best shot-blasted and sprayed with specialist paints, although the after-market offers a wide range of custom wheels which many will find preferable.

CHROMEWORK

A word of caution: some of the cheaper items of trim which are widely available can turn out to be very poorly made. Don't be surprised if your 'bargain' bumpers are ready-scratched and rusting, and don't be surprised if they are so poorly shaped that fitting them is at best a nightmare and at worst an impossibility. Anticipate finding that bolt holes are in the wrong positions and that extra holes must be drilled. If you can afford top quality trim, then buy it.

An alternative to buying cheap bumpers is to have your own re-chromed, but here again the quality achieved by some chrome plating companies is very poor. Find a company which is recommended by previous customers whose chromework has stood the test of time, and always deal with the actual company which carries out the work – some 'chrome plating specialists' turn out to be no more than agents.

Remove the bumper brackets from the bumpers, fit the brackets loosely to the car and then re-fit the bumpers – if you try to fit the whole assembly in one go, there is a strong chance that the brackets will scrape new paint from their mounting plates and from the apertures in the wings through which they fit, and you don't want the car to begin rusting before the restoration has finished! If you have new bumpers, then firstly drill holes in the front one for mounting the number plate. There is some degree of adjustment in the bumper bracket mounting holes, to allow careful placement; check that the bumpers are parallel to the ground and square to the bodywork before final tightening. If a bumper is not central when fitted (if it sticks out further one side than it does the other) check the mounts then the symmetry of the mounting holes in the bumpers. If no explanation can be found, then the problem could be that the two wings have different shapes!

The chrome strips along each side of the car and down the centre line of the bonnet simply clip onto their fastenings; if any seem loose, they can be gently pinched up with heavily padded mole grip jaws. If there is paint on these or other items of trim, wipe it off with a rag dampened with thinners, and allow the thinners to fully

199

These bumpers hailed from distant shores and were a real pain to fit. Firstly, a long bolt was run through them to close up the two inch or so gap between them and the mounting brackets, then a G-clamp was used to hold them there whilst the proper bolt was fitted.

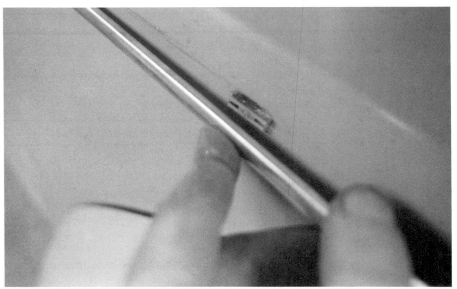

The chrome side strips simply clamp on to these nylon fixings; if the strip won't grip, give it a gentle squeeze with padded mole grips.

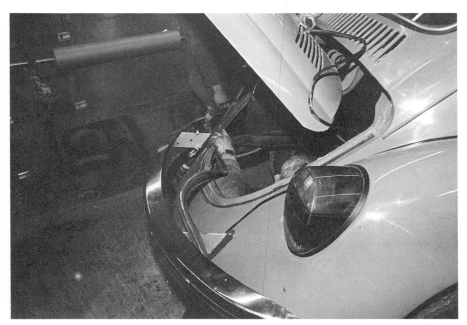

Fitting the engine bay seal is not fun. It is accomplished most easily by prising open one of the lips and closing it up with a hammer after the seal lips have been inserted into place.

evaporate before they are fitted. It is best to allow the paintwork to harden for at least a day or two and preferably for a fortnight before the chrome trim is fitted.

The longer you can leave the paintwork to harden before fitting the lights – especially the headlights – the better. If your car has replacement front wings then you might find fitting the headlight units difficult and only possible after the bowl rim has been gently re-shaped with a padded planishing hammer.

The engine lid seal can be fed into its retaining strip, using Swarfega as a lubricant if necessary – don't use washing up liquid as a lubricant, because this normally contains industrial salts! The luggage bay seal is more difficult to fit; push the three moulded rubber fixings per side into their holes and pull from below using long-nosed pliers until they are securely fastened – ensuring that the strip across the back is not twisted! Then ease the strip into its retainers, using a small (blunt) screwdriver and taking care not to puncture it. With both seals, leave plenty of slack at the corners so that the seal is able to lie flat, then trim off the surplus.

Before fitting the luggage compartment handle, ensure that the release cable is doing its job properly: if you close the bonnet without checking this, you could discover that the only way to open the lid is to grind away the handle! You will need to adjust the catch using a screwdriver and spanner so that the lid is gripped firmly but not so firmly that the release lever in the glove compartment cannot exert enough pressure to operate it! Start by screwing the catch fully downwards, then screw it back in stages until the lid is held firmly and the release lever operates without too much force being needed.

'BOXING UP'

This motor trade expression (which the author picked up from Terry Ball) basically describes putting the collection of largely trim components back into and onto the completed bodyshell, and it can be a time of great frustration or equally of joy, depending on whether you can remember where you placed each item for storage and how it fits!

Do remember that freshly-applied paint stays relatively soft for some time – and that it can easily be damaged until it hardens in perhaps two week's or so time. When you are leaning over the front wings and working in the luggage compartment, for instance, remove any sharp objects such as keys from your pockets to prevent damaging the paintwork; if you wear a belt, then be aware that the buckle could dent or scratch the paint surface. You can obtain specially made

padded protectors for wings to prevent this damage from occurring.

Although the restoration is almost at an end, don't rush boxing up. Apart from the risk of damaging paintwork, you could also risk damaging the items of trim.

Carefully examine every component which is to be fitted for signs of your own or previous over-spray. This can be removed with a rag wetted with thinners, mild cutting compound or, alternatively, it may be gently scraped off. A resprayed car looks so much better if all of the external chrome and rubber is free from paint that you cannot be too careful when cleaning these components. Pay especial attention to the chrome strips and badges, and to the wing beading.

CASE HISTORY – RVJ 403H ('Project')

This car was acquired as an MOT failure by Beetle Specialist Workshop on behalf of the author at a price of £200 (spring 1993). The obvious faults which had lead to the MOT failure included rotten heater channels, rotten rear body mount brackets and some rot in the floorpans; the rear bumper mountings and the bases of the A posts also required attention. The most attractive aspect of the car – a 1970 1500cc – was that it had not previously seen major structural repair. This is unusual, and indicates that the car has spent much of its life garaged.

Like many Beetle owners, the author decided that RVJ 403H was too formal a title for his own car and, after considering 'Harvey Jay' (RVJ), he named it 'Project'.

Most Beetles of 23 years of age will have either been re-panelled or, more usually(!), extensively plated. Project had some bodyfiller, including one huge lump of the stuff which had been reinforced with chicken wire, around the heelboard – but no evidence of welded repairs whatsoever. Major welded repairs to a car which has not been previously welded are always easier than to a car which has. I have seen no less than seven layers of patches (each overlapping the underlying patch) welded into a Beetle wheelarch, and dealing with this particular car had taken a very experienced restorer several times as long to deal with as Project.

The object of the exercise was to combine elements of professional and DIY restoration in order to create a strong and sound car which would not require major attention for many years – but at a budget price. Cost-cutting meant restricting the extent of the professional

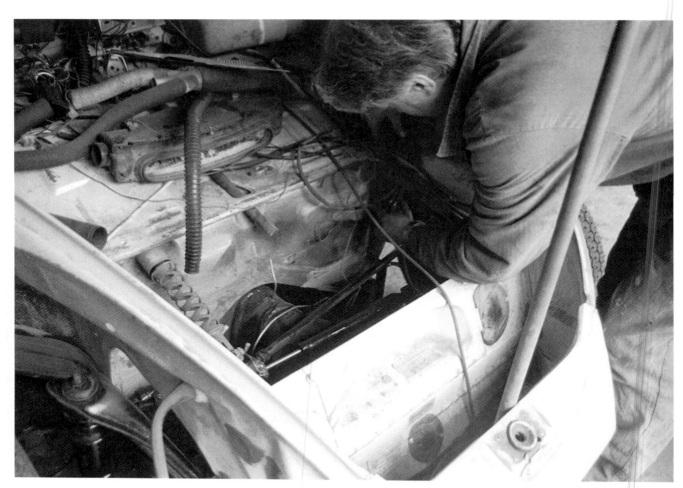

ABOVE LEFT
Boxing up commences. For an experienced pro like Terry, this takes no time at all; expect to spend many happy hours wondering which bit goes where on your own car.

BELOW LEFT
'Project' poses for a 'before' photograph. The car looks a little rough around the edges but its appearance belies the rot which has infested the heater channels and rear body mounting areas. The latter appeared quite sound until the mud had been scraped off.

RIGHT
The jacking point on 'Project' is thoroughly rotted. Being made of heavier section steel than the adjacent heater channel/sill assembly, it does not take much imagination to visualise what sort of state the latter will be in!

BELOW
While the bodyshell is off the chassis, it has been wheeled out of the way on a pair of trolleys – if you can obtain or build some – do. They're invaluable.

ABOVE
Terry applying the chassis black. If you decide to roll the chassis over in this manner, do firstly drain the transaxle oil and get someone to help with the lifting.

OPPOSITE ABOVE
Raising the bodyshell onto plastic milk crates with steel poles brings many parts of the body to a more comfortable working height and allows the chassis to be wheeled in and out from underneath. This may look precarious but the bodyshell sans floorpan is not too heavy.

LEFT
With the chassis rolled onto its side, the author applies plenty of seam sealer before chassis black is sprayed on. The rust-proofing consisted of weld-through spray to protect the overlapping part of the joint, Bonda-Prima followed by seam sealer to protect the underside, and chassis black on top of the lot. Hopefully, that little lot should keep Mister Rust at bay for years.

FAR LEFT
The top of the welded seam between the chassis spine and the floorpan edges was treated with Bonda Prima.

work to unavoidable and heavy (the author suffers from back problems) tasks such as bodyshell-off work, but carrying out the less important but time-consuming work on a DIY basis. Further cost reductions were made by buying as many spares second-hand as possible (seats etc.), and by utilising various components which the author happened to possess, including an old set of seat belts from an MG Midget and a battery from a Mini!

It was decided that the serious rot (which required the body to be lifted off the chassis assembly) should be dealt with by BSW, and the mechanical and cosmetic aspects of the restoration would be undertaken by the author at home. This arrangement is especially worthwhile for anyone working on a tight budget, because it ensures that the important structural work is carried out to the highest standards (so that the car is strong and will not require similar attention for many years), and it allows the remaining build-up to progress as and when funds allow. If you don't set a tight time-scale for the rebuild, then it is surprising how many necessary spares can be acquired either as special offers or second-hand at low prices from VW shows, through classified advertisements or even by buying an MOT failure car with good mechanicals, and so on.

ABOVE
After cleaning and de-greasing the floorpan tops, Terry sprays on chassis black, which will hopefully keep rust at bay for many years.

LEFT
Last job before the bodyshell is lowered back onto the chassis is to fit the 'Z' bar.

ABOVE RIGHT
Project has been fitted with a cut down quarter panel base repair section; Terry is welding on a plate with captive nuts for wing mounting.

BELOW RIGHT
The rot was severe but thankfully not too extensive in the heelboard/inner wing area on the nearside.

The workshop time needed to carry out all structural welding plus mechanical and boxing up work to MOT standard was estimated at eighty hours. The author booked forty hours' workshop time, which was estimated as the minimum time scale to complete the body-off structural welding and reassemble the car to a driveable state.

With the major work by BSW completed, the car was trailered home to the author's garage for painting and boxing up. As with his previous restorations, the author chose cellulose paint, not only for its relative ease of use but also because it looks right on a car of this vintage.

Two small welded repairs had to be carried out; the base of the flitch panel was rusted thin and was pulling out from under the A post lip, and the nearside door had an area in the centre which had rusted thin and which was therefore covered in perforations. The flitch repair was made up easily from sheet steel, folded and welded in without mishap before being 'tinned', lead loaded and finally flushed over with bodyfiller. The door repair was more problematical.

When a large, flexible panel such as a door skin is welded, the heat generated is liable to cause the panel to buckle – and this proved to be the case. After a rectangular hole had been cut from the panel with an angle grinder, a replacement piece was butt welded in, using the MiG welded at its gentlest setting. With the job completed, a concave dent was apparent in the centre of the panel. This was expected, but what was not anticipated was the fact that when the dent was pushed back out, several new and smaller dents appeared elsewhere in the door skin.

The author beat the skin flat as best he could, then used copious amounts of filler to achieve a fair surface, the idea being to acquire a replacement door at one of the 1993 Beetle shows or perhaps to obtain and fit a new skin at a later date.

All areas to be sprayed were taken back to bare metal or sound paint, then treated to two coats of high-build filler-primer. The feathered edges of surrounding paintwork in some instances immediately blistered, indicating one of two things. Either the paint itself was contaminated (possibly with silicones) or – more probably – at some stage the car had been given a barrier coat to isolate the existing paintwork from the new. Barrier coats might typically be used on synthetic-painted surfaces which have been flatted prior to respraying in cellulose, and they keep the powerful cellulose thinners away from the underlying paint. The blistered areas were allowed to harden and then flatted back, then given a barrier coat – neat Tractol proved ideal – before further (successful) applications of high build primer.

The primer was allowed to harden and then flatted

back to give the topcoats something to grip, then the topcoats were applied.

During the spraying, the usual problems of using too small a compressor and hence getting air-dry spray were encountered. The final coat sprayed on was almost pure thinners, which encouraged the surface of the existing paint to 'flow' and gave a better finish. Two weeks after the paintwork was completed, it was cut back to reveal fundamental flaws.

The roof section paintwork – apart from a few dents and scratches – was found to be thick enough to merely flat with 1000 grit, cut and polish, and the engine lid, much of the sides of the car and luggage compartment were similarly dealt with. However, in treating those few small dents and scratches, disaster struck.

At some time, the original topcoat of the car had been over-painted with a bright blue paint of unidentified type. On top of this were further layers of cellulose. In the course of sanding down the small repair areas, the author revealed small areas of said blue paint which, when covered with further cellulose, caused an immediate reaction which lifted the cellulose from the surface in a large bubble. In other areas where the blue paint had not been revealed the same thing happened, presumably because either tiny scratches from the flatting down had reached the paint, because the paint had contaminated the existing topcoat or because the cellulose thinners used softened the very thin layer of cellulose paint and permeated through to the aforesaid bright blue paint.

Various types of paint which happened to be lying around the workshop were tried as barriers, and eventually the author resorted to neat Tractol. This was sprayed over the problem areas, but caused yet further problems.

The author's spray gun was spitting – giving small areas of overspray which the author did not attach any significance to. However, when the topcoat had been applied and left for two weeks to harden, initial cutting immediately revealed thousands of tiny red spots in the new surface. Tractol doesn't shrink as much as cellulose when it dries (especially when used neat), and so each tiny spot lay just under the surface of the topcoat, ready to break through the moment cutting compound was wiped over it. The cellulose had to be flatted properly and another coat applied.

Flatting the cellulose revealed more areas of the bright blue paint which reacted so badly when top-coated – too widespread to be treated individually as before. One possible though drastic solution would have been to take the whole roof back to bare metal and begin again, but this would have still left the problem of the blue paint at the edges – no matter where these were. The chosen solution was to order a proper barrier paint

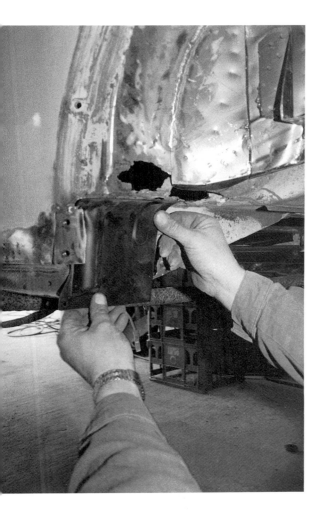

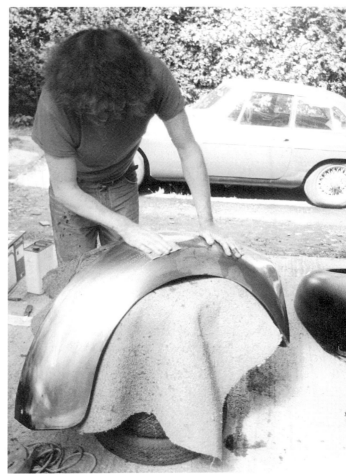

ABOVE LEFT

With everything cleaned back to bright metal, Terry offers the sill closing panel. The hole above it in the inner wing is in a non-structural area and will be patched.

ABOVE RIGHT

Numerous substances — mainly elbow grease — and methods were utilised to remove the black primer from the new wings. This is wet 'n dry which the author is using wet far too close to that extension lead! The sticking plaster on his left hand is testimony both to the sharp edges one finds on repair and replacement panels, and the author's foolish reluctance to wear stout leather gloves.

ABOVE

Paint contamination, probably caused when rubbing down exposed a layer of incompatible paint which reacted with the cellulose. Eventually, proper barrier paint was applied to these and other areas.

REACTION CAN OCCUR WHERE PROBLEM PAINT IS EXPOSED

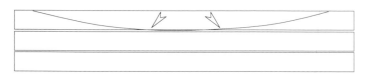

THINNERS CAN SOFTEN TOP COAT AND REACT WITH UNDERLYING PAINTWORK

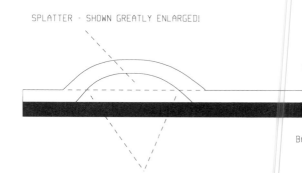

SPLATTER - SHOWN GREATLY ENLARGED!

WHEN THE TOPCOAT IS CUT BACK, A SMALL CIRCLE OF PAINT APPEARS

ABOVE LEFT
Reaction with existing paintwork need not only involve that which lies on the surface. Rubbing down can expose problem paints, and cellulose thinners can work their way down to get at it!

ABOVE
Tractol worked as a barrier coat, but splatter resulted in tiny dots of paint which did not shrink like cellulose and broke through the surface of the topcoat when it was flatted.

BELOW
Like those at the front, the rear wheel arches were given plenty of paint protection.

RIGHT
Stone chip on the front of the bonnet not only guards against flying stones, but in this case it also helped hide minor damage to the front of the bonnet!

BELOW
After masking, the inner wing has been sprayed with stone chip. The door and quarter panel have been sprayed with high-build primer. This should if possible be left for two weeks before flatting and top-coating.

(Bar Coat) from local suppliers Bancrofts, to cover the entire roof with this, then to apply two coats of filler-primer and finally to topcoat it.

A protracted bout of stormy weather then put a stop to work before the pre-paint preparations were complete. When a suitable day eventually dawned, the author was in such a bad state of mind that he failed to properly flat some areas and was rewarded with some very uneven areas around the bases of the quarter panels which were all too obvious when the topcoats had been applied.

The front valance and luggage lid were blessed with lavish applications of filler where a frontal collision had left small dents. The dents were beaten out and the bare metal sprayed – the results weren't bad, and far better, in fact, than when the filler had been in position! The lower portion of the bonnet was treated to two coats of stone chip – a paint which goes on thick and sets hard so that stone chips don't go through to the metal. This was top-coated along with the rest of the bonnet.

A gentle cutting of the dashboard paint did wonders for car's interior.

Boxing up

With the spraying finally finished, the author then spent a couple of days going over the interior and exterior paintwork, cutting back or touching up all of the blemishes in the existing paintwork. Areas which would be tricky to mask off for spraying, such as the bottoms of the A posts and visible portion of the heater channel within the doorstep, were brush painted. When you brush on cellulose, put on enough thicknesses so that you can cut back to give a nice, even surface after the paint has hardened. The author also took the opportunity to clean all external trim items before they were re-fitted to the car.

The rear wing beading proved a nightmare to fit, because the only available beading was intended for a front wing! Some tailoring with a pair of scissors was necessary so that the wing bolts aligned with the cut-aways in the beading, but even so, the job was only completed after two or three attempts. The author is not possessed of particularly great patience, and knows full well that if his efforts to do something are frustrated for any length of time, a loss of temper shortly follows, which in turn leads to damaged components. The solution is to walk away and leave it.

The author had a spare battery which unfortunately was the wrong shape to be gripped by the standard

fittings and, after some deliberation, an extension for the clamp was fabricated which held the battery very firmly. The alternatives, which included welding another length of threaded rod to the floorpan to bring the existing clamp closer to the battery, were ruled out because they would have had to be ground away when the author could afford to buy the correct battery!

With Project resplendent in its L50B Diamond Blue paint, the rusted old bumpers looked very out of place, and so new bumpers as well as running boards were ordered, along with black and silver pressed alloy number plates which were appropriate for a car of this age. Again, the new components made other fittings look decidedly tatty, and so new screen rubbers front and back were acquired and fitted.

The author foolishly decided to economise when buying bumpers, and settled for a cheap imported variety. These came ready rusted and with chrome which looked as though it would not see a full year before it started to blister. Worse, when offered up to the brackets (which were loosely bolted in place on the car) only two bolt holes were anywhere near their respective holes in the brackets. The two centre holes were just under two inches away from the bracket, and had to be pulled in with long bolts, clamped with a G clamp, only then could the standard bolts be fitted. The strain which pulling the bumper into shape placed on the brackets was immense and, if the author had fastened the brackets to the bumpers before fastening them to the car, they could not have been forced into the wing slots.

Cheap running boards were also acquired, and proved every bit as unsatisfactory as the bumpers. The main problem was the bolt slots which, on one side of the car, were over half an inch away from where they should have been, necessitating the enlarging of the slots to a ridiculous degree before the boards could fit.

The fuel gauge was not functioning. The first check was to earth the tank terminal via a 6W bulb then directly, to no avail, showing that the gauge itself was the problem. A replacement speedometer – for 1970 cars the fuel gauge is an integral part of this although the fuel gauge is separate on most earlier cars – was sought.

Eventually, it was all down to the MOT preparation work. This involved setting up the handbrake, checking all electrical equipment, windscreen wipers and washers, and so on. When you have successfully prepared a car for the MOT a few times, the work is a breeze. You obviously cannot test the brakes properly without a set of rollers, but if you jack up each wheel in turn, get an accomplice to apply the brakes and use your 36 mm socket and extension bar to try and turn the lifted wheel, you'll get a pretty fair idea of how effective the brakes actually are!

The evening prior to the actual MOT test, the nearside sidelight refused to work. The lamp unit was removed and the problem revealed as worn spring contacts. Unfortunately, in trying to re-shape the contacts, the author inadvertently touched them together, which blew the fuse. It is strange how, when you're under pressure, you can overlook the most obvious cause of a fault and try to find a cause elsewhere. So the author did not even stop to consider whether a blown fuse might be the culprit, and started tracing the feed wire back, testing with a lamp to see whether he could find power. Then he noticed that the rear light had also stopped working and, after stripping and reassembling the unit, remembered that the sidelight circuit was fused. The 16 amp fuse was replaced, and Project again had sidelights. However, the brake lights now refused to illuminate. This time, the author began tracing the fault by looking at the fuse, which had blown. The neighbour who had come to the rescue with the 16 amp lights fuse now kindly supplied two 8 amp fuses, the first of which popped as the author re-tested the brake lights. Because the rear lamp cluster had been removed and replaced, the author began by looking here, and discovered that, on replacement, the spade end connector of the stop lamp feed wire had touched and managed to scratch the paint on the wing, causing a direct short to earth. The cure was to bend the tab and to insulate the spade connector, after which it was all systems go for the MOT test the following morning. The 'fairytale end' to this restoration was an MOT pass at the first attempt.

As with any 'new' classic car, the author gave Project a number of local 'shakedown' runs to find out what problems might be looming and find any existing ones which had not yet come to light. The car had a tendency to jump out of first gear on the over-run (initially suspected to be due to a worn selector mechanism, but later traced to a wrongly located gearshift lever base plate) and there was a transmission whine in fourth gear. Taken together, the two problems hinted at a gearbox stripdown or exchange. A slow oil leak became apparent as a black patch on the garage floor; this was traced to a leaking rocker tube seal. When changing down from third gear into reverse – embarrassingly right outside the local garage – the author discovered that the gearshift plate was not correctly situated, and the plate was moved to save further embarrassment!

Project had its perfect public debut at the 1993 British Volkswagen Festival (highly recommended) – an annual event which happily occurs within ten miles of the author's home, so that the journey there and back amounted to little more than another shakedown run!

The author had moved to Project from a 1966 MGB

LEFT
Because the resultant holes were so large, the author made up rectangular washers to spread the load.

RIGHT
The author fitting the footwell side carpets. After abortive attempts with ordinary glue, he opted for impact adhesive.

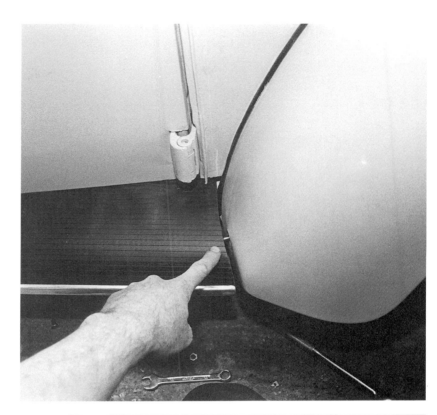

LEFT
The cheap running boards had mounting holes so far out of alignment that drastic surgery was needed to get them anywhere near.

RIGHT
Getting the gaps at either end of the running boards was not easy.

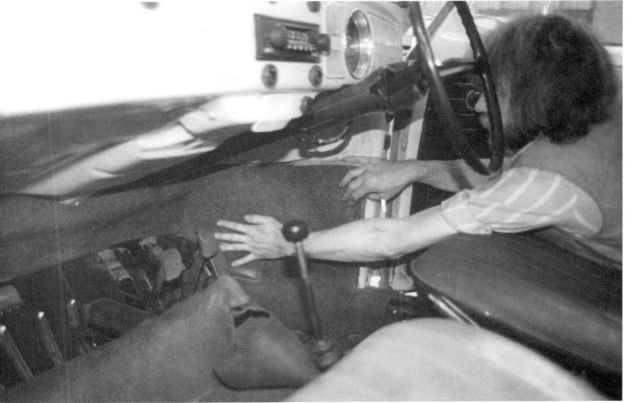

LEFT
The result of all that hard work. Appropriate black and silver number plates and black wing beading make a Beetle look much sharper.

BELOW
Project's engine. Hardly show standard, but nicely clean and business-like.

GT, a veritable old war-horse of a sports car which can still show the young colts a thing or two on the open road, and proceeded to drive Project at much the same speeds. Despite this fairly harsh treatment, Project regularly returned between 30 and 31 miles to the gallon (87 kpl), and went and still goes like a little rocket.

Project is now in daily use. The car is far from perfect – perfect cars attract vandals and thieves and anyway the author's natural preference is for comfortable rather than concourse. Future projects include transaxle removal and overhaul, plus perhaps a few tasteful minor modifications. However, because a 1970 1500cc Beetle is to be considered quite a desirable classic car in standard trim, the car may well remain stock.

You may see Project at one of the UK Beetle shows – not cosseted on a roped-off trade stand bathed in artificial light, or polished and preened and placed out in the concourse showring – but out in the public car park away from the neon and glitter alongside all the other cherished Beetles. The author is the scruffy one and has a taste for strong lager.

PROFESSIONAL RESTORERS

Just as in any other trade or calling, there are both good and bad Beetle restorers, ranging from deservedly highly reputable companies to the worst examples of back-street cowboy bodyshops. It can be difficult for the newcomer to tell which end of the Beetle restorer spectrum he or she is dealing with; the worst restorers are often the most talented bodyfiller sculptors, and a car restored by such a business might look good for a year or two before rust spreads underneath the layers of filler with the inevitable result that the filler drops out!

The best way to judge a restoration business is by inspecting cars restored by the business, but cars which were restored two, three or more years previously. The best place to see a selection of cars which have been restored by different businesses is at one of the many Beetle summer shows.

Few owners of top-quality professionally restored Beetles will be able to resist showing their cars off to you if you take an interest, and few aggrieved owners of badly restored cars will be slow in naming the company which bodged their car. Most Beetles are by now quite old enough to have had some body repair or restoration work carried out and, if you attend one of the larger shows which can attract thousands of visitors and their Beetles, you have a wealth of experience – good and bad – to draw upon!

The author always recommends that you begin your search for a restorer reasonably close to home, so that you can keep in touch with the workshop staff as the restoration progresses and perhaps call in once or twice to ensure everything is flowing smoothly and that your car is actually being worked on. The second rule in choosing a restorer is to only consider Beetle specialists; general restorers – however good – might not be familiar with the Beetle spares scene. They could waste countless hours making up replacement panels which are readily available or waste a lot of your money by buying over-priced components for which far cheaper sources are to be found.

Don't expect to take up too much of the restorer's time. Do remember that all car restorers are plagued by the occasional time-waster who overstays his welcome, asking question after question, requesting endless estimates but never actually getting around to commissioning the work.

Don't turn up to view a restoration business without an appointment, because you won't be made very welcome! However, arriving an hour or so before the appointed time might allow you to see the workshop in its natural state before it is readied for your inspection; if you see huge tins of bodyfiller lying around, new panels being welded on top of rusted metal or being stored in damp conditions then draw your own conclusions!

Look at the tools used by the business; poor quality sockets or spanners, for instance, will probably 'round' nuts and cheap damaged screwdrivers will distort screw heads! Try to judge whether there is any semblance of order in the workshop; if tools are strewn about the place then the restorer could spend almost as much time trying to find lost tools as in restoring the car!

You then have to discuss with the restorer exactly what work you wish to be carried out, and it is as well to be armed with a list of jobs which you know to be necessary. Some rogues will happily underestimate the amount of work which will have to be carried out in order to present you with an attractively low-priced estimate (the final bill, of course, will be far higher); others might try to take advantage of you and include work which is not really necessary.

Make certain that both you and the restorer are absolutely clear about the results you expect. If you want absolutely flawless paintwork, for instance, then emphasise the fact, because the pre-paint preparation will take far longer (at an obviously increased cost) than for a standard respray, and final examination, cutting and so on will also take much more of the restorer's time.

The restorer will examine your Beetle, and draw up an estimate for the work; this should list all components and consumables to be used, and detail labour charges. You won't get the estimate there and then (if you are given an estimate on your first visit then it's obviously not going to be very accurate), but the restorer will usually post it to you within the week.

Obtain at least two or three estimates before commissioning any work, just to give you a comparison. Unduly high or low estimates should be treated with some degree of caution; there could be a perfectly reasonable explanation why the estimate is so far from the norm, but the chances are that the business is either charging top whack or underestimating in order to secure the business. If one estimate is markedly higher than the average, it is worth discussing why this should be so with the restorer; it could turn out that the estimate is purposely on the high side to cover unforeseen extra work and, if the job is completed ahead of time then the restorer could present you with a far smaller final bill!

Check the prices quoted for components; you might be able to shop around and acquire these more cheaply to save money. If the estimate from your chosen restorer is still beyond your means, ask whether you can carry out part of the preparation work (initial strip-down, etc.) at home and deliver the bodyshell/chassis on a trailer.

Good restoration companies are always in demand and might not be able to start work on your car for some time because the workshop is booked up for months in advance; if a restorer can take your car at short notice then be wary unless a plausible explanation such as a cancelled restoration (this does happen) can be proven.

Payment usually consists of a non-returnable deposit (on commission of the restoration rather than on its commencement) followed sometimes by progress payments and sometimes by just one bill on completion. The deposit should not exceed 10 per cent or so of the estimate (if an unduly large deposit is requested then there is always a chance that the business is about to go bankrupt and is trying to raise cash by whatever means), and progress payments, if requested, will usually be a third payment when a third of the work has been completed, and so on.

The deposit should be used by the restorer to buy in components and materials for the restoration, and progress payments should also be used for this purpose. If a large deposit or progress payment is demanded, check that it does not exceed the costs of materials used.

Many DIY restorations end up at the premises of professional restorers for finishing, for a variety of reasons. Not all restorers will be happy to 'pick up the pieces' of a failed or terminated DIY restoration, and the prices quoted will usually reflect this. From experience, restorers know that putting right someone else's mistakes always takes longer than doing the job correctly in the first place, so you must expect to have to pay a fair price.

Project ready to set out on another adventure.

6 · MODIFICATIONS

This book is concerned primarily with restoration, and this chapter is no more than an introduction to various modifications, describing many popular modifications but not how they are carried out.

There are several excellent works on Beetle modifications, some limited to a single aspect such as engine performance mods and others, such as Keith Seume's Beetle Custom Handbook, which covers all aspects of the subject, and the author recommends that these are consulted before any modifications covered here are implemented on the reader's own car. It is also strongly recommended that professional advice is sought at all stages during the planning and implementation of any modification because, as any motor insurer will confirm, a modified car is potentially a more dangerous car – not just because it goes faster or is used in hostile terrain, but because much of the work which is carried out is ill-advised and some to a poor standard.

On the subject of motor insurers, it is essential that you inform your own insurer of any material alterations made to your own car. It is unfortunate that any mention of suspension, braking, bodywork or engine/carburation modifications will usually result in a sharp rise in premium prices or even a flat refusal to insure you and the vehicle. Some may be tempted not to disclose modifications.

If you fail to disclose modifications and are subsequently involved in any accident which requires the insurers' agents to inspect your car (and discover your mods) then they will deem the policy null and void – you will not have been insured. With legal costs being sky-high, and the unprecedented size of compensations for motor accident victims being awarded today, you could find yourself liable for hundreds of thousands of pounds. Insurers need no motivation other than getting out of having to pay the amount themselves to go over your car with a fine tooth-comb to try and discover any undisclosed mods and void your cover. Honesty is the *only* sensible policy.

ENGINE MODIFICATIONS

The flat four engine of the Beetle must be one of the most modified engines of all time and, because many of the leading lights in the field of boxer motor modification were and still are based in the United States, the various modifications tend to follow American thinking and be far more radical than those of UK enthusiasts and performance preparation businesses.

Whereas in the UK most performance modifications tend to be fairly conservative efforts involving blueprinting ports to manifolds, fitting up-rated cylinder heads and the like, in America the 'you can't beat cubes' philosophy finds people fitting much larger capacity engines, bolting turbochargers and superchargers onto the VW lump to produce power in the order of 150–200 bhp.

Most ordinary road-going examples of the Beetle could gain a small but worthwhile power increase simply by being set up properly, so that they run at their most efficient. Any MOT testing station in the UK must by law posses an exhaust gas analyser, which shows how well an engine burns fuel. With this equipment, the carburation can be set very accurately so that the engine uses fuel efficiently and, coupled with setting the timing, you may be rewarded by both a slight power increase and better fuel consumption.

The simplest power increases come from allowing the engine to breathe more easily, by fitting a better air filter(s) and exhaust, or perhaps swapping the existing fuel delivery for a twin-carb set-up, which entails obtaining not only the carburettors but also two new inlet manifolds. Fitting a pair of twin downdraught carburettors (with two separate inlet manifolds) means that the fuel supply to each cylinder can be adjusted separately and that the fuel mixture can be delivered in more accurate quantities.

More substantial power increases can be obtained in one of two basic methods. You can fit a host of special components (more on these later) to get more from your existing engine, but the sensible way to go about things is to fit a larger capacity engine.

When an engine is highly tuned, it usually has to have a faster tickover, it is usually far less tractable and the car less pleasant to drive in ordinary conditions. Power is increased, but the usable rev band is reduced, so that the low-down torque of the flat four which is an essential part of the character of the Beetle can be lost. Furthermore, wear of engine components is usually increased and reliability decreased. By opting for a larger capacity unit in standard or only slightly modified trim, you retain the character of the car, the reliability and driving experience, but have a useful gain not only in power but also in torque.

Larger capacity engines can be obtained by exchange (which gives the benefit of an overhauled bottom end), from a breaker's yard or through outright purchase. Alternatively, you can strip your own engine and install new cylinders and pistons, which gives you the (recommended) option of overhauling the complete engine at the same time.

If money is no object then you could consider fitting an engine from another manufacturer, of which the most obvious is a flat six Porsche. In the UK, all Porsche cars (including the 924 which is a thoroughly competent and desirable road car but not by any stretch of the imagination a supercar in the manner of the hotter 911s and 944s etc.) suffer from being banded into the very highest insurance risk grouping. Expect to have to pay through the nose for motor insurance if you fit such an engine!

Not only German cars have boxer motors; Alfa Romeos (notably the AlfaSud) and Subaru cars also utilise the flat four, albeit in water cooled form. Kits are available from specialist dealers to fit these and other liquid cooled engines to the VW transaxle. The most obvious obstacles are gaining sufficient clearance within the engine bay and finding somewhere to fit a radiator! The specialists in this field are Laser Cars Ltd. (Tel. 0256 895188 – address at rear of book), who produce (and recommend) the AlfaSud conversion kit, plus kits for Ford OHC, CVH, Essex 3 litre and V6 (2.3 and 2.8 litre), the highly regarded Fiat Twin Cam, the VW Golf and the Rover V8! Apart from the AlfaSud, all of these conversions require that bodywork modifications are made to the rear of the car in order to accommodate the engines. Consult Laser Cars for full details.

The other route to more power is the use of performance components: high lift camshafts, ported or large valve cylinder heads, lightened flywheels and the like. Such components usually perform one of two basic functions; either they move more mixture into and out of the cylinders or they strengthen the engine to take the extra forces generated in an uprated engine. The various

components should be carefully selected only after seeking professional advice from a performance engine preparation company, so that they complement each other. The science of building performance engines is such a complicated business that it is outside the scope of a book primarily concerned with aspects of restoration.

There are some excellent books available on the subject of Beetle engine tuning and modification; the author strongly recommends that anyone who wishes to obtain more than a modest power increase from their existing engine studies these works. In addition, it is well worth following any advice offered by the suppliers of uprated engine/carburation component suppliers. If you obtain all of the components from a single supplier then you have the opportunity to ask the supplier to ensure that those components are all fully compatible and will work to their most efficient in the combination supplied. If you were to alternatively buy a camshaft from one supplier, pistons from another and uprated cylinder heads from a third supplier, you have no way of knowing whether the components will complement or fight against each other.

Best of all, consult a performance engine preparation company which will have engineering facilities and a rolling road on which they can properly set up engines to give their best.

SUSPENSION MODIFICATIONS

It seems that playing around with ride height is synonymous with the Beetle – some owners lower the ride height of their cars for enhanced cornering performance on the asphalt, whilst others take the opposite route and raise the ride height to gain precious extra ground clearance for off-road use.

There are two types of Beetle suspension; the earlier cars were all fitted with a torsion bar front end and swing axles at the rear, whilst later cars have McPherson struts at the front and independent semi-trailing arms at the back.

As already described earlier in this book, swing axle rear suspension does have a drawback – namely, positive camber of the rear wheels which can suddenly increase as the rear of the car 'jacks' itself up on hard cornering and throws the vehicle into massive oversteer (in other words, the start of a spin!). Another drawback applies to off-roaders, because when they raise the ride height of the car to increase ground clearance, they increase the positive camber of the rear wheels. The solution is to convert the car to the trailing arm rear suspension.

Meet the Giraffe. This was in a former life a competition trials car which was fitted with a GRP convertible Baja style body and many mechanical modifications such as reduction boxes on the axle shafts by BSW, and then resumed trialling.

Before describing the conversion, it must be stated that it need only be considered by owners who intend to either drive at high speed off the public highway (competition driving on tarmac) or who intend to raise the ride height substantially in the case of off-roaders. For standard road cars which are not driven by suicidal maniacs, the swing arm rear suspension is fine! It is further recommended that the work is carried out by an experienced professional, because the slightest error can turn your car into a death trap.

The most common 'donor' of necessary components for the modification is a Type 3 – the Variant. This car does not enjoy quite the classic status of the standard Beetle and is much more likely to be scrapped for spares rather than repaired. Basically, the job entails very carefully cutting the trailing arm brackets from the Type 3, and welding them to your own car. Diagonal arms, hub assemblies and of course double jointed drive shafts must also be obtained. The positioning of the trailing arm brackets on the torsion tube and the engine/transaxle mounting arms must be precise and, for this reason, it is strongly recommended that the work is entrusted to a professional who has previous experience of the conversion. Because the conversion is most often carried out to competitions trials cars, those who compete in this sport with Beetles should be able to recommend a workshop to undertake the conversion on your own car. Even better, seek a professional restorer who takes part in off-road trials and who will have carried out the conversion many times on his fellow competitors' cars. Terry Ball at BSW is a successful trials driver and an accomplished swing axle to diagonal arm converter.

Lowering the suspension

That lowered Beetles have better road holding and handling is generally true. The desirability of lowering your own car is counterbalanced with the costs involved (including increased insurance premiums), the dangers of upsetting the suspension geometry and, of course, the problems of reduced ground clearance.

At the rear end, lowering simply involves re-positioning the spring plates on the torsion bar ends or moving the torsion bar inner end (as described in Chapter Four). Alternatively, adjustable devices can be fitted which allow you to alter the ground clearance; these may be preferable, as they allow you to set the clearance to suit specific conditions. Do check (this applies equally to the front of the car) that the dampers' range of travel is still sufficient to accommodate the full suspension travel.

The solution at the front for torsion bar cars (with McPherson Struts simply fit the appropriate springs) is to fit adjustable lowering devices, which are welded into position. The drawbacks are that the track rod angles are altered (which increases bump steer), that the castor is altered, which makes the car feel very twitchy and, as in the case of rear end lowering, that the dampers may have to be replaced because they cannot accommodate the new range of suspension movement.

Bump steer is caused when a suspension is compressed or extended to the extent that the angle of the steering track rods is altered substantially. This lessens or increases the horizontal distance between the steering box or rack and the steering arm attached to the wheel, causing the wheel to toe out or in – so steering the car and, of course, lessening grip because the tyres are fighting each other. Special kits of components are available to upturn the track rod ends and so counteract this effect.

The reduction in castor angle (the angle between the hub assembly and the vertical) caused by lowering the front end greatly reduces the self-steering effect (the natural inclination of the steering to return to dead-ahead following a corner). It makes the car react markedly to slight movement of the steering wheel and hence gives the car that twitchy feel. The solution is to fit widely available castor shims between the lower beam and the chassis frame head.

Raising the suspension

It is common practice to raise the ride height of Baja conversions, although on cars which are to be used predominantly on the road, the best solution is to fit adjusters, because the high centre of gravity of a raised Beetle compounds all known handling and road holding deficiencies! Alternatively, the ride height can be altered less drastically by careful choice of wheels and tyres. As with lowering, the author recommends that specialist manuals detailing the work are consulted and that professional advice is sought.

Wider wheels and tyres

There is a great temptation when looking for that 'road-hungry' Cal look to fit extra wide wheels and tyres. Whilst these increase road grip, they do have drawbacks (in addition to being more expensive). Firstly, steering effort – especially at low speeds – will be increased. Secondly, wider wheels and tyres will place greater strain on the wheel bearings and to a lesser extent on the entire steering and suspension system, necessitating more frequent examination and replacement of the wheel bearings. Lastly, before fitting wider wheels (and the same applies to wheel spacers which increase wheeltrack) do check that the tyres will not foul any part of the bodywork or suspension, both at full lock in either direction and at all points of suspension travel. Wider wings will normally have to be fitted.

Before using a car with modified suspension on the road the author recommends that the suspension is checked out by a professional, to ensure that you have not inadvertently altered some vital characteristic of the geometry.

OTHER MODIFICATIONS

Unlike cars with liquid cooled engines, engine temperature gauges are not fitted to the Beetle. However, the oil in the Beetle engine passes through a cooler radiator hidden away in the fan shroud and plays the same role in cooling the engine as does the liquid coolant in other cars. An oil temperature gauge shows any rise in oil temperature which could be caused by a number of faults – some of which can quickly prove terminal for the engine if you continue to run it in that state.

Two types of after-market oil temperature gauge are available; some fit in place of the engine oil drain plug and others in place of the dipstick. The latter gives the more accurate reading, because the bottom of the crankcase is where cooler oil falls, whereas the dipstick hole mounted model registers the temperature of hotter oil higher up in the crankcase. Also worthwhile is an oil pressure gauge; this can warn you of drops in oil pressure as soon as they commence – the alternative is to rely on the low oil pressure warning lamp, but by the time this registers a drop in oil pressure, the engine could be suffering the consequences. Both oil temperature and oil pressure gauges come with fitting instructions. If in doubt, get an auto electrician to carry out the work.

Whilst on the subject of engine cooling, some people are tempted to remove the two flaps in the fan housing which cut cool air supply to the cylinder fins when the engine is cold, along with the thermostat and linkages. Firstly, *never* disconnect the thermostat alone, because if you do so then the flaps will remain permanently closed in the engine will overheat – when this happens, seizure is not far away!

Temper any desire to remove the cooling flaps with the thought that engine wear is at its greatest (in normal day to day running) whilst the engine is cool. If you remove the flaps then the engine will be running in a cold state for longer and engine wear will generally be higher, even if you take it easy until the engine is warmed. The work is thus not recommended.

KITS AND CUSTOMS

The majority of (though by no means all) Beetle customs and kit car designs are influenced by the Californian sun, sea and surf youth culture of the late 1950s and throughout the '60s. Perhaps it was the fact that the Beetle was cheap to run, repair and maintain, compact and simple to work on in comparison with the typically large and relatively sophisticated American gas-guzzler which so endeared the Beetle to the enthusiasts who began customising Beetles all those years ago: perhaps the Porsche 356 connotations helped more than a little.

Three broad styles emerged. The Baja is the fast off-roader and evolved from Beetles which were modified for use in off-road desert racing events which were held on the Baja peninsular, and hence the name. The seemingly immortal Beach Buggy is the recreational representative of the trio and has been going strong in the UK for a staggering 25 years, out-lasting many a production car. The California 'Cal' Beetle is the 'street custom' member of the three and has been with us in one form or another for longer than even the Beach Buggy, and today the industry which manufactures and sells the necessary conversion kits for Bajas, Buggies and Cal lookers appears to be larger and stronger than ever before. There seems no end in sight for the customised Beetle.

But there is more. The mechanical similarities between the Beetle and 356/911 ranges from Porsche have resulted in the availability of a number of kits which can transform the humble Beetle into one of a number of quite convincing replica Porsche sports cars. In addition, there are a number of individually styled and stunning sports car kits, stylish enough to convince casual observers that they are viewing an exotic and very expensive Italian creation rather than a well-dressed Beetle.

The Beetle is a car which especially lends itself for conversion to kit or component cars, not least because of its strong chassis/floorpan assembly which is, on all but the most rotten of examples, usually strong enough to be used – perhaps following welded repairs to the floor edges or floor sections replacement – as a chassis on which the kit car can be built. This saves the kit manufacturer the problems of designing and building a separate chassis (something which is necessary for most monocoque car based kits) and it helps to keep the prices of mainstream Beetle kits lower than those for almost any other car.

Almost as important as the chassis/floor assembly of the Beetle is the fact that the bodywork simply bolts onto (and off) it. Whereas with most cars, even if the floorpan/transmission tunnel/sill structure was strong enough to be used, removing the body from the floorpan would entail a terrific amount of cutting with all the attendant dangers from razor-sharp metal edges, in the case of the Beetle it is quickly and (sometimes) easily achieved without damaging either the floor or the bodywork. The new body – or its metal internal skeleton – can then be bolted into place, rather than bonded.

The simplicity of the Beetle's air cooled engine, the robustness of its suspension and transmission, all conspire to make the car as close to the ideal kit base car

as possible. The fact that vast numbers of Beetles exist ensures a steady supply of cars for customisation or for kit building.

The first question to be addressed by anyone who wants a custom Beetle is whether to opt for the easy route of buying an already built and road-going car, or whether to buy in the components and do the necessary conversion work themselves. Both have their attractions and drawbacks.

If you buy a kit which someone else has built up and which is already taxed and tested for the road, then you must be especially wary when trying to assess the build quality. Some people look upon the kit car as a cheap method of getting a rotten old Beetle back onto the road, but because building a kit properly is *not* cheap, corners are sometimes cut to keep the build within a tight budget. Some people may simply cut costs by not buying essential 'accessories' such as a hood or bumpers; others will cut costs by re-using tired old brake pipes or fuel lines, scored brake drums or a dubious wiring loom. Some of these 'economies' can leave the car in a dangerous condition, irrespective of whether the car in question has been granted a certificate of roadworthiness.

The mounting costs of carrying out a kit build to a higher standard lead to many would-be builders offering their cars for sale before they have been completed, and these make tempting buys because these vendors usually have to sell their part-built kits at a whacking loss. Again, be especially thorough when assessing the build quality of work carried out so far.

The only way to acquire the kit you want in the condition you want is to build it yourself. Because most kits are made specifically for the front torsion bar suspension cars, you will normally be starting out with an old Beetle. Old Beetles usually have a predominance of old and tired components, so that the mechanical aspect of the build up costs will be roughly the same those incurred in a straight restoration. The difference in overall costs between a kit build and a restoration will be the difference between the cost of the kit and accessories, and the bodywork restoration cost.

Baja

The Baja is generally considered to be the easiest and cheapest popular customisation for a Beetle. Baja kits consist of a number of GRP panels which are bolted or bonded onto a slightly modified Beetle bodyshell. The supplied GRP panels include wheel arches which are invariably far wider than standard and which look silly with skinny wheels and tyres fitted, so budget for larger wheels and tyres.

The Baja looks at its best when the suspension is raised substantially to provide great ground clearance in true off-roader fashion. At the rear, ride height alteration is merely a matter of adjustment, but at the front, you will have to buy in components and carry out modifications.

The downside to raising the rear of a Beetle with swing axle rear suspension is of course that you are also raising the roll centre and most importantly the transaxle. This alters the camber of the rear wheels, making it more positive the higher the bodyshell is raised and, of course, exacerbating the problems caused by positive camber of the outside wheel when the rear roll centre rises (the so-called 'jacking effect') on a tight corner. Off-road, positive camber is no great problem because there is normally enough space to allow the driver to apply opposite lock and drift the car sideways to deal with the violent oversteer which results from a raising of the roll centre on hard cornering. On the road where this manoeuvre cannot be undertaken in safety, however, be very careful when negotiating bends in a car with raised suspension and a swing axle.

Bajas based on swing axle Beetles and which are meant for road use (as most in the UK appear to be) should be raised as little as possible at the rear (and preferably fitted with a camber compensator) or possibly raised at the rear only fractionally by the use of larger diameter wheels with smaller diameter wheels at the front. This gives the road-going Baja an authentic chunky look whilst keeping the roll centre low – the only negative effect on handling and road-holding would be due to the softer springing effect of wider tyres. Alternatively, switching the rear suspension to the diagonal trailing arm type will remove the positive camber problem altogether.

Before carrying out any suspension modifications to a Baja, it is recommended that you consult the kit manufacturer and gain recommendations according to the intended use of the car, i.e.. on or off road. If the manufacturer is vague, then perhaps his experience of Bajas is limited to making moulds and you may be better advised to buy from someone who not only moulds body panels but also drives Bajas!

Beach Buggy

There are two basic types of Beach Buggy, the short and standard (long) wheelbase. As their names suggest, the standard wheelbase car is rather longer than the shorter

The GP Beach Buggy – the original, and still going strong here in the UK some 25 years after first launched.

(original) Buggy. Which you prefer will depend on whether you require the extra carrying capacity of the long wheelbase version or prefer the more traditional looks of the short wheelbase Buggy.

If you prefer the short wheelbase car, then irrespective of whether you buy a part-completed, a finished car or a kit, there arises the question of the strength of the shortened chassis. The quickest and easiest way to shorten the Beetle chassis is to make two cuts straight across the car from sill to sill, then to butt weld the two halves together as depicted in the illustration. This method does not give the strongest possible chassis; if off-road use is anticipated for the completed car (and who could resist using a Buggy off-road?) then remember that is far from unknown for a chassis which has been shortened in this manner to break its back.

The second illustration shows a better way of shortening the chassis. This method takes a lot longer and entails far more welding, but the resulting chassis is far more robust and – if the quality of the welding is up to scratch—well able to withstand the roughest of usage.

Terry Ball of Beetle Specialist Workshop has built many Beach Buggies, and in addition to making the longer cuts shown in the illustrations, he spot welds a strip of steel around the inside of the spine, to give even greater strength.

Cal lookers

The California looker is the last of the three great 'traditional' Beetle customs, and is based on a lowered ride height to give a road car with better than standard grip and aggressive looks to match! Building a Cal looker is an entirely different business from building a Baja or Buggy, because the only panels which have to be bought in are wider or flared wings which enable wider wheels and tyres to be fitted.

BODY STYLING PANELS AND KITS

The fact that the Beetle bodyshell is not structurally too important means that all panels – with the exception of the flitches of McPherson strut cars – can, if desired, be replaced with alternatives made from GRP. In comparison with steel pressings, GRP mouldings have very low development, equipment and production costs, and many small companies consequently manufacture custom GRP moulded Beetle body panels – and even complete bodyshell mouldings.

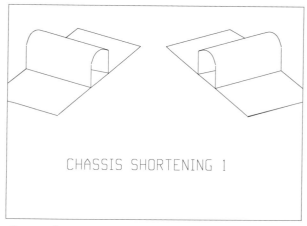

Chassis Shortening 1: This is the obvious and easiest way to shorten a chassis/floorpan assembly but the chassis will be weak.

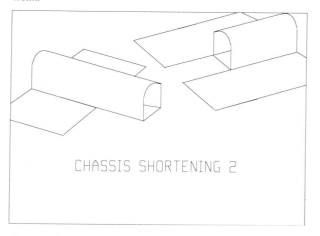

Chassis Shortening 2: By staggering the cuts through the spine and the floorpan, there is more welding to be done but the resultant chassis will be stronger.

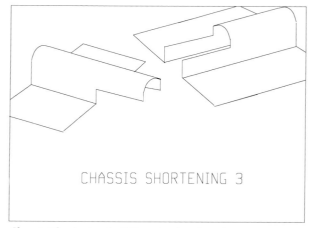

Chassis Shortening 3: If the spine is cut as shown, even more welding has to be carried out, but the chassis will be very strong. Terry Ball at BSW recommends spot welding a strip of steel to the inside of the cut spine before welding the two halves of the assembly together.

Some of these panels, such as flared wings, simply bolt on, but the majority are affixed by bonding directly to steel. The GRP itself is a mixture of glass filaments and (commonly) polyester resin to bond them together. The production of panels starts with the manufacture of the 'original' plug – a full sized model of the panel, which can itself be made of a wide range of materials. The plug is highly polished and then covered with a release agent – a thin layer which isolates the plug and prevents resin from bonding directly to it.

The female mould, from which the actual panels will be produced, is then made on the plug. A gel coat, which is a layer of resin, is painted on, followed by layers of glass fibres which are whetted out with resin. When the glass and resin have been built up to the desired thickness, wood or steel reinforcing is normally bonded on to the mould to give it rigidity. The plug is removed when the GRP has cured (hardened by a chemical process).

Producing GRP panels simply involves polishing the mould, painting on a release agent followed by the gel coat (which can contain pigment so that the panel is self-coloured), then glass fibres whetted out with resin.

The benefits of GRP for making body panels are low set-up and production costs, plus the fact that the low initial costs are quickly recouped, which makes it financially viable to produce the panels in small numbers. The downside to GRP is that the panels are less inclined than steel to distort and absorb energy in a collision, and that their resin content is flammable.

The most attractive of styling kits are cabriolet conversions. Some of these comprise closing panels which are bonded onto the remnants of the steel bodyshell after the roof has been cut away, others are complete GRP bodyshells which bolt onto the chassis/floorpan assembly in place of the original bodyshell. The former are invariably cheaper to buy and fit, although it goes without saying that your bodyshell should be structurally very sound and all welded repairs must be carried out before GRP is bonded on – subsequently welding in the vicinity of flammable GRP is *not* recommended!

The original Karmann Ghia Beetle Cabriolet had strengthening longitudinal steel members and the author would recommend that any cabriolet conversion began with the fitment of similar strengtheners.

The addresses of many of the companies which manufacture or retail GRP body styling panels and GRP bodyshells are in the appendix of this book. Before choosing any such customisation, it is recommended that you visit a Beetle gathering, look at the various customs to assess build quality and talk to owners of the customised cars to ascertain the degree of difficulty in carrying out the work.

BEETLE-BASED KIT CARS

The kit car manufacturing business seem in a constant state of flux, with manufacturers moving address, selling their kit moulds to other companies, going into liquidation or being taken over by other companies with frightening regularity. To obtain the latest information on the availability of kits, look in one of the kit car magazines; the publishers of these magazines also publish annual directories listing the majority of kits on the market.

The kit cars included here are those which represent a particular style or type (there are in some instances other kits with similar looks), and for which the manufacturers could be contacted at the time of writing; you will find a far greater selection of kits on the second-hand market and indeed by consulting Beetle and kit car periodicals. There are undoubtedly many Beetle-based kit car bodyshell moulds lying unused and unloved in the dark corners of workshops, because manufacturers are inclined to update their kits so that, instead of being based on the VW chassis, they incorporate their own chasses. This allows the use of more recent engines and transmissions.

There are essentially two types of Beetle-based kit car. The more traditional variety is based on the Beetle chassis assembly, and usually comprises a simple GRP bodyshell which bolts on in place of the standard body. Although the kits are thus usually low-priced, don't forget that interior trim, body fittings and so on usually have to also be acquired, and the final build costs can in some instances be far more than and in some instances a multiple of the kit price. As an example, most kits look positively silly when fitted with standard Beetle wheels and tyres, and so you should budget for new larger wheels and tyres.

More recently, kit manufacturers have offered kits based on their own chassis – usually constructed from steel tubing – which utilise only elements of the suspension, the transaxle and the engine. These kits will normally cost more than those which use the Beetle chassis, and the costs of specialised other components can bump up these prices.

Madison

The Madison is a GRP kit with stunning 1930/40s sports/tourer looks. Designed by John Jobber of GP Projects, the Madison was originally Beetle-based but is at the time of writing only available for other donor cars in the UK. The Beetle variety is still manufactured in France, however.

So the opportunities to buy a Beetle-based Madison

in the UK sadly appear to be limited to buying second-hand. In addition to a full mechanical check, buyers should be very careful when assessing both the build-up quality and especially the state of mechanical/electrical/fuel components with a view to fire hazards.

GP Buggy

This is the original Buggy which originally came to the UK back in 1966, and some early examples survive to this day! At the time of writing, the GP Buggy is being manufactured by 1965 British Saloon Car Champion Roy Pierpoint, who states that he was attracted to the car because it is such fun to drive.

Both long and short wheelbase versions of the Buggy are available. The short wheelbase version is the original and, in the opinion of the author, the better looking of the two, although the practicality of the LWB version will endear it to many people – not least because the chassis does not have to be shortened, because of its load-carrying potential and because a full hardtop is available to turn it into a van.

The Beach Buggy should prove one of the easier and less expensive kits to build, and a good build manual is available.

GT Mouldings – Kyote 2 and bugle 2 Beach Buggies

The Kyote is a long wheel base Buggy which incorporates many components from the standard Beetle – such as lights – to keep build costs low. The bodyshell is a one-piece moulding, which avoids the need to fabricate or fit a separate dashboard.

The Bugle 2 is a short wheel base Buggy which allows the fitment of many standard Beetle components, including lights and switches.

'A thing of beauty is a joy for ever,' if you look after it. The GP Spyder.

GP Spyder

If there's one kit car which is guaranteed to turn every head it is the GP Spyder – even those who see no virtue in classic or sports cars can appreciate the lines of this beauty. Two versions are available, the original Beetle or Porsche powered Spyder has now been joined by one powered by the Golf engine.

The GP Spyder is one of the best quality Beetle-based kits, and a build-up will be priced accordingly.

Laser Cars – UVA Fugitive

The Fugitive comprises a tubular space frame chassis and little in the way of bodywork – it offers the most spartan motoring for those who want to get back to basics and have some serious on or off road fun! A four seater version has now been added to the established two seater.

Chesil Speedster

A Porsche 356 lookalike good enough to fool most people! The kit comprises GRP body panel mouldings and has a built-in frame which bolts to a shortened Beetle chassis/floorpan assembly. The kit is of a high quality and build costs will not be low.

Eagle SS

A sleek and stylish sports car which looks a million dollars but costs a fraction of the price of any similarly exotic production car. The car is so different from a Beetle that you can expect to have to buy in many components – upholstery, electrical etc. – because Beetle varieties will look totally out of place, that is if they will fit at all!

APPENDICES

Data, Lubricants and Fluids

The figures given here relate to popular recent Beetles; it is essential that you cross-check with a workshop or service manual which is specific to the model and year of your own Beetle. On some cars, details of fuel requirements can be found on a plate on the filler cover, and details of tyre pressures on the glove compartment lid.

Engine oil 20W 50	4.4 pints (2.5 litres) Multigrade SAE
Transaxle oil 80	4.4 pints (2.5 litres) EP Gear oil SAE
Fuel	
1200/1300	9.2 gallons (42 litres) 87 RON
later 1300/1500/1600	9.2 gallons (42 litres) 91 RON
TYRE INFLATION	
5.60–15 PR Crossply	16 psi front, 24 psi (26 psi full load) rear
155 SR15 Radial	18 psi front, 27 psi rear
Maximum load	880 lbs (400 kg)
Maximum trailer unbraked	880 lbs (400 kg)
Maximum trailer braked	1433 lbs (650 kg)
Maximum roof rack load	110 lbs (50 kg)
Turning circle	32 ft (9.6 m)
Kerb weight	1821 lbs (890 kg)
Ground clearance	5.9 ins. (15 cm)

Torque Wrench Settings

ENGINE

Spark plugs	25 lb ft (3.5 kg m)
Oil strainer plate	5 lb ft (0.7 kg m)
Oil drain plug	25 lb ft (3.5 kg m)
Engine to transaxle	22 lb ft (3.0 kg m)
Cylinder head	23 lb ft (3.2 kg m)
Rocker gear to cylinder head	18 lb ft (2.5 kg m)
Crankshaft pulley	33 lb ft (4.5 kg m)
Generator pulley	43 lb ft (6.0 kg m)
Flywheel to crankshaft	253 lb ft (35.0 kg m)
Con rod to crankshaft	24 lb ft (3.3 kg m)
Crankcase halves M8	14 lb ft (2.0 kg m)
Crankcase halves M10/12	25 lb ft (3.5 kg m)
Oil pump	14 lb ft (2.0 kg m)
Fan to generator	43 lb ft (6.0 kg m)

Clutch/Transmission

Oil filler plug	14 lb ft (2.0 kg m)
Oil drain plug	14 lb ft (2.0 kg m)
Clutch to flywheel	18 lb ft (2.5 kg m)
Transaxle/frame bolts	166 lb ft (23.0 kg m)

Rear Suspension/Brakes

Hub nuts	253 lb ft (35.0 kg m)
Wheel bearing cover bolts	43 lb ft (6.0 kg m)
Damper mounting bolts	43 lb ft (6.0 kg m)
Wheel cylinder bolts	18 lb ft (2.5 kg m)
Master cylinder bolts	18 lb ft (2.5 kg m)
Brake unions	11–14 lb ft (1.5–2.0 kg m)

Front Suspension/Brakes

Caliper bolts	29 lb ft (4.0 kg m)
Backplate bolts	36 lb ft (5.0 kg m)
Wheel bearing locknut	51 lb ft (7.0 kg m)
Torsion arm grub screws	33 lb ft (4.5 kg m)
Damper lower nut	25 lb ft (3.5 kg m)

Steering

Steering wheel to column	36 lb ft (5.0 kg m)

SPECIALISTS' ADDRESSES

Inclusion in this list should not necessarily be taken as a recommendation of a company or service, except where specifically stated.

ACC Ltd. Unit 3, Kingsley Street, Kirby in Ashfield, Notts NG17 7BA   *Tel.* 0623 751486
(Workshop, bodyshop, spraying, customs)

Ace Auto Spares 230 High Road, Chadwell Heath, Essex RM6 6AP   *Tel.* 081 599 8356
(Spares supply)

AC & V Auto Supplies Unit 8, Matalline Industrial Estate, Winster Grove, Shady Lane, Great Barr, Birmingham B44 9EG
Tel. 021 366 6356
(Workshop, bodyshop)

Allshots Beetle Centre All shots Farm, Woodhouse Lane, Kelvedon, Essex CO5 9DF   *Tel.* 0376 83295
(Workshop, bodyshop, spares supplier)

Arnie Levics Ltd Leigh Road Garage, Street, Somerset BA16 0HA
Tel. 0458 42677
(Workshop, performance engines)

ARS 42 Townsend Road, Chesham, Buckinghamshire HP5 2AA
Tel. 0494 792412
(Workshop, bodyshop, custom parts)

Autobahn Ltd Units 16–17, Morton Street Industrial Estate, Failsworth, Manchester M35 0BN   *Tel.* 061 683 4707
(Spares, panels, mail order)

Autobarn Manor House Farm, Kersoe, Pershore, Worcestershire WR10 3JD.   *Tel.* 0386 71080
(Importers and suppliers of new bodyshells, chassis/floorpan assemblies, genuine repair assemblies/chassis/panels and spares)

Autocavan 103 Lower Weybourne Lane, Badshot Lea, Farnham, Surrey GU9 9LG.   *Tel.* 0252 333891
(All Beetle spares, performance components. Mail order. Autocavan are one of the largest Beetle spares stockists in the UK with local depots in Belfast, Ipswich, Rochdale, Exeter and Poole. The company wholesales to many independent retail outlets. Comprehensive price lists)

Autocraft Reynolds Building, Watnall Road, Hucknall, Nottinghamshire   *Tel.* 0602 681504
(Workshop, bodyshop, custom specialist)

Autocraft (Birmingham) 63, Oldbury Road, Greets Green, West Bromwich.   *Tel.* 021 520 5307.
(Workshop, bodyshop, spares, car sales)

Autoklass 100 Baker Road, Newthorpe, Nottingham MG16 2DP
Tel. 0602 459901
(Workshop, bodyshop, car sales)

Autoline Eagle House, Redstone Industrial Estate, Boston, Lincolnshire PE21 8AL   *Tel.* 0205 354500
(Distributors of Autoline brand products, including Dinitrol RC800 rust killer, Dinitrol 3125 cavity wax and Aluminium Anti-sieze – recommended in this book)

Autoparts 406 Blackburn Road, Accrington, Lancashire
Tel. 0254 384500
(Spares supplier)

AVW Unit 16 Cibyn Industrial Estate, Caernarfon, Gwynnedd, Wales LL55 2BD   *Tel.* 0286 673559
(Spares supplier, workshop)

AVW (Kent) 43–5 Wainscott Road, Wainscott, Strood, Kent ME2 4LA   *Tel.* 0634 722681
(Workshop, bodyshop, spares)

Barrett and Shore 724–6 Warwick Road, Tyseley, Birmingham.
Tel. 021 706 4969
(Spares supplier, car sales)

BCL Auto Parts 38 Jubilee Avenue, Paulsgrove, Portsmouth, Hampshire PO6 4QN   *Tel.* 0705 325945
(Spares supplier, workshop, bodyshop)

BD Car Trim Cornford Road Garage, Marton, Blackpool FY4 4QQ
Tel. 0253 761252
(Beetle interior trim)

Bears VW Supply Unit 1, Sandpits Industrial Estate, 18 Summerhill Street, Birmingham B1 2PD   *Tel.* 021 236 6216
(Spares Supply, workshop, bodyshop)

Beetle Centre Pottery Road, Nr Pier, Wigan.   *Tel.* 0942 491684
(Workshop, spares supplier)

Beetlelink Unit 7, Finns Industrial Park, Mill Lane, Crondall, Farnham, Surrey GU10 5RP   *Tel.* 0252 851 590
(Spares supplier, workshop, bodyshop)

The Beetle Sanctuary Wells-Next-The-Sea, Norfolk.
Tel. 0328 710221
(Workshop bodyshop, spares)

Beetle Specialist Workshop Ballard's Place, Eardiston, Tenbury Wells Worcestershire WR15 8JR   *Tel. 0584 70348*
(BSW should need no introduction to readers of this book! In addition to restoration, mechanical repair and servicing work, the company build kit cars, Bajas, Buggies and Cal Lookers. All staff are involved in competitive off-road trails, so a good source of info on off-roaders. All air-cooled VWs catered for (plus liquid cooled Type 2s). Also spares supply. Very helpful with technical information for customers)

Beetle Works Newport, South Wales.   *Tel. 0633 221953*
(Workshop, bodyshop)

Beetle World Ltd Court Lane Estates, Iver, Buckinghamshire SL0 9HL   *Tel. 0753 630300*
(Workshop, bodyshop, car sales)

Big Boys' Toys Unit 1, Motherwell Way, West Thurrock, Essex RM16 1NR   *Tel. 0708 861827*
(If it's Beetle goodies you're after – they've got it! Specialists in Cal Look and performance, but standard spares supply as well)

Bilbo's Trading Co. Marlfield, Eastbourne Road, South Godstone, Surrey RH9 8JQ   *Tel. 0342 892499*
(Type 2 specialists. Workshop. Bodyshop. Motor caravan conversions. Type 2s for sale)

BMG Autoparts Park House, Randalls Road, Leatherhead, Surrey KT22 0AH.   *Tel. 0372 378951*
(Spares supplier)

Bodystyle Glassfibre 71 Heath End Road, Nuneaton, Warks CV10 7JG.   *Tel. 0203 371749*
(Low cost GRP body panels, including Baja and soft top conversion kits)

Bugpack Britavia House, Southend Airport, Southend-on-Sea, Essex SS2 6YU   *Tel. 0702 530440*
(Spares supplier, performance spares)

Bugshack Milford, nr Godalming, Surrey.   *Tel. 0483 419763*
(Workshop, bodyshop, customs)

BVW Engineering 26 Queens Park, Aylesbury, Buckinghamshire HP21 7RS   *Tel. 0296 434499*
(Auto engineers. All boxer motors (including liquid cooled) catered for. Line boring, all machining)

Charles Barber & Sons 1–13 Station Road, Northwich, Cheshire CW9 5LR   *Tel. 0606 46061*
(Spares supplier, car sales)

Chesil Speedsters The Old Barn, Cogden, Burton Bradstock, Bridport, Dorset DT6 4RN   *Tel. 0308 897072*
(Manufacturers of Chesil Speedster 356 kits. Kits to completed cars. Jigged bodywork repairs)

Congleton Beetles Danemill, Broadhurst Lane, Congleton, Cheshire.   *Tel. 0260 279887*
(Workshop, bodyshop, car sales)

Continental Autospares 64 Haxby Road, York YO3 7JU   *Tel. York 610286*
(Spares supplier, mail order)

Continental Spares 435–7 Wells Road, Bristol   *Tel. 0272 776 544*
(Spares supplier)

Eagle Cars Ltd Unit 4, Hooe Farm Industrial Estate, Tye Lane, Warburton, Arundel, West Sussex BN18 0LU   *Tel. 0243 544673*
(Manufacturers of the Eagle SS kit car)

Eastwood Publications 16 Fore Street, Eastcote, Pinner, Middlesex HA5 2HY
(VW Trends magazine UK distributor)

Elite Vehicles 29 Green Hill Drive, Bramley, Leeds LS13 4JZ *Tel. 0532 637900*
(Bodykits)

E & M Motors Ongar Hall Farm, Brentwood Road, Orsett, Grays, Essex RM16 3HU   *Tel. 0375 892500*
(Workshop, bodyshop, spares supplier)

Europa Parts 32 London Road, Apsley, Hemel Hempstead, Hertfordshire HP3 9SB   *Tel. 0442 248894*
(Spares supply, workshop at Watford, branches at Watford and Hitchin)

European Autoparts 5 Kimber Road, off Garratt Lane, Wandsworth, London SW18 4NR   *Tel. 081 874 2124*
(Spares supplier)

European Motor Components Unit 5, New Meadow Road, Lakeside Industrial Estate, Redditch, Worcestershire B98 8YW *Tel. 0527 510513*
(OEM spares supplier)

Form & Function Keighley Business Centre, South Street, Keighley, West Yorkshire   *Tel. 0535 690702*
(Workshop, bodyshop, recon engines)

Francis Tuthill's Workshop Wardington, nr Banbury, Oxfordshire OX17 1RY   *Tel. 0295 750514*
(Workshop, bodyshop, specialist competition car body/mechanical work, Beetle sales)

Frost Auto Restoration Techniques Crawford Street, Rochdale, Lancashire OL16 5NU   *Tel. 0706 58619*
(Restoration tools specialist, mail order, catalogue)

German and Swedish 2 Space Way, North Feltham Trading Estate, Feltham, Middlesex TW14 0TH   *Tel. 081 893 1688*
(Spares supplier, mail order)

GP Buggies Hazlehead, 41, Woodend Drive, South Ascot, Berkshire SL5 9BD   *Tel. 0344 874831*
(Current manufacturer of original GP Buggy, first introduced into the UK back in 1966! SWB & LWB versions, good build manual. Very friendly and approachable!)

GP Projects Unit 49, Princes Estate, Princes Risborough, Buckinghamshire HP27 9PX.   *Tel. 0844 275 202 (Fax.230)*
(Manufacturers of the absolutely stunning GP Spyder kit car)

GT Mouldings 66 Mile Oak Road, Portslade, East Sussex BN41 2PL   *Tel. 0273 430505*
(Beach Buggies – Kyote, Manta Ray, Bugle – manufacturers, suppliers)

Haselock 22 Slingsby Close, Attleborough Fields, Nuneaton, Warickshire CV11 6RP   *Tel. 0203 328343*
(Workshop, bodyshop, spares supplier)

Herbie Heritage Unit 2, Newcroft, Tangmere, nr Chichester, West Sussex PO20 6HB   *Tel. 0243 778902*
(Workshop, bodyshop, spares supplier)

J & G Motors 94 Graham Road, Partslade, Brighton, West Sussex BN41 2WL   *Tel. 0273 430412*
(Workshop, bodyshop)

231

John Forbes Automotive 7 Meadow Lane, Edinburgh, Scotland EH8 9NR   *Tel.* 031 667 9767
(Workshop, spares supplier)

Johnsons The Engine Centre, Oxford Road, Kingston Bagpuize, Abingdon, Oxfordshire OX13 5AP   *Tel.* 0865 821408
(Spares supplier, specialist engine components, machining services)

Karly Kars Gambril House, Falfield, Wotton-under-Edge, Gloucestershire GL12 8DP   *Tel.* 0454 260111
(Workshop, bodyshop, engine builders)

Karmann Classics 96–8 Northease Drive, Hove, Sussex BN3 8LH   *Tel.* 0273 424330
(Genuine factory spares supplier, mail order)

Karmann Konnection 4–6 High Street, A13, Hadleigh, Essex SS7 2PB   *Tel.* 0702 551766
(Spares, mail order – one of the larger companies, good catalogue)

Kingfisher Kustoms Units 21/22 Mornington Road, Smethwick, Warley, West Midlands B66 2JE   *Tel.* 021 558 9135
(Workshop, bodyshop, kit supply and build)

Laser Cars Ltd 14, Ardglen Road, Evingar Trading Estate, Whitchurch, Hampshire RG28 7BB   *Tel.* 0256 895188
(Specialists in fitting non-VW engines into the Beetle – anything up to the Rover V8! Also suppliers of the UVA Fugitive kit car)

Limited Edition Warrington Road, High Leigh, nr Knutsford, Cheshire WA16 0RT   *Tel.* 0925 757575
(Workshop, bodyshop, spares supply – one of the biggest, good catalogue)

LR Superbeetles Gosbecks Road, Colchester, Essex
Tel. 0206 563433
(Workshop, bodyshop, spares supplier, car sales)

John Maher Unit 16 Albany Trading Estate, Albany Road, Chorlton, Manchester M21 1AZ   *Tel.* 061 881 5225
(Performance components)

Mega Bug Unit 1, Whitehart Road, Plumstead SE18 1DG
Tel. 081 317 7333
(Workshop, bodyshop, spares supplier, mail order)

Microgiant Unit 7, Westfield Close, Rawreith Industrial Estate, Rawreith Lane, Rayleigh, Essex SS6 9RL   *Tel.* 0268 782601
(Workshop, bodyshop, engine machining, standard to race spec)

D & M Middleton & Son Rawfords Mill, Checkheaton, West Yorkshire BD19 5LY   *Tel.* 0274 869950
(Manufacturers/suppliers of all Beetle interior trim)

Mister Beetle 141–3 Sprowston Road, Norwich, Norfolk NR6 6LZ   *Tel.* Norwich 426433
(Workshop, spares supplier, car sales)

Bernard Newbury 1 Station Road, Leigh-on-Sea, Essex SS9 1ST   *Tel.* 0702 710211
(Coachtrimmer)

North Cornwall VW Centre Fair Park Garage, Fairpark Road, Wadebridge, Cornwall PL27 7NS   *Tel.* 0208 814747
(Workshop, bodyshop, car sales)

Northampton VW Centre 138 Wellingborough Road, Northampton.   *Tel.* 0604 38985
(Spares supplier)

NRC The Carriage Works, Heath End Road, Nuneaton CV10 7JB   *Tel.* 0203 350766
(Workshop, bodyshop, spares supplier, customs)

Oxford Beetles Unit 1 Station Yard Grove, Wantage, Oxfordshire   *Tel.* 0235 770996
(Workshop, bodyshop, spares supplier)

Paris Beetles 23 Middleton Avenue, Chingford, London E4 8EF   *Tel.* 081 524 1338
(Cabrio conversion)

Peter Norris Unit 1, Ellerslie Square, 11, Lyham Road, London SW2 5DZ   *Tel.* 071 737 1795
(Workshop, bodyshop)

Peter Robinson (Chrome). 10 London Road, Worcester   *Tel.* 0905 764077
(Chromework. Peter is a Beetle owner himself and understands the needs of customisers).

Paintbox Kelvedon, Essex. CO5 9EN.   *Tel.* 0376 571957
(Workshop, bodyshop, Cal Look specialist)

Replacement VW/Audi Parts Centre 170–2 County Road, Walton, Liverpool L4 5PH   *Tel.* 051 525 1764
(Spares supplier)

Ron Turnbull Snowdon Road, Middlesborough, Cleveland TS2 1DB   *Tel.* 0642 248848
(Spares supplier, car sales)

Small Car Specialists The Old Pump House, Swift Lane, Bagshot, Surrey GU19 5NR   *Tel.* 0276 51918
(Workshop, bodyshop, spares supplier, custom)

Speedsters Cherry Tree Cottage. 2, Church Lane, Frant, East Sussex TN3 9DX   *Tel.* 0892 750875
(UK supplier of Apal Speedster 356 replica)

Stateside Tuning Unit 3, Enterprise Works, Alexandra Road, Enfield. Middlesex EN3 7EH   *Tel.* 081 805 4865
(Engine machining)

Stirling Garage Unit 9, Sterling Estate, Kings Road, Newbury, Berkshire RG14 5RQ   *Tel.* 0635 528953
(Workshop, bodyshop)

Streetside Unit 9, Hawthorne Industrial Estate, Warrington WA5 1BX   *Tel.* 0925 414184
(Workshop, spares supplier, race preparation)

Telford Beetle Centre Trench, Telford, Shropshire.
Tel. 0952 604483
(Workshop, bodyshop)

Teme Valley Race Preparation Ltd. Unit 1 Cromwell Works, Boraston Lane, Tenbury Wells, Worcs. WR15 8LS   *Tel.* 0584 811313   *Fax* 0584 810080
(All performance – road-going, rally or race – preparation work. Rolling road. Full machining facilities)

Terrys' Beetle Services Shirley Garage, Shirley Gardens, Hanwell, London W7 3PT   *Tel.* 081 567 3165
(Workshop, bodyshop, spares supplier)

Thames Valley Beetles 22 Great Knollys Street, Reading, Berkshire   *Tel.* 0734 595909
(Spares supplier)

Uro Automotive Unit 21, The Fort Industrial Park, Dunlop Way, Birmingham B35 7AR *Tel.* 021 749 4700.
BRANCHES: Swansea, West Thurrock, Glasgow, Manchester, South Ruislip, Bristol, Bradford, Bournemouth, Belfast, Edinburgh.
(Very large company specialising in all Beetle spares supply. Dealerships and many agents throughout the UK)

Urry Motors 145–9 Stanwell Road, Ashford, Middlesex
Tel. 0831 898857
(Workshop, bodyshop, spares supplier)

Vas Auto Services 3–4, Quayside Industrial Estate, Woodbridge, Suffolk. *Tel.* 0394 380876
(Workshop, bodyshop, modifications)

V-Dub Wybunbury, Nantwich, Cheshire. *Tel.* 0270 841971
(Workshop, bodyshop, customs)

Volksbits 800 Pershore Road, Selly Park, Birmingham B29 7NG
Tel. 021 472 1388
(Spares supplier, catalogue)

Volksdiscount London Road, Bishops Stortford, Hertfordshire
CM23 5NF *Tel.* 0279 507175
(Workshop, spares supplier)

Volksfolk Cowbridge, Boston, Lincolnshire *Tel.* 0205 367565
(Workshop, bodyshop)

Volkspares 104–6 Newlands Park, Sydenham, London SE26
Tel. 081 778 7766. Branches in and around London.
(Workshop, spares supplier)

Volksrod Unit 44 Wymeswold Industrial Estate, Burton on the Wolds, Loghborough, Leicestershire LE12 5TR *Tel.* 0509 881228
(Beach Buggy manufacturer)

Volkstop 211, Harden Road, Leamore, Walsall, West Midlands
Tel. 0785 714404
(Workshop, bodyshop, spares supplier)

Volkswares Autowagen House, 173 Loughborough Road,
Leicester *Tel.* 0533 669998
(Spares suppliers, mail order)

Volkswagen Yeomans Drive, Blakelands, Milton Keynes MK 14 5AN
(Publishers of Volkswagen Car and Driver magazine. Some historic (Beetle) content, but mainly concerned with current VW cars.)

Volksworld Link House Magazines. Dingwall Avenue, Croydon, Surrey CR9 2TA *Tel.* 081 686 2599
(Publishers of VolksWorld monthly magazine. Covers all aspects of Beetle ownership and driving. Much coverage of custom aspects and good DIY features. Also one-off DIY specials published from time to time)

Voltsvagen 3, The Birches, Charlton, London SE7 7PB
Tel. 081 305 0831
(Mail order only supplier of Snugbug electric heater and wiring looms)

Volkswork Unit 6P, Atlas Business Centre, Oxgate Lane, London NW2 7HJ *Tel.* 081 450 1004
(Workshop, bodyshop)

VWOC (GB) PO Box 7, Burntwood, Staffs WS7 8SB
(National club for all VW owners. Regional centres, local clubs, magazine, technical help etc.)

VWP Car Sales 22 Goring Road, Staines, Middlesex TW18 3EH
Tel. 0784 46910
(Car sales)

VW Centre Sutton Road, Leverington, Wisbech.
Tel. 0945 588931
(Spares supplier)

VW Motoring PO BOX 283, Cheltenham, Gloucestershire
GL52 3BT *Tel.* 0242 262723
(Monthly magazine devoted to all VW vehicles, but with high Beetle content)

VW Tools 338, Bradford Road, Liversedge, West Yorkshire
WF15 6BY *Tel.* 0924 402860
(Specialist VW tools supplier mentioned in this book, catalogue, mail order only)

WASP Unit 2B, Millfield Road Industrial Estate, Donnington, Lincolnshire PE11 4UR *Tel.* 0775 822022
(Workshop, bodyshop, spares supplier)

Wagenmaster Mill Road, West Walton, nr Wisbech, Cambridgeshire PE14 7EU Tel 0945 64650
(Workshop, bodyshop, engine and transmission specialist)

Westside Motors 34–6, The Broadway, Woodford Green, Essex
Tel. 081 505 5215
(Workshop, bodyshop)

Wizard Roadsters 373 Buckingham Avenue Trading Estate, Slough SL1 4LU *Tel.* 0753 551555
(Range of GRP body kits, cabriolet conversions and full GRP bodies)

ABOVE

As (we hope) a fitting and entertaining finale, we thought it would be a good idea to take a look at some radical 'restoration' work. These photographs from Mike Key, author of Custom Beetle (Osprey) are a reminder of just what can happen if you lose all self-control. Here we have a 1971 floor pan and running gear; front beam is a JC Performance with Sway-a-way adjusters and Jatech forged drop spindles, rear transaxle is a 1971 IRS unit. The hi-boy look body started from a 1961 convertible, dechromed, the windscreen chopped by 6 inches, the factory top replaced with a Carson lift off. Designed by D&D Specialities in Van Buren, Arkansas and finished by Terry Maheuron.

Tom Lubbock's 1970 1300 interior, with white vinyl Cobra seats, white door panels, four spoke wheel and centre console, aluminium billet winders, hand brake and pedals.

2110cc engine of Gary Berg's 1967 Bug, with 82 mm Gene Berg forged crank, Carillo rods, Eagle FK-87 cam, Clyde Berg modified dual port heads, a pair of 481DA Webers on Scat Track manifolds with Berg linkage and a Stinger electronic ignition system.

The stock ball joint front end on Gary Berg's car was narrowed and modified for a lower stance. Wheels are BRM magnesium originals, the windows are one-piece and the trim is de-chromed, to produce a very beautiful looking machine.

LWB pinstriped 1968 sand buggy, a Bug Pack frame with Dune Buggy headlights, air horns, chrome mirrors and stock VW turn indicators. Mustang seats from a '66, chrome roll bar, Grant steering wheel, Hurst shifter and a cluster of Stuart Warner gauges on the dash.

INDEX